C# Data Security Handbook

Matthew MacDonald
Erik Johansson

® Wrox Press Ltd.

C# Data Security Handbook

© 2003 Wrox Press Ltd

First published January 2003

Published by Wrox Press Ltd,
Arden House, 1102 Warwick Road, Acocks Green,
Birmingham, B27 6BH
United Kingdom
Printed in the United States
ISBN 1-86100-801-5

Trademark Acknowledgments

Wrox has endeavored to provide trademark information about all the companies and products mentioned in this book by the appropriate use of capitals. However, Wrox cannot guarantee the accuracy of this information.

Credits

Authors
Matthew MacDonald
Erik Johansson

Commissioning Editor
Benjamin Hickman

Technical Editors
James Hart
Benjamin Hickman
Christian Peak

Indexer
Michael Brinkman

Project Manager
Beckie Stones

Managing Editor
Emma Batch

Technical Reviewers
Richard Conway
Andrew Krowczyk
Eric Lippert
Ciaran Roarty
David Schultz

Production Coordinator
Neil Lote

Production Assistant
Paul Grove

Proof Reader
Chris Smith

Cover Design
Natalie O'Donnell

About the Authors

Matthew MacDonald

Matthew MacDonald is an MCSD developer, educator, and author. He's had a hand in nearly a dozen .NET books, including *Programming .NET Web Services* (O'Reilly), *User Interfaces in C#* (APress), and the forthcoming *.NET Distributed Applications* (Microsoft Press). He's also a frequent article writer, and regular columnist for Inside Visual Basic. In a dimly remembered past life he studied English literature and theoretical physics. Contact him at matthew@prosetech.com.

This book wouldn't have been possible without the vision and work of the Wrox team, including Benjamin Hickman, Beckie Stones, and my co-author Erik Johansson. The tech review team; Richard Conway Andrew Krowczyk, David Schultz and Ciaran Roarty provided invaluable comments on what was often dense and highly technical material. In particular I owe a heartfelt thanks to Eric Lippert for his deep insights into .NET security, and his quick e-mail responses to all my questions.

Finally, thanks must go to my family and wife Faria, all of whom support me tirelessly.

Matthew contributed Chapters 2-5 and Chapters 7 and 8.

Erik Johansson

Starting his professional career in the late 80's with Sweden as base, ABB gave Erik a solid foundation of high-end system development and delivery, stationing him for some time in Silicon Valley. Seeking new adventures, he embarked on a digital identification management project, where he led the development of a CA independent Internet-based identification platform for e-commerce.

To my loving wife Gunilla for the total support and understanding she has always given me, and to our cat, Matrix for also being there in time of joy as well as despair.

Erik contributed Chapters 1 and 6.

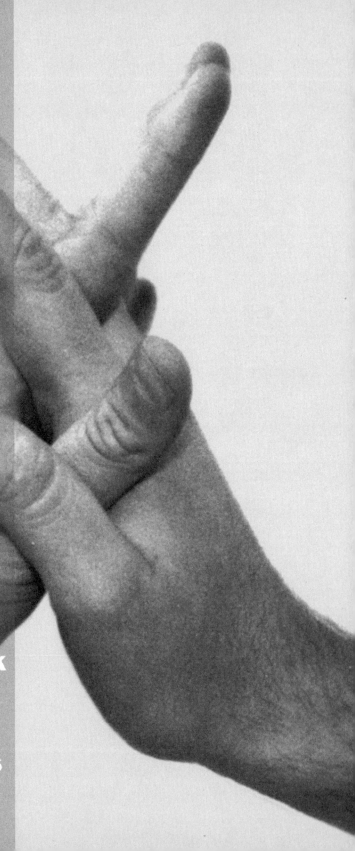

C#

Data Security

Handbook

Table of Contents

Table of Contents

C#

Data Security

Handbook

Introduction

Introduction

Put simply "When implementing a cryptographic system do it well or don't bother."
Cryptography isn't some sort of magic that you can use to make an application secure.
You have to understand the potential vulnerabilities if you are to be safe from attackers.
While most of the cryptographic algorithms implemented in the .NET Framework
security namespaces are essentially unbreakable by any reasonable definition, the vast
majority of flaws that lead to secret data being revealed to attackers are the results of
mistakes in the implementation of applications.

While the actual mathematics behind cryptography can be very complex, it isn't
necessary to understand them in any great detail. The important thing is to make
correct use of the .NET classes that implement these algorithms. Therefore, this book
will show you how to get the most out of the .NET Framework's cryptographic support,
focusing on practical issues and best practices.

Who is this Book For?

This book is aimed at practicing C# .NET developers who are creating distributed
applications or who need to store data in a secure manner. This book is aims to take
C# developers with little or no knowledge of cryptography to the point where they can
confidently implement their own secure applications.

What does this Book Cover?

This book covers the using symmetric and asymmetric cryptography with the .NET
Framework and Windows platform, then we go on to examine how to make practical
use of these technologies.

❑   **Chapter 1 – Introduction to Cryptography**
    This chapter examines the motivation behind using cryptography by
    looking at the threats that you need to consider in a modern distributed
    computing environment. The chapter introduces the various types and uses
    of cryptography supported by .NET.

❑ **Chapter 2 – Cryptography in .NET**
In this chapter, we take our first look at .NET's cryptographic services. We will explore the class model in detail, uncovering how it works with streams and cryptographic transforms, and how it can be extended with new algorithms and implementations.

❑ **Chapter 3 – Data Integrity – Hash Codes and Signatures**
In this chapter, you'll learn how to apply hashing techniques to ensure no one has tampered with your data. We'll explore basic hashing, keyed hashes, digital signatures, and the XML Signatures standard.

❑ **Chapter 4 – Securing Persisted Data**
In this chapter we examine protecting data that is stored for long periods in some sort of semi-permanent storage. Along the way, you'll see how to store encrypted data in files, XML documents, and databases. We'll also look at support for operating system features such as the encrypting file system (EFS), and what role these technologies can play in a secure application.

❑ **Chapter 5 – Securing Data Over the Wire**
In this chapter, we focus on how to use encryption and authentication to secure communication between components in a distributed system. We'll examine both automatic (transparent) encryption that is built into your transport format (for example, you might use SSL) and using the .NET Framework's cryptographic classes to selectively encrypt portions of the data before it is sent in a message.

❑ **Chapter 6 – Key and Certificate Management**
Key management is one of the most important aspects of cryptography, yet it is often the least well understood. This chapter will help you find out how keys are stored in Windows and how to access them using the .NET environment. We'll also examine the concepts behind digital certificates, what certificates really are, what to use certificates for, and how to manage certificates.

❑ **Chapter 7 – Cryptography – Best and Worst Practices**
To create secure code, the developer not only needs to understand cryptography theory and the concepts presented throughout this book, but attention to detail. This chapter looks at some good practices you should implement and worst practices you should avoid.

❑ **Chapter 8 – Designing Secure Applications**
This chapter presents an end-to-end example that pulls together multiple techniques from the earlier chapters. It demonstrates a "virtual hard drive" web service that allows users to securely store and retrieve any type of data on a remote server.

❑ **Appendix A – Transport Layer Security**

❑ **Appendix B – Generating Secure Randomness**

What do you Need to Use this Book?

This section details the software you will need to run the example code presented in this book.

❑ **.NET Framework SDK** – this is obviously required to develop and run the C# code presented in this book. Although not absolutely necessary, using Visual Studio .NET is recommended, especially when working with Windows Forms applications.

❑ **SQL Server 2000** – The examples of storing encrypted or hashed data in this book use SQL Server 2000 but in principle, these could be adapted to almost any database.

❑ **Microsoft Windows 2000** (or better) – a lot of cryptographic support is only available in the more modern versions of Windows. To get the most out of this book it is recommended that you at least have access to Windows 2000 Professional (with the high encryption pack, http://www.microsoft.com/windows2000/downloads/ recommended/encryption/), although Windows XP Professional (or in the future .NET server) would be better.

The .NET Framework only provides limited support for working with certificate stores on Windows. In Chapter 6, we use two additional libraries that provide additional support for working with certificates.

❑ **CAPICOM** – this provides a simple COM interface to much of the Windows Cryptographic API. CAPICOM 2.0 is available for download from http://www.microsoft.com/downloads/search.asp?. Choose Keyword Search and use CAPICOM as the keyword.

❑ **Web Service Enhancements for .NET** – This .NET library is principally aimed at web services developers but we make use of the added certificate support that it offers; it is available from http://msdn.microsoft.com/webservices/building/wse/.

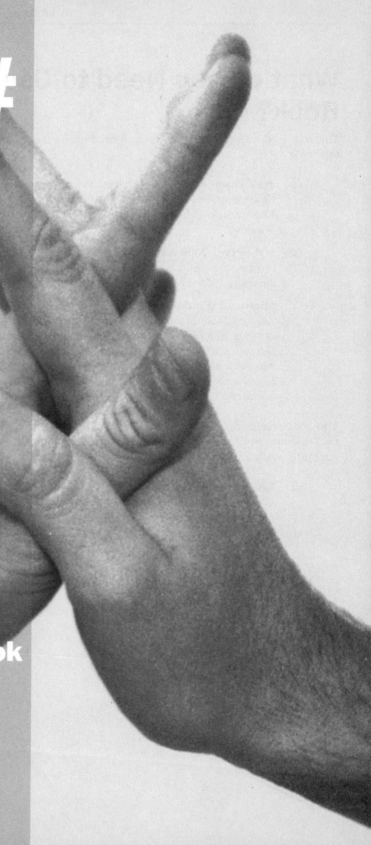

C#

Data Security

Handbook

1

Introduction to Cryptography

Do you ever think of where your e-mail goes when you click send in your e-mail client? No? Well you're probably not alone leaving the technical aspects of transferring the message to the intended recipients to your software, but there are reasons to take an interest. E-mail, it turns out, is not as reliable or trustworthy as most of us like to pretend. Messages traveling between e-mail users can be intercepted and read as easily as a postcard. Not only that, but they can be altered, replaced, or forged without any of the parties being aware. Now, obtaining access to a network in order to cause such mischief isn't trivial, but compromised servers, DNS attacks, and even abuses by people in a legitimate position of authority, such as a system administrator, all make such security breaches possible. So if we want to conduct private business, or be assured that e-mails we receive really do come from who they claim they come from, and haven't been altered in transit, then we can't rely on e-mail to provide the facilities. These are all problems of **data security**. The solutions are to be found in the arcane mathematical science of **cryptography**.

Although e-mail messaging is an obvious case where data security risks are prevalent, the same goes for sensitive information located in your trustworthy old company intranet. There are countless cases where confidential information has been stolen from internal file systems and sold to competitors. People spend a lot of time worrying about attacks from outside their network, but a significant number of security breaches (or successful attacks, depending on your perspective) are inside jobs. With this in mind, you should consider the security of internally accessible information as well as protecting yourself from outside attacks.

Cryptography is not a panacea. Unless it is applied correctly, the assumed protection is no more than an illusion. Many of the crucial aspects of implementing a cryptographic system are handled by convenient tools and services available in many software and programming environments. But we can't simply run a program, or call an API, and expect, like a magic wand, to make our data security problems go away. Cryptography is a complex science, and we need to tread carefully. The .NET Framework has most of the facilities you need when securing data and this handbook is of course all about how to make best use of them – we'll look at how we can use those facilities to create systems that offer genuine security benefits.

Brief History

Cryptographic techniques have been in use for thousands of years. In pre-digital days, encryption operated on text. Nowadays, we can encrypt anything that we can represent in binary digits, through digital cryptography, but two key cryptographic terms are still used from earlier times. The message we want to encrypt is known as the **plaintext**; the encrypted message is called the **ciphertext**.

Early cryptographic techniques were character-based, like substitution or transposition ciphers, or word-based, like codes. Substitution ciphers replace each plaintext character with a ciphertext character (for example, A maps to G, B maps to K, etc.), and transposition ciphers basically shuffle all plaintext symbols around, according to some predefined rules. Codes are based on whole words/phrases and require a codebook or similar to translate the codes into understandable sentences. Codes only define mappings from symbols to a certain set of words, so are not often applicable outside a certain field, and are not a general cryptographic technique.

Cryptography slowly evolved from these basic principles during the following centuries, but improved substantially in the 15th century when Leon Battista Alberti from Italy published the first poly-alphabetic cipher. This polyalphabetic cipher was much harder to break than the substitution and transposition ciphers, and was still in use during the American Civil War.

The serious study of cryptography and number theory led to the discovery of the perfect cryptosystem early in the 20th Century. It's called the **one-time pad**, and it really cannot be broken at all. Using a completely random sequence of symbols (the pad) the same length as the text you want to encode, you encrypt each symbol in the text with the corresponding symbol in the pad. The resulting text is completely undecipherable without the pad itself. The pad is destroyed after having been used to encrypt and decrypt one message – it is used one time only, hence the name.

Like almost all mathematically perfect things, there's a catch. This solution is not practicable for most cryptographic applications, because the person sending the message and the person receiving it must both have access to exactly the same pad, which is exactly the same length as the message. The problem is, the pad must be kept just as secret as the message we wanted to send in the first place – how can we transmit the pad, if we couldn't transmit the message? Nonetheless, one-time pads can be (and are) used for certain specialized high-security applications. Two copies of a number of pads are distributed in advance to the two parties, and each is used once, and destroyed immediately after use.

All such character-based ciphers were typically performed using mental calculation and a pen and paper. By the time of World War II (1939-1945), electromechanical machines were beginning to perform complex polyalphabetic cipher algorithms, making complex cryptosystems available for even quite simple message transmission. A famous example of such a machine, which used rotors to perform encryption and decryption, was the German Enigma.

The effort to break such ciphers led directly to the development of computer technology, and that led to the development of digital cryptography. With digital systems, cryptographers turned their attention from encrypting characters to encrypting binary data – in other words encrypting numbers, and they were able to bring a lot of mathematical ideas to bear that simply hadn't been relevant to the previous encryption paradigm. At the same time, a lot of existing character-based techniques had direct digital equivalents, including one-time pads.

1976 was a great year for mathematical cryptography, because of two major events. First, IBM and the US NSA (National Security Agency) invented the Data Encryption Standard (DES) algorithm that is still in wide use today – it may no longer be regarded as the most secure algorithm in existence, but it is a benchmark by which others are judged. Second, Whitfield Diffie and Martin Hellman published the paper *New Directions in Cryptography*, which introduced the world to asymmetric cryptography, or Public Key Cryptography (PKC) as it is also called. Modern digital cryptography picks up from this point, and these techniques are the basis for what we do today.

Basics of Cryptography

Although modern cryptography is based on math, it isn't necessary to understand all of the complex numerical methodology behind it to make good use of it. This section will actually not go into any mathematical operations at all, it will discuss cryptographic terminology and simple applications.

The ancient attempts at cryptography were designed to keep information secret, but secrecy itself is not enough if you want communicate securely with someone else. This has naturally been identified in history, and modern cryptography now manages:

❏ **Secrecy** – keeping information secret

❏ **Integrity** – knowing information hasn't been tampered with

❏ **Authentication** – knowing the origin and destination of information

❏ **Non-repudiation** – knowing that information, once sent, cannot be retracted or denied

So cryptography isn't entirely about rendering data useless to someone without the right key, but can also be used to make sure data hasn't changed over time, that an entity really has the necessary credentials to access something, and to prove that an entity actually did perform a certain action. All these features add up to a great toolkit for you to apply in your business to make sure things happen exactly as they are intended.

Definitions

Cryptography has been practiced for many years, originally in a secretive and rather closed community. As you'd expect, then, it is as riddled with jargon as computer science is. There are some basic definitions discussed here that are almost impossible to avoid even for the simplest applications that need cryptography. They will be explained later in more detail; this list is just a warm up and may help you through the next sections.

❏ **Plaintext** – All data that is processed by some cryptographic algorithm is called plaintext before it has been processed. It doesn't matter if it really consist of plain text, an image or anything else.

❏ **Ciphertext** – As plaintext is the data before processed by a cryptographic algorithm, ciphertext is the product of an encryption process.

❏ **Encryption** – The process that scrambles data (plaintext) into a lump of apparently incoherent data (ciphertext). Also called **enciphering**.

❏ **Decryption** – The opposite of an encryption process. It restores ciphertext to plaintext again. Also called **deciphering**.

❏ **Cipher** – A cryptographic algorithm that can encrypt and decrypt data is called a cipher. As a cipher can both encrypt and decrypt, it is said to be a two-way or reversible algorithm.

❏ **Key** – A key is a parameter used by many ciphers to control the result. Two different keys will produce different ciphertext from the same plaintext.

❏ **Message digest** – A small fixed-size byte representation of a plaintext of any-size. An algorithm that produces such a message digest is called a message digest algorithm. A message digest algorithm is not reversible; it is one-way only.

❏ **Hash** – Another name for a message digest. A hash algorithm may also be called a hash function. Generating a hash may be referred to as hashing.

Two other terms deserve a bit more discussion: cryptographic protocols, and cryptanalysis.

Cryptographic Protocols

A cryptographic protocol is a strict procedure definition that describes how cryptography should be applied in a certain scenario. When two parties agree to exchange data using cryptography, they must agree on a protocol. The protocol sets out what each party must do at each stage in the interaction in order for the protocol to continue. So, a party might have to encrypt a message, or generate a random number, or transmit a message to another party.

To help describe protocols, cryptography literature uses a number of traditional actors, who help us act out cryptographic scenarios:

❑   **Alice** – first participant, a typical user

❑   **Bob** – second participant, also a typical user

❑   **Eve** – eavesdrops on information sent between the participants

❑   **Mallory** – malicious active attacker

❑   **Trent** – trusted arbitrator

Alice, Bob, Eve, Mallory, and Trent have an illustrious history in the literature, and they'll be playing their part in this book too.

Cryptanalysis

As cryptography is used to keep information confidential (or maintain its integrity, or authenticate someone, or guarantee non-repudiation), there are of course people who are bent on reading the confidential information (or changing it, or impersonating someone, or claiming they didn't do something they did, or did something they didn't). The science of discovering how to breach cryptography is called **cryptanalysis**. A cryptanalyst seeks to '**break**' the ciphertext or the algorithms by **analyzing** anything available like parts of ciphertext or plaintext, in order to recover either the plaintext or the key (which probably will give them the plaintext eventually). Cryptanalysts may also analyze protocols and algorithms for weaknesses that can be exploited by the participants, so that they can obtain information they shouldn't, or feed inaccurate information to another person.

Cryptanalysis is a crucial branch of cryptography – it ensures that weak algorithms and protocols are discovered, and abandoned. The algorithms and protocols used in cryptographic applications today have been subjected to enormous cryptanalytical efforts and been found to withstand them. It's only through continual cryptanalysis that we are able to claim any cryptosystem is actually secure.

One of the fundamental principles of modern cryptography is that a cryptosystem can only be deemed secure if the information we want to keep secret remains secret, even when an attacker has complete access to the details of its implementation, the protocol and algorithms in use, and any messages exchanged between the participants. There is no security in obscurity; using a custom protocol we developed and our own home-made algorithms offers no guarantees of security, just because we keep them secret. On the contrary, we should only use published protocols and algorithms that have been subjected to rigorous cryptanalysis; this will ensure that we benefit from the efforts of other people, who are almost inevitably more talented cryptologists than we are.

Cryptographic Functions

Let's look now at those basic cryptographic functions we mentioned before:

- ❑ **Secrecy**
- ❑ **Integrity**
- ❑ **Authentication**
- ❑ **Non-repudiation**

Secrecy

Secrecy is important in a number of circumstances. If we're storing data we don't want others to see, or transmitting it to a specific person or group and mean to keep it from anyone else, we need a way to ensure secrecy. Let's examine a scenario where secrecy might be required.

Information Exchange

In the information exchange scenario, Alice writes and sends an e-mail to Bob.

Figure 1

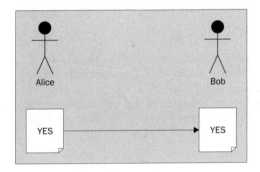

1. Alice creates a text message

2. Alice sends the message to Bob

3. Bob reads the message

In this case, the message reaches Bob without being read or tampered with on the way.

Since an e-mail is no more than a plain text file (binary attachments are encoded to text), where all content may be read or decoded by anyone that get hold of it, it poses several different security risks:

❑ The content may be read by someone unintended

❑ Any part of the e-mail may be altered by someone with ill intent, like the sender address, the recipient address list, the content, timestamps, etc.

❑ The recipients may not be whoever you think they are

❑ The sender may not be whoever you think they are

There is more than one way to read messages that travel across the different networks around the globe, and while it may not always be as simple as it sometimes may sound in the press, the possibility for malicious or just curious parties to read unprotected e-mail is very real. In this case, Alice sends the same message as before to Bob, but this time Eve listens in what is called a passive attack.

Figure 2

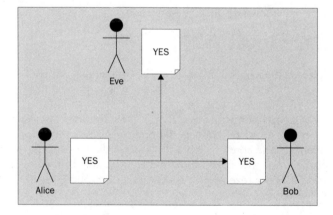

1. Alice creates a text message

2. Alice sends the message to Bob

3. Eve reads the message

4. Bob reads the message

Even though the message content isn't altered on the way, just having Eve listening in may have disastrous consequences depending on the information.

Let's now introduce a new malicious party, Mallory, who intercepts and alters the message from Alice to Bob.

Figure 3

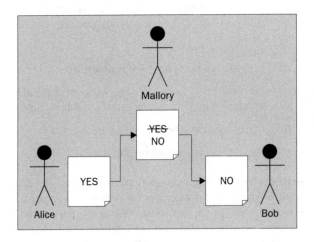

1. Alice creates a text message

2. Alice sends the message to Bob

3. Mallory intercepts and alters the message

4. Bob reads the altered message

Mallory not only reads the original message, he also alters the content before relaying it to Bob.

The obvious way to keep information secure from unauthorized disclosure is to encrypt it. The encryption process renders the original plaintext into apparently meaningless ciphertext. The core of such a process is called a **cryptographic algorithm** or **cipher**. A cipher must be reversible to be able to recover the plaintext from the ciphertext, and the reverse process is called decryption. Figure 1 illustrates how a typical cipher works:

Figure 4

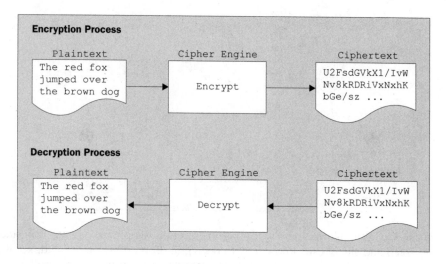

It's clear that the ciphertext, although it appears meaningless, must actually be meaningful to the cipher engine. The cipher engine must know an algorithm to convert the plaintext into a particular ciphertext message that it also knows how to convert back into the original plaintext. The relationship between the ciphertext and the plaintext needs to be a secret, in order to keep the plaintext secret.

Information Exchange Protocols

Let's take this and apply it on the information exchange scenario to see if Alice and Bob can use it to communicate without having to worry about Eve or Mallory. This simple example will show how we begin to develop and analyze cryptographic protocols.

Alice and Bob will use a simple cryptographic protocol in this instance:

1. Alice encrypts her plaintext message with an agreed cipher

2. Alice sends the ciphertext to Bob

3. Bob decrypts the ciphertext with the same agreed cipher

Now, what happens when Eve and Mallory try to interfere? First, let's look at the eavesdropping case:

Figure 5

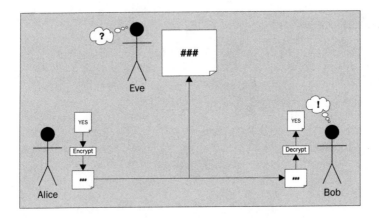

As you can see in the illustration, Eve cannot interpret the simple message to Bob since it is encrypted and she doesn't know how to decrypt it. Bob on the other hand, knows how to decrypt it and can therefore read it. So, cryptography can clearly be used to protect information being exchanged between two or more parties from passive attacks. Let's see if we can use secrecy to protect the information from active attacks as well.

Figure 6

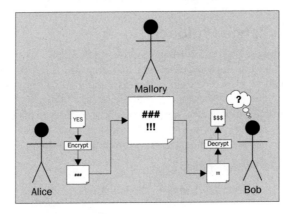

Although it is an improvement, secrecy cannot prevent ciphertext from being tampered with. It does however provide some protection anyway since Mallory cannot produce a ciphertext that will become meaningful plaintext to Bob after he decrypts it, unless he knows how Alice encrypted the plaintext to begin with.

It is important that Alice and Bob are clear on the agreement to secure the data this way, it is otherwise possible for Mallory to fake a message to Bob anyway, even though he can't read the original message from Alice:

Figure 7

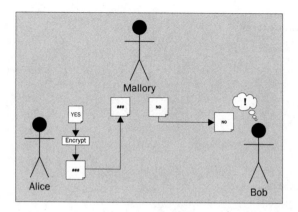

This particular example maybe is a little dramatic since it isn't likely Mallory will fake a NO to Bob without knowing anything about the content in the original message, but it does underline the importance of Bob knowing for sure the message from Alice is supposed to be encrypted!

This emphasizes the role of cryptographic protocols. If Bob and Alice are to effectively communicate, without Mallory getting in the way, they must agree – and stick to – a clear protocol. If the party they're dealing with deviates from the protocol, or can't fulfill a part of the protocol, then it should set off alarm bells that maybe Mallory has been trying to interfere.

Introducing the Key

A cipher is used to encrypt plaintext to get ciphertext and to decrypt ciphertext to recover the plaintext, but if it always encrypts the plaintext the same way every time, it isn't very secure. It won't take very long before such a cipher is useless since anyone with access to the cipher is able to decrypt the ciphertext. Remember we said we always wanted to use published algorithms, and not rely on security through obscurity. The choice of the mechanism used to perform encryption and decryption should not really form part of the secret part of our protocol. If Eve or Mallory in the above scenarios were to work out the algorithm being used by Alice and Bob (which cryptographic experience tells us is only a matter of time, if Alice and Bob keep on using the same algorithm) their attempts to read or replace the messages could be successful.

For a cipher to produce ciphertext that no one else can decrypt, even if they know what the cipher mechanism is, it needs a user-defined parameter to the encryption or decryption process, and that parameter is called a **key** in cryptography. The key (or keys in some algorithms) is the single most important part of a cipher except the algorithm itself, and all ciphertext is only as protected as the decryption key is.

Figure 8

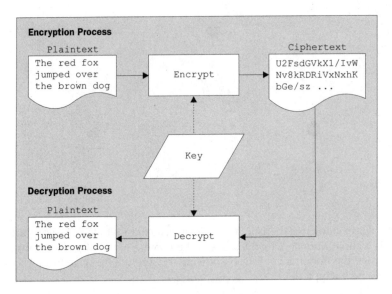

The key is, then, an input into both the encryption and decryption processes, and allows the same cipher to produce a different effect each time it is used, simply by using a different key. This enables us to use one robust algorithm, and vary our key, keeping the key secret, but not worrying whether Eve or Mallory find out which algorithm we're using.

With a key, the scenario where the message sent from Alice to Bob is encrypted would then look like this:

Figure 9

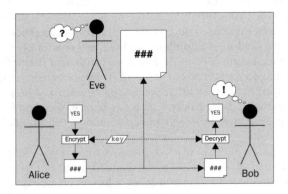

This example makes it clear that Eve cannot read the message since she doesn't have the key, but let's also have a look a the related case where Mallory tries to fool Bob by altering the message even though he doesn't have the key.

Figure 10

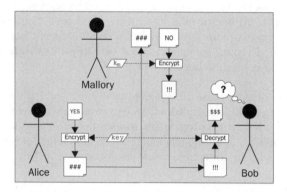

Mallory can't read the message from Alice, and if he tries to fake an encrypted message to Bob, he will have to use another key than that which Alice and Bob use. When Bob decrypts the ciphertext from Mallory, it will only be garbage.

What Mallory actually does in this case is pretty pointless since Bob isn't fooled, and if he is looking to disrupt the communication between Alice and Bob, he can as well send any random data to Bob.

Now, one thing you'll notice is that Alice and Bob both need to use a key, and as we said, they need to keep it secret to ensure the message is kept secret as well. This looks like a chicken and egg problem; if they couldn't send the message without Eve or Mallory getting hold of it, how can they send the key without the same thing happening? The key's just another message, after all. We'll look at how Alice and Bob can come to have the same key without having to send it in a message later in the chapter. We'll also see that in some cases, Alice and Bob don't need the same key – just two keys that are closely related.

Single key systems are called symmetric ciphers. Dual key systems are asymmetric ciphers. Let's look now at how both of these basic cryptographic tools are employed.

Symmetric Ciphers

The example where the message from Alice to Bob is encrypted is a typical example where a symmetric cipher is well suited. These are called symmetric because the same key is used to both encrypt and decrypt, that is, if the key k is use to encrypt `'plaintext'` into `'NajDs78a'`, the key k is also used to decrypt `'NajDs78a'` to recover `'plaintext'`. Symmetric ciphers are also called **secret** or **session** keys because all communicating parties must secretly share these keys, sometimes through a session of some kind. They are sometimes called **one-key** and **single-key** as well, because the same key is used both to encrypt and decrypt.

There are two categories of symmetric ciphers that are designed with slightly different areas of application in mind, namely **block** and **stream** ciphers. Symmetric ciphers may also operate in different **cryptographic modes** depending on the exact usage. The modes differ regarding security, efficiency, and fault-tolerance. For example, a mode that increases security for a cipher may also propagate an error from one iteration to another.

Block Ciphers

Block ciphers process plaintext or ciphertext one block at a time. Operating on chunks of data allows for complex cryptographic techniques to be applied – the larger the block, the greater the security possible. However, the larger the block, the more complex the maths becomes, and the slower the process of encrypting or decrypting gets. In modern cryptography, block sizes of 8 to 16 bytes have been proven to represent a compromise manageable and secure size. The ciphertext blocks are always equal to the plaintext blocks in size, and the remaining bytes of the last plaintext block (if the plaintext isn't evenly dividable by the block size) have to be **padded** before encryption.

To illustrate padding, lets say we want to encrypt the plaintext 'This is a sample text to illustrate padding' using a block cipher with a block size of 8 bytes. Since the plaintext length is 43 bytes (using 8-bit characters), the algorithm will have to use 6 blocks and we'll end up with a remainder of 5 bytes in the last block that the plaintext doesn't fill out.

Figure 11

In this case, the last 5 bytes are padded using the '#' character. The cryptographic library in .NET includes automatic padding, but you should always make certain since insufficient padding can in the worst case help adversaries to recover the key.

Having broken up the plaintext into blocks, there are several ways to process the blocks to generate ciphertext (with analogous inverse techniques for decryption). They are known as block cipher **modes**.

ECB – Electronic Code Book

The ECB mode of operation is pretty straightforward. Encryption means each plaintext block is processed with the key as the only other input, producing a ciphertext block. Decryption is simply operating the process backwards. This mode is fairly easy (from a cryptanalyst's perspective, relative the other modes) to analyze when the plaintext consists of predictable patterns like simple text, because every plaintext block will always transform into the same ciphertext block given the same key. This means that if the same block of characters occurs twice in the same message, or in two messages encrypted with the same key, then the same block of ciphertext will occur in both cases. This can give cryptanalysts clues about structure, which can help them guess at the underlying plaintext, which can vastly accelerate their discovery of the key. Typical examples that help cryptanalysts are the common salutations in letters and memos, like 'Hi' or 'Hello', or any static data-chunks that occur at well-defined points in a message like an e-mail header, letterhead, or footer. Consequently, the ECB mode produces much more secure ciphertext on random plaintext than it does on structured, character-oriented text.

Figure 12

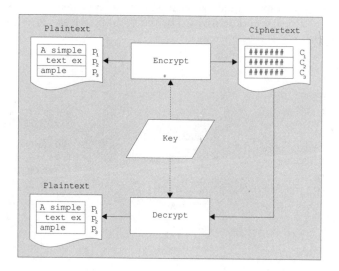

CBC – Cipher Block Chaining

This mode takes care of the problems caused by ECB's consistent transformation of matching blocks by combining sequential blocks together. This means that the ciphertext for any particular block ultimately depends on the ciphertext for every preceding block, which means that the same block of plaintext appearing twice in the same message, or in two different messages, but preceded by different plaintext, will generate two different blocks of ciphertext. But there's one problem this leaves. We talked before about how message headers are often identical from one message to another; this means that often, the same plaintext block might occur in different messages, preceded by exactly the same sequences of plaintext blocks.

This means messages with identical headers could end up encrypting to ciphertexts with identical sequences of blocks at the start. We overcome this using an Initialization Vector (IV). The purpose of the IV is to add security to the ciphertext by acting as an input to the encryption of the first block. Using different IVs for every message makes it possible to use common headers without compromising the security since they are altered according to the IV before encryption. The IV doesn't have to be secret, so it may very well be sent together with the ciphertext unencrypted. This often surprises people new to cryptography, but it's true – the IV should not be treated as another key; it's just a random value that adds security but contains no data.

So how does CBC work? The first plaintext block is XOR'd with the IV, then encrypted. The second block is XOR'd with the first ciphertext block, then encrypted, and so it continues. Each of the following blocks is XOR'd with the previous ciphertext block before encryption. The plaintext block and IV or previous ciphertext block are XOR'd before the encryption which means that the IV affects the resulting ciphertext as much as the plaintext. Changing the IV for the same plaintext results in different ciphertext.

This mode is well suited for normal plaintext like documents, images and spreadsheets because of the enhanced security provided by the IV and feedback from the previous iteration.

Figure 13

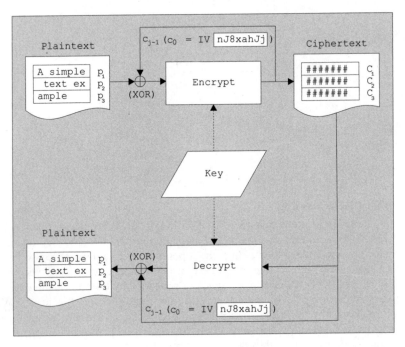

The diagram illustrates how each plaintext block is first XOR'd with the IV (first block only) or feedback (previous ciphertext block) before it is encrypted. c_0 represents the IV value (nJ8xahJj in this example) that is XOR'd with the first plaintext block, and c_{j-1} represents the feedback ciphertext blocks used for all plaintext blocks after the first one.

Decryption takes the IV and XORs it with the first decrypted ciphertext block to recover the first plaintext block, and all following ciphertext blocks are XOR'd with the previous ciphertext block to recover the rest of the plaintext.

Now that you see how each ciphertext block is reused in the same way as the IV is used for the first block, it is also apparent that it doesn't have to be kept secret. Otherwise you would have to protect all ciphertext blocks as well!

Stream ciphers

Block ciphers operate most efficiently when the data to be processed is already in memory, in a large buffer. They can divide the buffer into blocks, and process each in turn. But sometimes, we don't have all the data we want to encrypt available immediately; it might still be coming in across a network, or we might be waiting for the user to type the next character. In these circumstances, we might not have a full block's worth of data to process all at once. For these purposes, we can use stream ciphers.

True stream ciphers do not have a key in the sense block ciphers do, they use something called a running-key or keystream generator instead. The keystream generator can output a constant stream of random bits, each of which we can XOR with a single bit from our plaintext. This results in a single bit of ciphertext. To decrypt, we need an identical keystream, and we can again XOR each bit of ciphertext with a bit in the keystream, to recover the plaintext. The task of a stream cipher is therefore to produce a stream of bits that is apparently random and unpredictable, but the stream must also be completely reproducible in order to decrypt the ciphertext.

Figure 14

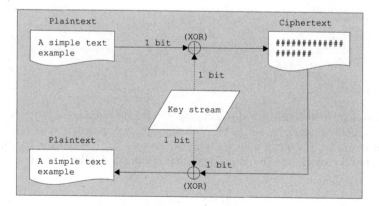

It is possible to gain stream cipher properties by operating a block cipher in certain modes that use a single key to produce a keystream. Two such modes are CFB and OFB.

CFB – Cipher Feedback

This operation mode is similar to CBC but it allows us to reduce the number of processed plaintext bits in each block operation. These reduced blocks are called 'units' or 'sections' and can actually be as small as a single bit. However, it is still necessary to execute a full block size transformation of each section, so this system results in reduced performance compared with the ECB or CBC modes. This mode is also called a self-synchronizing stream cipher.

Figure 15

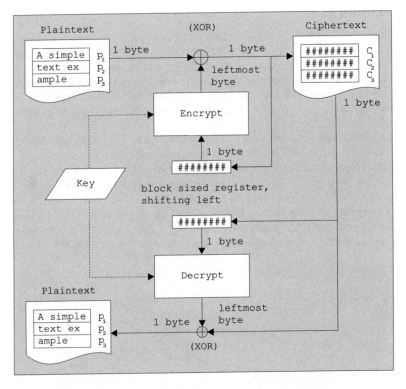

This diagram may look somewhat discouraging, but it isn't as bad as it may seem. This mode may actually operate on single bits, but that isn't very practical since a full block encryption operation is executed for each bit, which more or less renders the cipher a factor equal to the block size (in bits) slower than if operated in ECB or CBC mode.

The example above uses a cipher block size of 8 bytes and a CFB unit size of 1 byte, which also means a register size of 8 bytes will be used since the size of the register is equal to the block size. The cipher initializes the register with an IV, as in the CBC mode (this one doesn't have to be protected either), and then processes one byte at a time. The register is encrypted and the leftmost byte of the encryption result is XOR'd with the plaintext byte. The ciphertext byte is then left shifted into the register before the next encryption.

The decryption works the other way around, also starting off with a register initialized with an IV (the same as used at encryption) and processing a byte at a time.

A cipher operating in this mode can easily encrypt data as it is typed by a user, one character keypress at a time.

OFB – Output Feedback

This stream cipher mode is very similar to CFB, but it differs in the way feedback bits are used. Where CFB uses feedback from the ciphertext, OFB uses feedback bits from the encryption computation before XORing them with the next plaintext bits. This mode is also called a synchronous stream cipher.

Figure 16

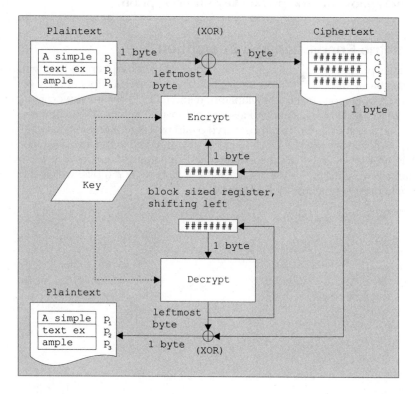

Asymmetric Ciphers

Having looked at single key systems, as we said before there are some systems that use two keys. These **asymmetric ciphers** use two different, but mathematically related keys such that plaintext encrypted with one key can only decrypted with the other key. Not even the key used to encrypt the data can be used to decrypt it.

Asymmetric cryptography is often called 'public key cryptography'. Rather than having a single key that must be kept secret between two parties, public key cryptography has one key, the private key, that must be kept secret by a single party, and a second key, called the public key, that can be given freely to anybody who wishes to communicate with them.

This mechanism makes it possible to communicate securely with entities over the Internet without any previous contact; this is the technology behind secure web communication, which has enabled electronic commerce.

> **With some asymmetric algorithms, it is possible to use either one of the keys to encrypt data to be decrypted with the other key. In general, though, the public key is used for encryption and the private key for decryption.**

Asymmetric Encryption and Decryption

Asymmetric ciphers work slightly differently from symmetric ciphers. Where symmetric ciphers treat keys and data as basically lines of bits, asymmetric ciphers carry out mathematical operations (such as multiplication and modulo arithmetic) on numbers, so we have to divide binary data into a series of binary numbers. These binary numbers serve as blocks for asymmetric cryptography. To get numbers that can work together, it's necessary that the block length is always equal to the length of the key. If the key is 1024 bits (128 bytes), the plaintext and ciphertext blocks will be 128 bytes as well. The following examples use a key length of 32 bytes = 256 bits, which is rather shorter than most asymmetric ciphers use.

Figure 17

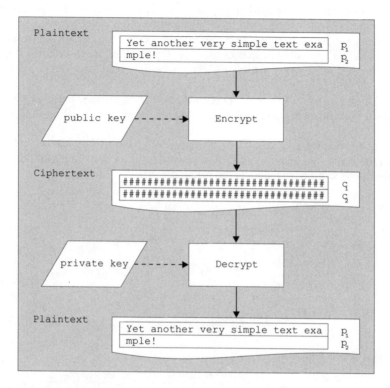

Using a public key to encrypt data is secure, because even though the public key may be known even to malicious eavesdroppers, it cannot be used to decrypt data. Only the private key, which is kept securely by one user, can decrypt the message. So Bob can encrypt a message with Alice's public key, secure in the knowledge that only Alice, not Eve or Mallory or even Bob himself, can read the message.

Integrity

It is sometimes important to make sure published information does not change over time, like a contract or software modules. This is called **data integrity** in cryptographic terms and often works as a complement to securing information from public view. In some cases, like the software module case, the sole purpose is to guarantee the content of the module hasn't changed since it was deployed or even created. .NET itself uses an extensive cryptosystem based on asymmetric cryptography to ensure that strong-named assemblies aren't modified after their creation.

Cryptographic algorithms that provide data integrity are called hash or message digest algorithms and the process of applying them is similar to the encryption process with one major difference; the encryption process is a two-way reversible process whereas a hash or message digest is one-way only. The results or products of a hash or message digest computation are called hashes or message digests, and are a small fixed-sized representation of the plaintext, which will always be the same for a certain plaintext.

Essentially, hashes provide one-way encryption. You can't recreate the plaintext from the hash, but you can verify if two plaintexts are the same by comparing their hashes.

In order to be useful for cryptographic purposes, each hash value must be relatively unique, in the sense it is extremely difficult to write a different meaningful plaintext that results in the same hash value as the original.

Figure 18

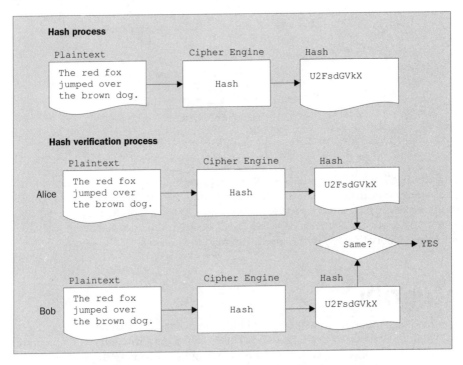

In the illustration above, Alice writes a message, computes a hash and sends the message and hash to Bob. Bob also computes a hash from the message and compares the hash with the one he got from Alice. If they match he knows the message is intact.

Let's see how hashes fit into our basic information exchange scenario.

Figure 19

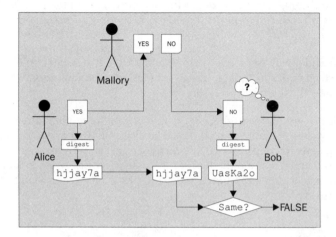

In this case, Mallory somehow doesn't get hold of the digest that is sent to Bob along with the message. Bob must have the digest as well to be able to verify the message integrity by comparing the digests with each other. Since Mallory only intercepts and alters the message, it is easy for Bob to see that the message has changed by computing a message digest from the message himself, and comparing the result with the digest sent by Alice. However, it is likely that Mallory could also get hold of the digest, and then he can forge the digest as well.

Figure 20

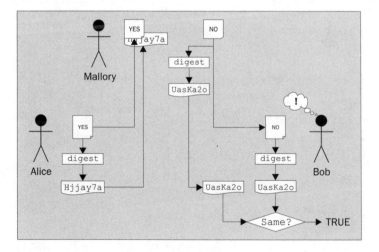

In this case, Mallory intercepts both the message and the digest value. He then forges a new message and computes a new digest for that message and then sends them to Bob. Since the digest is produced from the forged message, Bob cannot determine it has been forged.

So we need to find a way to secure the hash and ensure that it can't be duplicated. There are two techniques for doing this, called Message Authentication Codes, and Digital Signatures. We'll look at both shortly.

Hashes can also be useful for storing data that you want to be able to compare to other data, but don't want to be able to read. A classic example is a password file. There's no need to store passwords in plain text in a database; we can store hashes of the passwords, and then recalculate the hash of the user password when it is entered, and see if the hash matches the hash in our password file. If the hashes match, the password is correct.

MAC – Message Authentication Code

A MAC is a symmetric cryptographic technique that provides a secure message digest format. A MAC is calculated just like a hash, but with the addition of a cryptographic key to protect the hash value from being tampered with. With this technique, it is possible to trust the integrity of data even if it is sent over the Internet. The MAC technique plays an important role in Internet transport-level security protocols like TLS and SSL because of its superior performance compared with other techniques like digital signatures.

It isn't possible to forge a MAC without knowing the key the intended audience expects the MAC to have been encoded with, which makes it impossible for Mallory to fake a message and MAC to Bob. Let's have a look at the information exchange case where Mallory fakes a message to Bob again.

Figure 21

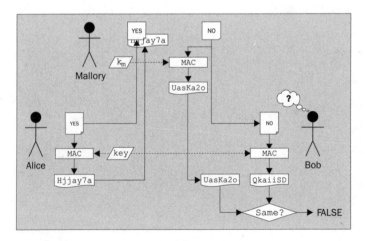

This case is similar to the case where the message is encrypted and Mallory tries to fake a message using a key of his own, which is pretty pointless if Bob follows the protocol he agreed upon with Alice since Bob easily can discover the MAC doesn't authenticate the message. Again, however, we're left needing to share a key between Alice and Bob, and they need to make sure Mallory doesn't get hold of the key.

Notice that the document data here isn't encrypted. There's nothing to stop you combining this protocol with our simple information exchange protocol and exchanging authenticated, encrypted documents.

Signatures

We looked briefly at public key cryptography earlier in the chapter. We said some asymmetric algorithms can perform encryption and decryption with either key. But then we talked about how the public key would be available to everybody (including Eve and Mallory), while we kept hold of the private key. In such circumstances, what possible benefit could there to encrypting with the private key? Since the public key can decrypt a message encrypted in that way, such a message could be decrypted by Eve and Mallory. So there's no point in such a scheme. Or is there?

We can't use this technique to keep data secret, but we can use it to prove that only one person – the holder of the private key – could possibly have encrypted a message that the matching public key decrypts. That's a powerful ability. For that reason, we don't generally refer to these operations as encryption and decryption, but rather as signing and verification.

How does a digital signature prove some plaintext data really was signed by a certain key? In order to be called a signature, it implies the result is a small piece of data that can easily attached to the data that was signed. So to call it signature, a certain process more or less must take place:

1. Run the data through a secure message digest algorithm, like SHA-1

2. Sign the message digest with your private key

This way you will always end up with a signature as long as the length of your key (provided the message digest product is smaller than your key). The technical strength of a signature is defined by the strength of the message digest algorithm, the reliability of the asymmetric cipher and the length of the key.

Figure 22

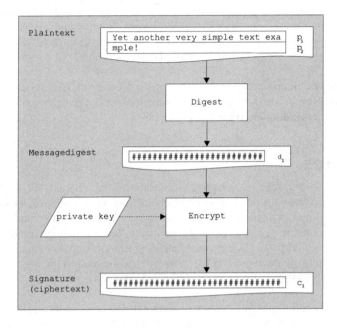

Verification

A signature is verified as easily as it is produced. You need a copy of the original message in the same state it was in when it was signed, the public key, and the signature.

Figure 23

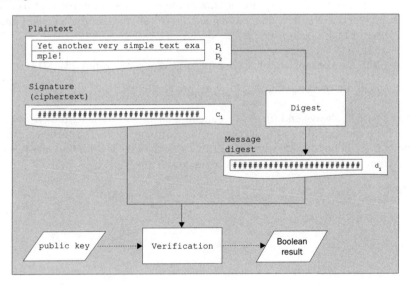

So using this technique, we can produce secure, non-forgeable message digests for our messages, and Alice doesn't have to share a secret key with Bob; to verify her signature, he only needs her public key. Mallory can't forge it because he doesn't have Alice's private key.

Secure Persistence Protocols

Let's look now at a slightly different encryption scenario – although a very common one. This deals with storing data securely on a storage medium that other users can access. This is a straightforward application where two symmetric keys, ks and ki, are used to protect the information (plaintext) called p in this example. Two different secret keys should be used to heighten security. Even if one key is compromised, it is still possible to detect active attacks.

Encrypting the data

Some cipher engines may let you run both MAC and encryption in one pass, but this example shows you each operation that must be taken to secure the data.

Figure 24

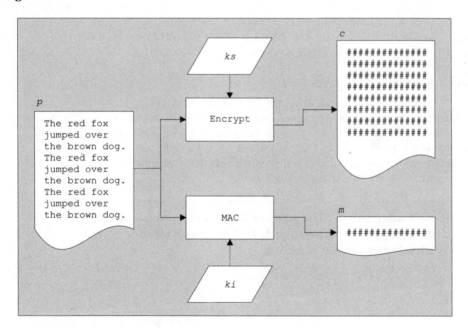

1. generate key (ks) for secrecy

2. generate key (ki) for integrity

3. produce a MAC (*m*) from plaintext *p* using *ki*

4. encrypt plaintext *p* using *ks* to get ciphertext *c*

5. secure the keys *ks* and *ki*

Securing the keys

As you probably already noticed, the weak link in this example is how the keys are secured. It is a common mistake when using cryptography the first time, but it is very important to make sure that the keys are sufficiently secure, or else the whole protection falls. Most operating systems, Windows included, provide a secure store for each user on a machine or network to keep keys in, and use the operating system's built-in security to ensure those keys are only accessible to the correct user. There are, however, a couple of techniques for securing keys outside the operating system that are worth investigating.

PBE – Password Based Encryption

Although not a perfect way to secure a key, passwords, or passphrases may be a suitable protection depending on the circumstances. There are a number of cryptographical techniques for deriving good keys from human-memorable passwords. However, cryptanalysts consider PBE-protected data as compromised at the same moment as the password becomes public. There are techniques to make it harder to guess passwords, but for the most part it is only a matter of time before a good cryptanalyst uncovers a key that is wholly password derived.

PKE – Public Key Encryption

A safer way to secure keys is to use the Public Key Encryption scheme. To use this scheme you need at least one set of asymmetric keys, the public key and the private key. The public key is used to encrypt the secret key you want to protect, and the private key is used to decrypt the key again. This way you only have to have one set of asymmetric keys, and you don't have to worry about where the PKE protected symmetric keys are stored, as they will be safe anyhow.

> **Consider storing the private key on removable media such as a floppy or a smartcard, and storing that media in a physically secure location.**

Decrypting the data

First we have to recover the symmetric keys, using PBE alone or PBE in combination with PKE.

Figure 25

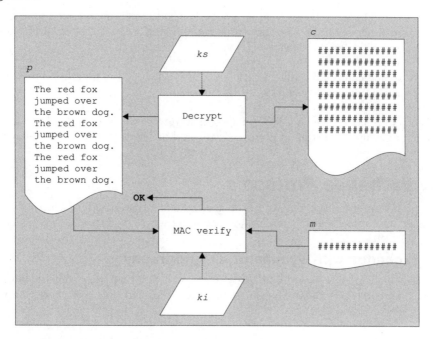

1. recover the keys *ks* and *ki*

2. decrypt ciphertext *c* using *ks* to get plaintext *p*

3. verify the MAC *m* using *p* and *ki*

Authentication

Regardless of technology, the principle is the same for all authentications. The requesting party, human, machine or otherwise must provide the right credentials to gain access to the requested information. The credentials may be something as simple as an IP address or a password, but may also be as sophisticated as a digital certificate combined with biometric equipment reading the iris of the one requesting access.

In our basic scenarios, Alice and Bob could generally be assured of who they were communicating with because only they held the secret keys. We glossed over the question of how they both came to acquire the same secret key; we must assume they've met in person at some point and agreed a key to use.

If Alice and Bob had never met, or if Bob accidentally let slip what their key was in idle conversation with Eve, meaning they had to switch to a new key, then they would have a problem. How could they possibly agree a key? Alice could mail a key to Bob, but how does Bob know the key that arrives isn't one of Mallory's tricks, or that Eve hasn't intercepted the key in transit so she can continue to monitor their conversations.

Even in our public key example, we assumed Alice had somehow managed to give Bob a copy of her public key, but how does Bob know what he thinks is Alice's public key doesn't really belong to Mallory?

We have an authentication problem here, and this is where Trent, the trusted third party, comes in to our discussions.

The problem of how Alice and Bob can agree a secret key without Eve finding out about it, or having to meet up in person is answered by the process of key exchange.

Key Exchange Protocols

There are several cryptographic protocols that cover this scenario, and we'll look at two – one using just symmetric cryptography, and one using some asymmetric techniques.

Key Exchange with Symmetric Cryptography

This protocol includes a trusted third party, Trent, who will hold the symmetric keys used to protect the information. It also assumes that Alice and Bob each share a secret key with Trent (KA and KB).

1. Alice asks Trent for a key to protect communication with Bob.

2. Trent produces a new symmetric key K and encrypts one copy of K with K_A to produce $E_{KA}K$ and another copy of K with K_B to produce $E_{KB}K$. The encrypted keys $E_{KA}K$ and $E_{KB}K$ are distributed to Alice and Bob respectively.

3. Alice decrypts $E_{KA}K$ with K_A to get K.

4. Bob decrypts $E_{KB}K$ with K_B to get K.

5. Alice and Bob use K to communicate safely.

This protocol has a single point of failure in Trent, as he holds all of the trust. If Mallory somehow breaks into Trent, it compromises all communication that uses Trent as trusted arbitrator. Also, all communication security is effectively inhibited if Trent is somehow made unavailable, by a DoS attack for example.

Neither Mallory nor Eve can listen in or alter the communication between Alice and Bob. There are attacks on this basic protocol, which we'll learn more about in later chapters.

This protocol becomes hard to manage in a very large network, because all clients need to have a separate secret key for communicating with Trent.

Key Exchange with Asymmetric Cryptography

This is a slightly more scalable protocol that does not require a previously distributed secret key for Alice and Bob, although they need Trent's public key. It goes like this:

1. Alice generates a public-private key pair.

2. Alice meets up with Trent and gives him a copy of her public key.

3. Trent signs Alice's public key with a note saying he knows it belongs to Alice.

4. Trent gives the signed key back to Alice.

5. Alice sends the signed key to Bob.

6. Bob verifies Trent's signature using Trent's public key. Bob trusts Trent, so he believes the key belongs to Alice.

7. Bob generates a secret key.

8. Bob encrypts the secret key using Alice's public key and sends it to Alice.

9. Alice decrypts the secret key with her private key.

10. Bob and Alice now share the same secret key, and can communicate with it.

In practice, the role played by Trent here is played by companies such as Verisign, who will sign a public key (creating what is known as a certificate) if you can prove that you are who you say you are. Verisign and other certificate authorities have widely distributed public keys, called root certificates, which can be used to verify the identity of anybody who presents a public key signed by them.

These scenarios show how Alice and Bob can establish a common key and be confident of who they share it with. Let's look at a couple more authentication scenarios which revolve around Alice proving her identity not to Bob, but to a computer:

Authentication Using One-Way Functions

1. Alice sends her password to the other the host

2. The host computes the hash value from the password

3. The host compares it with its password database

This is a simple protocol that works well with the current World-Wide-Web browsers, but it isn't secure at all since Alice credentials are sent in clear text. A secure channel like HTTPS (SSL/TLS) MUST complement this cryptographic protocol.

Authentication Using Public Key Cryptography

This protocol provides strong authentication but also requires computations to be made on the client side, which normally aren't included in the common operating systems, which means there must be special software installed in the client computer. It goes like this:

1. The host sends a random value to Alice

2. Alice signs the value with her private key, producing a signature

3. Alice sends the signature to the host

4. The host verifies the signature against the random value and Alice's public key

This last protocol mentions another key cryptographical concept – random numbers. We've talked a lot about protocols where one or other participant must generate a key, as well, and for that task, we also need a cryptographically sound random number. If you use ordinary 'random' numbers in cryptographical applications, you are creating weaknesses in your cryptosystem, because cryptanalysts can attack the mechanism which generates your 'random' numbers, and ultimately predict what the next 'random' number will be. Cryptographically strong random number generators are designed not to be prey to this weakness.

Non-Repudiation

As authentication proves the access rights for someone or something, non-repudiation proves someone really did perform an action or agree on a contract etc. It is sometimes difficult to see the difference between these two, and the techniques involved in non-repudiation may very well be used to authenticate someone. The difference is not as much in the technique as in the intended usage and the context in which they are applied. This is a typical case where a cryptographic protocol is very important.

Non-repudiation is intended to help solve disputes over digital agreements. Let's say Alice promised Bob to buy a first edition copy of *C# Data Security Handbook* from him for $1000 via e-mail, but after delivery she refuses to pay up. The only evidence of an agreement Bob has is an e-mail from Alice, which won't necessarily be evidence enough in court. Alice can claim Bob simply knocked up the e-mail in a copy of notepad. Alice would have a much harder time avoiding payment had the e-mail been signed with a digital signature according to a non-repudiatable cryptographic protocol.

Non-Repudiation Scenarios

In this scenario, Bob is selling Alice a car, which may lead to problems for either Bob or Alice if the other isn't honest. First we have a look at how it should work out in a perfect world (where cryptography wouldn't be necessary).

Figure 26

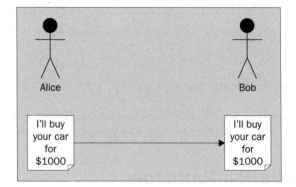

1. Alice send a message to Bob telling him she'll buy his car for $1000

2. Bob reads the message and delivers the car to Alice

3. Alice pay Bob $1000

This is how it should be, Alice and Bob are both honest people and both fulfill the agreement.

It is however possible for either of Alice and Bob to cheat the other depending on how the event unfolds. If Bob requires payment before delivery, he can easily take Alice's money and claim he never got it and therefore doesn't have to deliver his car to her. If Bob delivers his car before payment, Alice can state she already paid Bob and refuse to pay him anything.

This is solved by engaging a trusted third party that can record any agreements Alice and Bob have, like a kind of notary public.

Figure 27

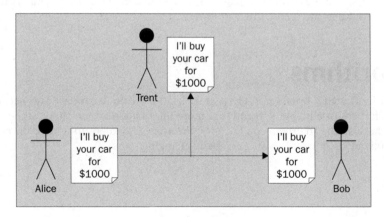

1. Alice sends a message to Bob telling him she'll buy his car for $1000

2. Alice sends the same message to Trent, the trusted third party

3. Bob reads the message and delivers the car to Alice

4. Alice pays Bob $1000

Now, it doesn't matter if Alice or Bob are dishonest or not. Trent has the evidence!

Engaging a third party that record all agreements and transactions between Alice and Bob makes it very difficult for either of them to repudiate any commitments or actions.

Non-Repudiation Protocols

There is a general protocol that lays out the most important aspects of non-repudiation, and it goes like this:

1. Alice writes a message M that she signs, producing the signature S_M.

2. Alice concatenates the signature S_M and an identifying header H to the message M to get a new message $M1$.

3. Alice signs the message $M1$ to get a new signature S_{M1} and sends $M1$ and S_{M1} to Trent.

4. Trent verifies S_{M1} and confirms that the header identifies Alice.

5. Trent concatenates a timestamp T to $M1$ to get a new message $M2$.

6. Trent signs $M2$ to get a signature S_{M2}, and sends $M2$ and S_{M2} to Alice and Bob.

7. Bob verifies Trent's signature S_{M2}, confirms the header identifies Alice and verifies Alice's signature S_{M1}.

8. Alice verifies Trent's signature S_{M2}, that the content is her original content, and that the timestamp T is correct.

Algorithms

We'll finish off with a briefing on the popular algorithms in use today. This section will only touch them briefly, but you can find more information about each of them and lots of others on the Internet. You are strongly advised to keep up to date on news in the security arena since this world is rapidly changing.

Export Considerations

Before January 2000, the US export restrictions on cryptographic software were extensive, not allowing the export of programs that use strong algorithms to other countries at all. Since most of the popular algorithms in use today come from US, this was a major problem. Now the restrictions have loosened up quite a lot, allowing export to all countries except a few embargoed destinations: **Cuba, Iran, Iraq, Libya, North Korea, Sudan, Syria, Serbia, and the Taliban controlled areas of Afghanistan.**

If you plan on using any US invented algorithms, you can distribute your software to any destination but those mentioned above. However, it is entirely possible that your own country disallows you from using encryption. France is one example of a country with very restrictive internal regulations regarding encryption, so you must verify the rules and regulation for each destination you plan on using encryption software, regardless of whether the software comes from the US or not.

Symmetric Ciphers

Some of the most popular symmetric key ciphers are listed below, but there are many others as well. To become popular, the cipher must more or less withstand time. The longer a cipher is used without any known compromises, the more popular it becomes.

❑   **DES – Data Encryption Standard**
Invented by IBM 1970.
Although this cipher probably is the most used one right now, it is not safe enough any longer. There are known successful attacks on this cipher, and it should therefore not be used anywhere high security is imperative.

❑   **Triple DES – Data Encryption Standard**
DES algorithm used three times (also called 3DES or EDE) by simply using three DES keys. The first one encrypts the plaintext, the second 'decrypts' the ciphertext from the first encryption and the third key encrypts the result from the decryption (hence the name EDE) thereby effectively increasing the key length three times. There are no known successful attacks on this cipher, and it may be used for high security encryption.

❑   **Rijndael – AES (Advanced Encryption Standard)**
Developed by Joan Daemen and Vincent Rijmen.
Submitted as a candidate to the AES program, this cipher was selected winner in May 2002. The cipher has of course been in focus since winning the AES title, and is implemented in more and more crypto libraries. This should be the natural choice for most symmetric cryptography applications today.

❑ **Blowfish – Blowfish**
Invented 1993 by Bruce Schneier.
Developed as a 'free to use' alternative to DES. This is a good alternative as long as the key is generated according to recommended guidelines (in practical terms this means keeping the number of rounds to 15 or higher).

❑ **RC2 – Rivest Cipher 2**
Invented by Ron Rivest and trademarked by RSADSI (RSA Data Security). Designed to be a drop-in replacement for DES, but significantly more secure using longer keys, 128 bit or higher.

❑ **RC4 – Rivest Cipher 4**
Originally published anonymously 1994. Invented and trademarked by RSADSI. This is a stream cipher that is being replaced by other options, like 3DES-CBC.

Asymmetric Ciphers

As with the symmetric algorithms, there are certain asymmetric algorithms that have become more popular than others. Some of the most widely accepted asymmetric algorithms are:

❑ **DH – Diffie Hellman**
Invented at Stanford University 1976
This is still a very popular key agreement and key exchange algorithm, being implemented in SSL for example.

❑ **RSA – Rivest, Shamir, and Adelman**
Invented 1977
Very popular Public Key algorithm used in most serious digital signature applications today. The RSA cipher is used in X.509 certificates.

❑ **DSS – Digital Signature Standard (DSA)**
Developed in 1991 by NSA (US National Security Agency)
Developed as the Digital Signature Standard and standardized (in US) later as DSS. The abbreviation DSA is still in use. DSS can only perform signing and verification, and cannot encrypt or decrypt data.

Message Digests, Hashes

❑ **MD2 – Message Digest 2**
Developed by Ron Rivest in 1989
There has been one known successful attack on this algorithm (it showed it was possible to find collisions, that is, meaningful plaintext other than the original that results in the same hash value), and it produces too small a hash value to suffice. There are better replacements of this algorithm listed next.

❑ **MD4 – Message Digest 4**
Developed by Ron Rivest in 1990
This digest is broken. Do not use it under any circumstance.

❑ **MD5 – Message Digest 5**
Developed by Ron Rivest in 1991
This is an acceptable algorithm in many cases, but there are more secure algorithms today.

❑ **SHA-1 – Secure Hashing Algorithm 1**
Developed by NSA (US National Security Agency) in 1995
This is the most commonly used hashing algorithm today, implemented in the TLS protocols and SSL. SHA-1 and it successors are also the preferred choice in digital signatures.

Message Authentication Codes

Some MAC implementations use a password or similar instead of a key, and some combine a key with a password. However, there is more or less only one MAC commonly used today.

❑ **HMAC – Hash-based Message Authentication Code**
Published by Bellare, Canetti, and Krawczyk in 1996
This specification more or less covers all combinations of the popular hashing algorithms and symmetric ciphers today. A very popular combination is 3DES-CBC and SHA-1

Summary

At this point (if you've been reading from the beginning), your head is probably spinning, right? Well, let's summarize the main points. A small number of widely accepted patterns cover a surprisingly large number of applications. The following two patterns are usually applicable; in effect, they are base patterns:

Persistent data encryption:

❑ generate two secret keys

❑ secure the integrity using one key (MAC)

❑ encrypt the data using the other key

❑ secure the keys

Ephemeral data encryption:

- ❏ generate two secret keys
- ❏ exchange the keys securely (a certificate is often practical in this case)
- ❏ secure the integrity using one key (MAC)
- ❏ encrypt the data using the other key
- ❏ transmit data and MAC

Always search for a commonly accepted protocol before trying to invent new ones. You may be fooled into believing there's nothing to it by the advances made in this area that put all the power of cryptography in your hands, but beware; it is a very complex science that should not be taken too lightly.

We'll be building many applications on these and other patterns throughout the book.

Cryptography is a vast science, and cannot be explained fully in only one chapter. You should have learned some basic principles and available algorithms as well as some practical areas of application. You are encouraged to learn more about cryptography theory and to keep up to date on the subject; there is no telling what tomorrow has in store in cryptography.

C#

Data Security

Handbook

2

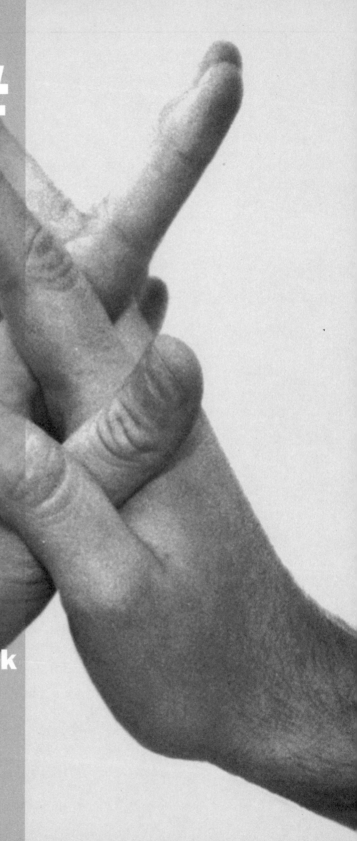

2

Cryptography in .NET

In the pre-.NET Windows world, using cryptography usually meant using the unmanaged Win32 CryptoAPI library, which was a chore for C++ programmers, and even more awkward for coders from other languages like Visual Basic. In .NET, cryptography, like so many areas of programming, is much more pleasant. Developers can use an elegant new cryptography model that is baked into the class library and remarkably extensible. Instead of calling an obscure function in an unmanaged library, you can now use a complete set of cryptography classes that wrap the intricacies of encoding data, computing hashes, and generating secure random numbers.

In this chapter, we take our first look at .NET's cryptographic services. We will explore the class model in detail, uncovering how it works with streams and cryptographic transforms, and how it can be extended with new algorithms and implementations. You'll also see fundamental examples that show how to use symmetric and asymmetric encryption to protect your data from prying eyes, and basic techniques to manage key information. In fact, this chapter introduces many of the techniques we'll return to throughout this book and build on to create practical applications.

First, let's take a high-level look at cryptography and the core namespaces.

The .NET Cryptography Model

The .NET Framework includes three cryptography namespaces:

- ❑ System.Security.Cryptography contains the core classes for all encryption tasks

- ❑ System.Security.Cryptography.Xml contains classes you can use, in conjunction with the System.Security.Cryptography classes, to encrypt and sign portions of an XML document

- ❑ System.Security.Cryptography.X509Certificates contains classes that allow you to retrieve certificate information

The first namespace, System.Security.Cryptography, is by far the most important, as it contains the basic functionality for all types of encryption, along with additional classes for creating hash codes (as discussed in the next chapter), generating secure random numbers (as discussed in *Appendix B*), and exchanging keys.

The core encryption classes in the System.Security.Cryptography namespace are divided into three layers. The first layer is a set of abstract base classes that represent a *type* of encryption algorithm, used for a particular cryptographic task. These include:

- ❑ AsymmetricAlgorithm (represents asymmetric encryption)

- ❑ SymmetricAlgorithm (represents symmetric encryption)

- ❑ HashAlgorithm (represents hash generation and verification)

The second level includes classes that represent a *specific* encryption algorithm. They derive from the encryption base classes, but they are also abstract classes. For example the DES algorithm class, which represents the DES (Data Encryption Standard) algorithm, derives from SymmetricAlgorithm.

The third level of classes is a set of encryption *implementations*. Each implementation class derives from an algorithm class. This means that a specific encryption algorithm like DES could have multiple implementation classes. In reality, there is only one provided out of the box in the .NET Framework (DESCryptoServiceProvider), but it's quite conceivable that another implementation that provides better performance could be created in the future, by Microsoft or a third-party vendor.

Figure 1

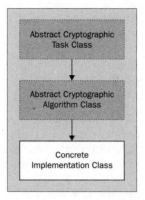

While some .NET Framework encryption classes are implemented entirely in managed code, most are actually thin wrappers over the CryptoAPI library. The classes that wrap CryptoAPI functions have "CryptoServiceProvider" in the class name (for example, DESCryptoServiceProvider), while the managed classes typically have "Managed" in the name (for example, RijndaelManaged). Essentially, the managed classes perform all their work in the .NET world under the supervision of the CLR, while the unmanaged CSP classes use unmanaged P/Invoke calls to the CryptoAPI library. This might seem like a limitation, but it's actually an efficient reuse of existing technology. CryptoAPI has never been faulted for its technology, just its awkward programming interface.

Figure 2

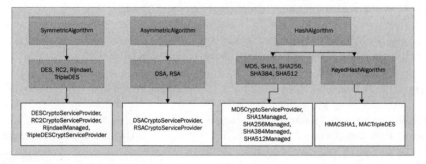

This three-layer organization allows almost unlimited extensibility. You can create a new implementation for an existing cryptography class by deriving from an existing algorithm class. For example, you could create a class that implements the DES algorithm entirely in managed code by creating a new DESManaged class and inheriting from the abstract DES class. Similarly, you can add support for a new encryption algorithm by adding an abstract algorithm class for it (for example, CAST128, which is similar to DES but not provided in the framework), and a concrete implementation class (such as CAST128Managed).

47

The encryption classes are one of the few examples in the .NET class library where the standard naming and case rules are not followed. This means, for example, that you'll find classes like `TripleDES` *and* `RSA` *rather than* `TripleDes` *and* `Rsa`.

The Abstract Classes

The abstract classes actually serve two purposes. Firstly, they define the basic members that encryption implementations need to support. However, they also provide some functionality you can use directly without creating a class instance, through the static `Create()` method. This method allows you to create an instance of one of the concrete implementation classes without needing to know how it is implemented.

For example, consider the following line of code:

```
DES crypt = DES.Create();
```

The static `Create()` method returns an instance of the default DES implementation class. In this case, the class is `DESCryptoServiceProvider`. However, the code above doesn't assume that this is true. Instead, it uses the basic members defined in the base `SymmetricAlgorithm` and `DES` classes to manipulate the new instance. The advantage of this technique is that you can code generically, without creating a dependency on a specific implementation. Best of all, if Microsoft updates the framework and the default DES implementation class changes, your code will pick up the change seamlessly. This is particularly useful if you are using a CSP class, which could be rewritten in a managed class equivalent in the future.

In fact, you can work at even higher level if you like by using the static `Create()` method in one of the cryptographic task classes. For example, consider this code:

```
SymmetricAlgorithm crypt = SymmetricAlgorithm.Create();
```

This creates an instance of whatever cryptography class is defined as the default symmetric algorithm. In this case, it isn't DES, but Rijndael. The object returned is an instance of the `RijndaelManaged` implementation class.

You can change these defaults; we'll look at configuring the .NET cryptography system later on, in the next section.

> **It is good practice to code generically using the abstract algorithm classes. This allows you to know which type of algorithm you use (and any limitations it may have), without worrying about the underlying implementation.**

Finally, you can use an overloaded version of the `Create()` method that accepts a string which identifies the algorithm by name. For example, the following code creates an instance of the default implementation of the DES algorithm, which is `DESCryptoServiceProvider`.

```
SymmetricAlgorithm crypt;

// The following two lines are equivalent.
crypt = SymmetricAlgorithm.Create("DES");
crypt = DES.Create("DES");
```

This technique is primarily useful if you want to use configuration settings in an `application.config` file to determine the type of encryption. You can read the name of the encryption algorithm to use from the file, and pass it to the `Create()` method.

CryptoConfig

The above examples raise a few interesting questions. Namely, where are the mappings between algorithm names and classes defined? And how are the default algorithms specified? At runtime, the `Create()` method uses the `CryptoConfig` class, which provides a static helper method called `CreateFromName()`. The `CryptoConfig` class uses the default mappings listed in the following table.

Simple Name	Algorithm Implementation
SHA	SHA1CryptoServiceProvider
SHA1	SHA1CryptoServiceProvider
MD5	MD5CryptoServiceProvider
SHA256	SHA256Managed
SHA-256	SHA256Managed
SHA384	SHA384Managed
SHA-384	SHA384Managed
SHA512	SHA512Managed
SHA-512	SHA512Managed
RSA	RSACryptoServiceProvider
DSA	DSACryptoServiceProvider
DES	DESCryptoServiceProvider

Table continued on following page

Simple Name	Algorithm Implementation
3DES	TripleDESCryptoServiceProvider
TripleDES	TripleDESCryptoServiceProvider
Triple DES	TripleDESCryptoServiceProvider
RC2	RC2CryptoServiceProvider
Rijndael	RijndaelManaged

You can use any of these names to specify an algorithm, or you can supply a string with the fully qualified class name. For example, with the default settings the following two statements are equivalent:

```
SymmetricAlgorithm crypt;

// The following two lines are equivalent.
crypt = SymmetricAlgorithm.Create("DES");
crypt = SymmetricAlgorithm.Create(
  "System.Security.Cryptography.DESCryptoServiceProvider");
```

Of course, you may need to take special care that you don't encounter a casting error. For example, the code above can create any implementation that derives from SymmetricAlgorithm. The following code, however, would successfully create the implementation class, but throw an exception when you attempt to store a reference in the crypt object.

```
SymmetricAlgorithm crypt;

// This won't work because RSA is an asymmetric algorithm.
crypt = SymmetricAlgorithm.Create("RSA");
```

If you specify a string that is not defined, you'll receive a CryptographicUnexpectedOperationException.

Configuring Algorithm Mappings

The CryptoConfig mappings can be modified easily, on a per-machine basis, by altering the computer's machine.config file (typically found in the C:\[WindowsDirectory]\Microsoft.NET\Framework\[Version]\CONFIG directory). Essentially, you do this by adding a <cryptographySettings> section to override the default settings. This element is not present by default, but can be added as shown here:

```
<configuration>
  <mscorlib>
    <cryptographySettings>
      <cryptoNameMapping>
        <cryptoClasses>
          <cryptoClass />
        </cryptoClasses>
        <nameEntry />
      </cryptoNameMapping>
    <cryptographySettings>
  </mscorlib>

  <!-- Other configuration settings go here. -->

</configuration>
```

In the `<cryptoClasses>` section, you can add additional `<cryptoClass>` elements to identify new algorithm implementation classes that you want to be included in the cryptography system. Nominated classes must be installed in the Global Assembly Cache. You can also add `<nameEntry>` elements to the `<cryptoNameMapping>` section to define the friendly string names for each class.

The following configuration settings define a new cryptography class for a hypothetical managed implementation of the DES algorithm, and assign the class a friendly name of ManagedDES. The settings also identify the strong name of the class, and its assembly (in this case named `ManagedDESAssembly.dll`). Note that a strong name always includes information about the assembly version, culture, and public key. You can retrieve this information by looking at the assembly in the GAC using Windows Explorer.

```
<configuration>
    <mscorlib>
        <cryptographySettings>
            <cryptoNameMapping>
                <cryptoClasses>
                    <cryptoClass ManagedDES="Wrox.Crypto.ManagedDES,
                    ManagedDESAssembly, Culture='en',
                    PublicKeyToken=a5d015c7d5a0b012, Version=1.0.0.0"/>
                </cryptoClasses>
                <nameEntry name="ManagedDES" class="ManagedDES"/>
            </cryptoNameMapping>
        </cryptographySettings>
    </mscorlib>

    <!-- Other configuration settings go here. -->

</configuration>
```

Note that the configuration settings do not identify that this class derives from DES, although this class certainly should.

Once you make these changes to register your custom cryptography class, you will be able to create it using the static `Create()` or `CreateFromName()` methods, as shown here:

```
SymmetricAlgorithm crypt = SymmetricAlgorithm.Create("ManagedDES");
```

If you want to ensure that this class replaces the `DESCryptoServiceProvider` class as the new default, you can add additional `<nameEntry>` elements. For example, consider this `<nameEntry>`, which overrides the default settings:

```
<nameEntry name="DES" class="ManagedDES"/>
```

Now, this code returns the custom `ManagedDES` class:

```
SymmetricAlgorithm crypt = SymmetricAlgorithm.Create("DES");
```

Finally, you can add this `<nameEntry>` to set the new algorithm as the default symmetric algorithm:

```
<nameEntry name="System.Security.Cryptography.SymmetricAlgorithm"
           class="ManagedDES" />
```

Now, this code will also return the custom `ManagedDES` class:

```
SymmetricAlgorithm crypt = SymmetricAlgorithm.Create();
```

Note that these configuration settings will apply to the current machine only. There is no way to set them in the application-file (and if you could, it would allow a program to circumvent the machine-set security settings, which could represent a dangerous security breach). You generally shouldn't rely on changing these defaults, because you won't want to modify the `machine.config` file on a client's computer.

High Encryption Support and Windows

Before delving any deeper into the encryption classes, it's worth discussing the support for different key sizes. In the past, due to the United State's restrictive cryptography export rules, Microsoft did not make certain (large) key sizes available, except through a separate download (which, in theory, would force the user to guarantee they were not a resident of a country to which the export restrictions applied). These rules were eventually loosened, and more recent operating systems and updates have included support for large key sizes.

All the managed classes support the use of strong (large) key sizes. However, encryption algorithms implemented on top of `CryptoAPI` require this to be available as part of the operating system. If the operating system does not have strong encryption support installed, an exception is thrown when you attempt to create a class with an unsupported key size. Windows XP and Windows .NET Server include support for strong key lengths without requiring any extra installation. However, this is not the case for all operating systems that support .NET:

❑ For Windows 2000 users, you can install Service Pack 2, which includes the High Encryption Pack. If you do not have Service Pack 2 installed you must install the Windows 2000 High Encryption Pack from http://www.microsoft.com/windows2000/downloads/recommended/encryption or upgrade to Service Pack 2 at http://www.microsoft.com/windows2000/downloads/recommended/SP2.

❑ For those few users still saddled with Windows NT 4.0, Service Packs are distributed in both standard and high encryption versions. If you do not have a high encryption service pack already installed, you can download the high encryption version of Service Pack 6a from http://www.microsoft.com/ntserver/nts/downloads/recommended/SP6.

❑ Windows ME and Windows 98 can acquire high encryption support by installing Internet Explorer 5.5, which includes the High Encryption Pack., or by installing the corresponding High Encryption Pack for your version of Internet Explorer at http://www.microsoft.com/windows/ie/download/128bit. Of course, these platforms only support running .NET applications, not developing them, which means its easy to forget at development time that your .NET applications might end up on such a system.

The Building Blocks

Before you can master the cryptographic classes, you need to understand a little more about the underlying plumbing. .NET uses a stream-based architecture for encryption and decryption, which makes it easy to encrypt different types of data from different types of sources. This architecture also makes it easy to perform multiple cryptographic operations in succession, on the fly, and independent of the actual block size of the algorithm. To understand how all this works, we need to consider two types: `ICryptoTransform` and the `CryptoStream` class.

The ICryptoTransform Interface

The ICryptoTransform interface is implemented by classes that can perform a blockwise cryptographic transformation. This could be an encryption, decryption, hashing, base 64 encoding/decoding, or formatting operation. The important detail about ICryptoTransform is that it performs its work on one block of data at a time. The InputBlockSize and OutputBlockSize properties define the size of this block in bytes, while the TransformBlock() method performs the actual task. TransformFinalBlock() takes the last block of data, and performs any additional work needed (for example, padding it with spaces). The CanReuseTransform property identifies whether an ICryptoTransform instance can be used again after one operation is ended by calling TransformFinalBlock().

Here's a code snippet that creates an ICryptoTransform for encrypting with the DES algorithm:

```
DES crypt = DES.Create();
ICryptoTransform transform = crypt.CreateEncryptor();

// You can now use the transform to encrypt a block of bytes.
```

The insight here is that various cryptographic tasks execute in the same way, even though the actual cryptographic function performing the transformation may be very different. Every cryptographic operation requires that data be subdivided into blocks of a fixed size before it can be processed.

You can use an ICryptoTransform instance directly but in most cases, you'll take an easier approach, and simply pass it to another class: the CryptoStream.

The CryptoStream Class

The CryptoStream wraps an ordinary stream, and uses an ICryptoTransform to perform its work behind the scenes. The key advantage is that the CryptoStream uses buffered access, allowing you to perform automatic encryption without worrying about the block size required by the algorithm. The other advantage of the CryptoStream is that, because it wraps an ordinary .NET Stream-derived class, it can easily "piggyback" on another operation, like file access (through a FileStream), memory access (through a MemoryStream), low-level network calls (through a NetworkStream), and so on. These features are extremely useful – for example, they allow you to encrypt network communication on the fly using a session key, encrypt several user-supplied values to an in-memory buffer, and so on. We'll look at applications of these techniques throughout this book.

To create a CryptoStream you need three pieces of information: the underlying stream, the mode, and the ICryptoTransform you want to use. For example, the following code snippet creates an ICryptoTransform using the DES algorithm implementation class, and then uses it with an existing stream to create a CryptoStream.

```
DES crypt = DES.Create();
ICryptoTransform transform = crypt.CreateEncryptor();

CryptoStream cs = new CryptoStream(fileStream, crypt,
   CryptoStreamMode.Write);

// Now use cs to write encrypted information to the file.
```

Note that the CryptoStream can be in one of two *modes*: read mode or write mode, as defined by the CryptoStreamMode enumeration. In read mode, the transformation is performed as it is retrieved from the underlying stream.

Figure 3

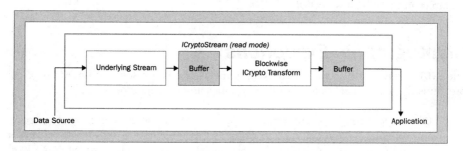

In write mode, the transformation is performed before the data is written to the underlying stream.

Figure 4

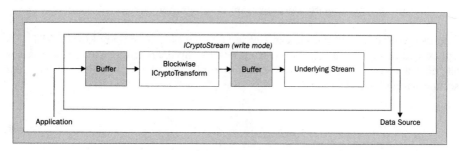

You cannot combine both modes to make a readable and writable CryptoStream. The Seek() method and Position property, which are used to move to different positions in a stream, are not supported for the CryptoStream, and will throw a NotSupportedException if called. However, you can often use these members with the underlying stream, as demonstrated later in this chapter.

> **A CryptoStream can be used when reading information from a stream, or when writing to a stream. Often, the reading operation uses the CryptoStream for decryption, while the writing operation uses it for encryption. However, this isn't a requirement. In some cases, it makes sense to perform decryption while writing a stream, and we'll use this technique in later chapters to simplify some byte size calculations.)**

The beauty of the CryptoStream is the fact that you can substitute it wherever you currently use an ordinary Stream object. We'll expand on this with a few practical examples in the next few sections.

Cryptographic Exceptions

The .NET cryptography defines two exception classes to represent the broad range of problems that can occur. Neither of them defines any new members.

❑ CryptographicException represents a generic error in a cryptographic operation. One common example is if you attempt to set invalid values for a property of an algorithm implementation class (such as specifying a key size that does not exist).

❑ CryptographicUnexpectedOperationException extends CryptographicException, and is used much less frequently. It represents an unexpected problem that, in practice, often occurs when you incorrectly specify a non-existant cryptographic service provider.

Of course, your encryption code can still see a much broader range of basic .NET errors if you misuse the encryption classes. For example, an InvalidCastException will occur if you try to reference an algorithm implementation class with a variable that uses the wrong base class type.

Symmetric Encryption

Symmetric encryption, also known as "secret key" encryption, uses a secret value to encrypt all messages. Symmetric encryption has the following characteristics:

❑ The strength of the encryption corresponds with the length of the key. The greater the key size, the harder it is for a brute force attack to succeed, because there are far more possible key values to test (twice as many for each bit of key data). Of course, greater symmetric key sizes also lead to longer encryption and decryption times.

❑ Symmetric encryption is simpler mathematically and thus much faster than asymmetric encryption. It is the best choice for dealing with large amounts of data.

❑ Symmetric encryption depends on a shared secret known to both parties. This value must be known prior to the encryption operation, and cannot be transmitted in the clear without compromising security.

As with all forms of encryption, the principle of symmetric encryption is that the encrypted information can be intercepted by a malicious party, but cannot be understood. All forms of encryption are subject to a brute force attack, but ideally, the type of symmetric encryption you use will not be able to be cracked without a brute force attack that is prohibitively expensive, or takes a long enough time that the information is no longer valuable.

A particular problem posed by the use of symmetric encryption is the fact that the same key must be used to encrypt the information as is used to decrypt the information. Depending on the application, there may be an obvious candidate for this shared secret (like a user password), or you may have to take additional steps to distribute the secret by another means. In the case where you are using encryption to secure distributed communication, it's common to combine asymmetric and symmetric encryption and use a dynamically generated secret, as described in Chapter 5.

Symmetric Algorithms

The following table lists the symmetric algorithms provided by the .NET Framework. For most purposes, the default recommended algorithm is Rijndael.

Algorithm	Abstract Algorithm Class	Default Implementation Class	Valid Key Size (bits)	Default Key Size (bits)
DES	DES	DESCryptoServiceProvider	64	64
Triple DES	TripleDES	TripleDESCryptoService Provider	128, 192	192
RC2	RC2	RC2CryptoServiceProvider	40–128	128
Rijndael	Rijndael	RijndaelManaged	128, 192, 256	256

DES, TripleDES, and RC2 are all implemented using the CryptoAPI, and thus for key sizes over 40 bits, need the high encryption pack on Windows 2000 or earlier. Note also that the key length for DES and TripleDES includes parity bits that don't contribute to the strength of the encryption. Thus, TripleDES with a 192-bit key only uses 168 bits, while a 128-bit key uses 112 bits. In DES, the 64-bit key uses only 56 bits. As a rule, any encryption with less than 100 or so bits should be considered fairly weak, which means DES should not really be used where it can be avoided. For additional information about the relative strengths of these algorithms, consult a dedicated book or Internet resource about encryption theory (like Bruce Schneier's *Applied Cryptography* ISBN 0-471-11709-9).

The SymmetricAlgorithm Class

All the classes in the previous table are derived from SymmetricAlgorithm, and thus support a few basic properties, including:

- ❏ BlockSize is the size of the basic unit of data that can be encrypted or decrypted in one operation with this algorithm. Longer data must be broken into successive blocks, while shorter data must be padded with extra bits to reach the size of a block.

- ❏ Key is the secret value used to encrypt and decrypt data. It's represented by an array of bytes.

- ❏ KeySize is the number of bits allocated to the secret key.

- ❏ IV is an initialization vector, which is also represented by a byte array. It provides an additional input into the encryption process and increases security, as we'll see shortly. The initialization vector, like the key, must be known by both the encryptor and decryptor. Unlike a key, however, it doesn't need to be kept secret, and you can simply transmit it along with the message. The IV is always the same length as the block size.

❑ LegalKeySizes and LegalBlockSizes return an array of KeySizes instances, which indicate what key and block sizes can be used with the specific algorithm.

All of these properties, aside from Key and IV, are read-only. In addition, the SymmetricAlgorithm class also provides the following methods:

❑ Create() is a static method used to generate the default algorithm implementation class, or an instance of a class that provides a named algorithm.

❑ CreateEncryptor() and CreateDecryptor() generate ICryptoTransform objects that can be used to manually encrypt and decrypt byte data, one block at a time.

❑ GenerateKey() and GenerateIV() create random Key and IV values. These methods are not usually required, because random values are created when you create the algorithm implementation class.

❑ ValidKeySize() tests if a specified bit length is valid to use as a key with the current algorithm.

❑ Clear() releases all resources held, and removes the key information from memory. It is equivalent to calling Dispose().

Some derived classes, like DES and TripleDES add IsWeakKey() and IsSemiWeakKey() methods that allow you to test for keys that result in encrypted data that is easier to decipher than it should be. If you take a document encrypted with a weak key, and encrypt it again with the same weak key, you will end up with the unencrypted source. For example, with TripleDES in 128-bit mode, if the first 64 bits are the same as the last 64 bits, the key is weak. It's not necessary to explicitly test for weak keys, because you will automatically receive a CryptographyException if you attempt to use a weak key. Randomly generated keys using the GenerateKey() method or the initial class values will never be weak.

> **It's a good idea to call Dispose() after using an object for encryption or decryption. This method is overridden for all algorithm implementation classes, so that it automatically calls Clear(). Clear() overwrites the sensitive parts of memory where the key was stored, protecting against a memory dump attack.**

Chaining

There are two properties provided by all SymmetricAlgorithm classes that we haven't yet addressed. This includes Mode, which determines how multiple blocks are encoded, using one of the values from the CipherMode enumeration.

As discussed in Chapter 1, one limitation of block-based encryption algorithms is that the same block of information will always generate the same block of encrypted data. This behavior can be used to attack your encryption, especially if you are frequently encoding blocks of the same data. To strengthen your encryption, you can use a chaining mode that takes a value from a previous block, and uses it when processing the subsequent block. This way, subsequent instances of the same block of data will result in different ciphertext.

There are five different `CipherMode` values, not all of which are supported by all symmetric encryption classes. The two most common values are:

❑ `CipherMode.CBC` uses Cipher Block Chaining, and is the default chaining mode for most algorithms, and the most secure. Before a block is encrypted, it is combined with the ciphertext of the previous block by a bitwise exclusive OR operation. This ensures that even if the previous block contains many similarities, the encrypted data will differ. Processing time is increased because of the additional step.

❑ `CipherMode.ECB` uses Electronic Codebook mode and encrypts each block individually. If there are any blocks of data that are identical (in the same message or in a different message encrypted with the same key), they will be transformed into identical encrypted blocks. This mode is the least secure, although it does theoretically allow you to decrypt only a portion in the middle of a message, or decrypt the remainder of a message if a part of it is corrupted. It also requires slightly less processing, and provides faster encryption for large messages.

Incidentally, now that we understand chaining, we can also understand the role of the initialization vector (IV). In CBC mode, there won't be a feedback value to use for the first block, because no blocks have been processed yet. Instead, the initialization vector will be used. The IV is an important element of chained symmetric encryption, and should not be underestimated. While using chaining ensures that if the same block of data occurs twice in the same message, it will be encrypted as different ciphertext, the IV allows us to ensure that if the same block occurs in two different messages encrypted with the same key, it is still encrypted as a different block of ciphertext. If you always used the same key and initialization vector, and you always began your message with the same data (for example, a `From` line in an e-mail), your encrypted messages would all start with the same ciphertext. The IV makes the encrypted text differ.

Obviously, the IV needs to be known by both encryptor and decryptor. However, it is not necessary to treat an IV like a second key – it is perfectly safe simply to precede your encrypted message with the IV. This will allow anybody in possession of the key to decrypt the message correctly, but won't give any additional data to a malicious third party who intercepts the message, but does not possess the key.

Padding

Most data can't be evenly divided into blocks. In most cases, there will only be enough data to fill the last block partially. In this case, the final block must be padded to its full size. How this padding is performed depends on the value of the `Padding` property, which can take any value from the `PaddingMode` enumeration, as described here:

❑ `PaddingMode.None` does not use any padding at all. An exception will be thrown if you try to encode a partial block.

❑ `PaddingMode.PKCS7` uses the PKCS #7 padding system. PKCS is the set of "Public Key Cryptography Standards", which set out cryptographic protocols for all kinds of communication scenarios. This scheme pads a block with a sequence of bytes, each of which is equal to the total number of padding bytes added. For example, if 3 bytes of padding need to be added, each byte will be set to "03", and the padding string that is added to the last block before it is encrypted will be "03 03 03". At least one byte of padding is always added, so the last byte in the message always tells you how many bytes of padding were added. If the message finishes on the end of a block, a whole block of padding is therefore added. This is the default padding mode.

❑ `PaddingMode.Zeros` simply sets all padded bytes to zero, which could lead to an error if the data legitimately ends with a zero value. For example, if 3 bytes of padding need to be added, the padding string is "00 00 00".

`PaddingMode.PKCS7` is the default. There is no practical advantage to using any other value.

Retrieving Key Data and Defaults

The following code shows a simple Console application that creates an instance of the `RijndaelManaged` algorithm implementation class, and displays information about its default settings. It also prints out the numeric value of each byte in the key and initialization vector, which is generated automatically when the class is instantiated.

```
// EncryptionDefaults.cs

using System;
using System.Security.Cryptography;

class EncryptionDefaults
{
    static void Main(string[] args)
    {
        // Create an instance of RijndaelManaged.
        Rijndael crypt = Rijndael.Create();
```

```
        // Display basic information about this algorithm.
        Console.WriteLine("Block size: {0}", crypt.BlockSize);
        foreach (KeySizes keySize in crypt.LegalKeySizes)
        {
          Console.WriteLine("Max key size: {0}", keySize.MaxSize);
          Console.WriteLine("Min key size: {0}", keySize.MinSize);
        }
        Console.WriteLine();

        // Display basic information about the defaults used.
        Console.WriteLine("Size of current key: {0}", crypt.KeySize);
        Console.WriteLine("Mode: {0}", crypt.Mode);
        Console.WriteLine("Padding: {0}", crypt.Padding);
        Console.WriteLine();

        // Display information about the
        // automatically generated Key and IV.
        Console.WriteLine("Key: {0}", BitConverter.ToString(crypt.Key));
        Console.WriteLine("IV: {0}", BitConverter.ToString(crypt.IV));
        Console.ReadLine();
    }
}
```

Note that to output the byte arrays to the console, we're using the static
`ByteConverter.ToString()` method. This outputs a byte array as a hyphenated
sequence of two-character hexadecimal values.

The output for this code will be similar to this:

```
Block size: 128
Max key size: 256
Min key size: 128

Size of current key: 256
Mode: CBC
Padding: PKCS7

Key: A3-7E-E1-3F-35-0E-E1-A9-83-A5-62-AA-7A-AE-89-93-A7-33-49-FF-E6-
AE-BF-8D-8D-20-8A-49-31-3A-12-60
IV: F1-8A-01-FB-08-85-9A-A4-BE-45-28-56-03-42-F6-19
```

Binary Data and Text Encoding

Encryption is always performed on a binary data. For the most part, you feed this data in as a byte array (containing unencrypted bytes), and retrieve it as another byte array (with the encrypted data). This process is straightforward if your data is already in binary format – for example, if you are reading a large image out of a file. However, what about primitive types like strings, integers, and decimals? You need to convert these types to a binary representation before you perform the encoding.

One way to do this is to use the System.BitConverter class we just used to convert byte arrays into strings. It also provides an overloaded GetBytes() method that can convert numeric types into byte arrays.

```
// Convert a number into a byte array.
int number = 102343;
bytes[] data = BitConverter.GetBytes(number);

// You can now write these bytes to a CryptoStream for encryption.
```

GetBytes() can't be used with string data. The problem is that there is more than one way to represent a string in binary form, depending on the text *encoding* that you use. The most common encodings include:

❑ **ASCII**, which encodes each character in a string using 7 bits. ASCII encoded data can't contain extended Unicode characters.

❑ **Full Unicode (or UTF-16)**, which represents each character in a string using 16 bits.

❑ **UTF-7 Unicode**, which uses 7 bits for ordinary ASCII characters, and multiple 7-bit pairs for extended characters. This encoding isn't regularly used.

❑ **UTF-8 Unicode**, which uses 8 bits for ordinary ASCII characters, and multiple 8-bit pairs for extended characters. This is the recommended standard – it's a compact format that supports extended Unicode characters. It's also the default for all .NET classes. It is only the most efficient form if your text consists mainly of ASCII characters, however.

For the multi-byte Unicode format, where each character is represented by two bytes of data, you must choose which order to write the two bytes in; The default Unicode encoding uses Little-Endian byte order, and a separate Big-Endian Unicode encoding is provided that orders the bytes the other way around.

.NET provides a class for each type of encoding in the System.Text namespace. Each encoding class provides a GetBytes() method that converts strings to byte arrays, and a GetString() method that performs the reverse operation.

```
// Convert a string into a byte array using UTF-8 encoding.
string text = "sample text";

System.Text.UTF8Encoding enc = new System.Text.UTF8Encoding();
bytes[] data = enc.GetBytes(text);
```

Often, when performing encryption you'll work at a slightly higher level by using writer and reader objects, like the `BinaryWriter` and `BinaryReader` classes from the `System.IO` namespace. They perform the conversion from ordinary data types to binary representation seamlessly (using UTF-8 encoding for strings by default). These classes are more convenient to work with when writing multiple pieces of data, and they support binary encoding of the decimal data type (which isn't provided through `BitConverter`). You'll see an example of this technique in the example in the next section.

Encrypting and Decrypting a Stream

To perform a simple encryption task, we simply need to bring together all the details we've discussed, including transforms, streams, and encryption algorithms. First, let's consider the code required to convert a string into binary data, encrypt it into a simple memory stream, and then decipher it. We'll dissect this code in detail.

The first step is to create an encryption object and a `MemoryStream` where the encrypted data will be stored:

```
// EncryptionTest.cs

using System;
using System.IO;
using System.Security.Cryptography;

class EncryptionTest
{
  static void Main(string[] args)
  {
    // Create an instance of RijndaelManaged.
    Rijndael crypt = Rijndael.Create();

    // Create an in-memory stream.
    MemoryStream s = new MemoryStream();
```

Next, you must generate a `CryptoStream` that wraps the `MemoryStream` and performs encryption. This `CryptoStream` works in write-only mode.

```
    // Create a cryptographic stream for encryption.
    CryptoStream csWrite = new CryptoStream(s,
      crypt.CreateEncryptor(), CryptoStreamMode.Write);
```

> **The objects created by the `CreateEncryptor()` or `CreateDecryptor()` implement the `ICryptoTransform` interface and are completely independent. They have all the information they needs to encrypt or decrypt data. This means that if you modify the original algorithm implementation class (for example, changing the key), the changes will not influence these objects.**

Next, we use the `StreamWriter` to encode a text into a bytes, and write it to the `CryptoStream`.

```
// Write a value to the stream (which will then be encrypted).
StreamWriter w = new StreamWriter(csWrite);
w.WriteLine("Here is a string with some secret data!");

// Make sure the CryptoStream has everything.
w.Flush();

// Finish encoding the last block.
csWrite.FlushFinalBlock();
```

At this point, the information is stored inside the `MemoryStream` in encrypted format. As a demonstration, you can retrieve this data, convert it to a string, and display it. This data won't correspond to a real string of course—instead, it will include extended and unprintable characters depending on the value of each byte,

```
// Now move the information out of the stream,
// and into an array of bytes.
Byte[] bytes = new Byte[s.Length];
s.Position = 0;
s.Read(bytes, 0, (int)s.Length);

// Display this encoded information.
System.Text.UTF8Encoding enc = new System.Text.UTF8Encoding();
Console.Write("Encrypted data: ");
Console.WriteLine(enc.GetString(bytes));
```

Finally, we can decrypt the information using another `CryptoStream`, this one in read mode. The `CryptoStream` is wrapped by a `StreamReader` that converts the decrypted binary data into a string.

```
// Now decipher the information in the memory stream.
s.Position = 0;
CryptoStream csRead = new CryptoStream(s,
   crypt.CreateDecryptor(), CryptoStreamMode.Read);
```

```
        StreamReader r = new StreamReader(csRead);
        string deciphered = r.ReadToEnd();

        // Display the decoded information.
        Console.Write("Decrypted data: ");
        Console.WriteLine(deciphered);

        Console.ReadLine();
    }
}
```

This simple console application produces something resembling the following output:

```
Encrypted data: ?♂P-EdK►¡∟g?↔5AyOGx▼←◄v^wx,↓JXV§
Decrypted data: Here is a string with some secret data!
```

Of course, the output differs every time you run the program, as the key and initialization vector are generated dynamically at run time. However, there's no reason that you can't add code that manually sets the Key and IV property to a fixed value.

Note that there are several best practices used here that you can follow in your own code:

❑   The Write() method of the CryptoStream only accepts bytes. To avoid having to convert your data to byte arrays manually, and to avoid encoding problems, simply use the StreamWriter class, which automatically encodes strings using UTF8 encoding unless otherwise specified.

❑   Once you have written information to the CryptoStream, call Flush() on the StreamWriter() to ensure there is no buffered information that has not yet been written (alternatively, you can set the StreamWriter.AutoFlush property to true).

❑   Once you have flushed the writer, call FlushFinalBlock() on the CryptoStream to ensure that the last block of data is padded and encoded.

❑   If you need to reuse a stream don't close it. You can use the Position property of the underlying stream to move to another location, although remember you cannot use the Position property of the CryptoStream.

If you fail to call Flush() or FlushFinalBlock(), you may discover that you lose information in some situations, depending on the block size of the algorithm, the amount of data to encode, and the buffering used.

Encrypting to a File

To create a more practical example, consider the following application, which encrypts data, and stores it in a file. The application consists of a single Windows form (simpleFileReader.cs), which includes a textbox and two buttons.

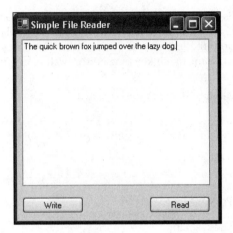

An instance of RijndaelManaged encryption class is stored as a form member variable. This is required because the same instance must be used both to encrypt data and decrypt it, unless you go to additional steps to persist the Key and IV.

```
Rijndael crypt = Rijndael.Create();
```

When the Write button is clicked, the data in the textbox is stored in a file, and encrypted at the same time using a CryptoStream in write mode:

```
private void cmdWriteFile_Click(object sender, System.EventArgs e)
{
    // Create the encryption transform for this algorithm.
    ICryptoTransform transform = crypt.CreateEncryptor();

    // Open a file for writing to.
    FileStream fs = new FileStream("c:\\testfile.bin",
        FileMode.Create);

    // Create a cryptographic stream.
    CryptoStream cs = new CryptoStream(fs, transform,
        CryptoStreamMode.Write);

    // Create a text writer.
    StreamWriter w = new StreamWriter(cs);
    w.Write(txt.Text);
```

```
        w.Flush();
        cs.FlushFinalBlock();

        w.Close();
    }
```

When the Read button is clicked, the data is retrieved from the textbox and decrypted using a `CryptoStream` in read mode. The retrieved data is displayed in a message box, and then entered into the textbox. In this case, the same `crypt` object is retained for both operations, and so the same key is used for both encrypting and decrypting.

```
private void cmdReadFile_Click(object sender, System.EventArgs e)
{
    // Create the encryption transform for this algorithm.
    ICryptoTransform transform = crypt.CreateDecryptor();

    // Open a file for reading from.
    FileStream fs = new FileStream("c:\\testfile.bin", FileMode.Open);

    // Create a cryptographic stream.
    CryptoStream cs = new CryptoStream(fs, transform,
      CryptoStreamMode.Read);

    // Create a text reader.
    StreamReader r = new StreamReader(cs);
    string text = r.ReadToEnd();
    r.Close();

    MessageBox.Show("Retrieved: " + text);
    txt.Text = text;
}
```

Generating Keys and Using Salt

So far, we've assumed that you want to use the key and initialization vector that is created by default when the class is instantiated. This is certainly not always the case. Sometimes, you might want to use another value, like a user password. Unfortunately, this type of information is rarely sufficient as a key, for the following reasons:

❑　It's usually too short.

❑　It uses a limited set of characters (alphabetic characters and numerals) rather than the full set of possible byte values.

❑　It often uses ordinary words or names, making it susceptible to a dictionary attack (where an attacker tries to decrypt a message by trying every word in the dictionary).

One solution is to use the `PasswordDeriveBytes` class, which generates a cryptographically sound key from a password, with the help of a cryptographic service provider. Of course, to ensure a truly strong key, it's best to also use a salt value, which is a random byte value that plays a similar role to an initialization vector. If you use a non-zero salt value, you will also have to supply this value when creating a key to decrypt the data. Again, it doesn't need to be kept secret, and just ensures that different keys can be generated by the same password. Like an IV, it can be passed along with the encrypted data.

> **A password derived in this form is still subject to a dictionary attack, because the same password and salt will always lead to the same series of bytes (assuming the attacker has access to the same `PasswordDeriveBytes` code) – although the attacker will have to generate the derived bytes for every possible password, rather than using a pre-calculated dictionary. In any case, the derived key is cryptographically strong, and ciphertext generated with this key cannot be easily subject to frequency analysis attacks and the like.**

Here's an example that uses the `PasswordDeriveBytes` class, along with the `RNGCryptoServiceProvider` to generate a random salt value. You'll learn more about the `RNGCryptoServiceProvider` in *Appendix B*. For now, it's just important to understand that it creates random numbers using a technique that makes it almost impossible to predict number sequences (unlike the `System.Random` class).

```
Rijndael crypt = Rijndael.Create();

byte[] salt = new byte[8];
RNGCryptoServiceProvider rng = new RNGCryptoServiceProvider();
rng.GetBytes(salt);

PasswordDeriveBytes pdb = new PasswordDeriveBytes(
  "OpenSesame", salt);

byte[] key = pdb.GetBytes(16);
crypt.Key = key;
crypt.IV = new byte[16];
```

We call `GetBytes()` to derive a key of a required length from the provided password and salt.

Base64 Transformations

A `CryptoStream` can wrap any `Stream`-derived object, including another `CryptoStream`. In this way, you could encrypt the same set of data multiple times (which will not necessarily improve the encryption strength and can even decrease it). A more useful reason to chain together `CryptoStream` instances is to use the `ToBase64Transform` and `FromBase64Transform` classes provided in the cryptography namespace.

By default, when you encrypt data, the resulting byte array uses any valid value (from 0 to 256). Some consequences of this include the fact that you cannot safely embed this encrypted data in an HTML page or XML document (because it may contain special characters), or use it as part of a SOAP message when communicating with a web service. To overcome this problem, you can perform a Base64 transformation. In Base64 encoding, each sequence of three bytes – 24 bits – is divided into four chunks of six bits each. Each of these chunks has one of 64 values, each of which is mapped to a printable character in the range {A-Z, a-z, 0-9, +, /}. These characters are then converted to a sequence of four bytes. Each Base64 encoded byte has one of the 64 possible values, all of which map to characters that can be safely displayed, e-mailed, or included in XML data. As a side effect, Base64 encoded data is 33% larger, since 3 source bytes become 4 output bytes.

In an encryption scenario, you would apply Base64 encoding *after* encrypting the message, thereby removing any bytes that map to special characters. Consider the earlier example with the simple file encryption application. In this case, we must attach two `CryptoStream`s, in reverse order (because we are attaching them to the final output, the `FileStream`).

Figure 5

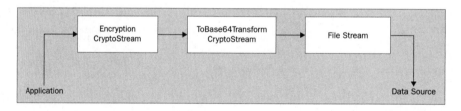

Here's the code:

```
private void cmdWriteFile_Click(object sender, System.EventArgs e)
{
  // Open a file for writing to.
  FileStream fs = new FileStream("c:\\testfile.txt",
    FileMode.Create);
```

```
    // Create a stream for converting to Base64 encoding.
    ICryptoTransform transformEncode = new ToBase64Transform();
    CryptoStream csEncode = new CryptoStream(fs, transformEncode,
      CryptoStreamMode.Write);

    // Create a stream for encryption.
    ICryptoTransform transformEncrypt = crypt.CreateEncryptor();
    CryptoStream csEncrypt = new CryptoStream(csEncode,
      transformEncrypt, CryptoStreamMode.Write);

    // Create a text writer.
    StreamWriter w = new StreamWriter(csEncrypt);
    w.Write(txt.Text);

    w.Flush();
    csEncrypt.FlushFinalBlock();

    w.Close();
}
```

The resulting document looks like this:

```
IuCP6bMgihL2B21i21AWT1U2+ABmJtB7q+3SYQovHNv6WVxomEo92w4XbS2u3bxM=
```

When retrieving the data, the information must be converted back to its native representation, and then decrypted.

```
private void cmdReadFile_Click(object sender, System.EventArgs e)
{
    // Open a file for reading from.
    FileStream fs = new FileStream("c:\\testfile.txt", FileMode.Open);

    // Create a stream for converting from Base64 encoding.
    ICryptoTransform transformDecode = new FromBase64Transform();
    CryptoStream csDecode = new CryptoStream(fs, transformDecode,
      CryptoStreamMode.Read);

    // Create a cryptographic stream.
    ICryptoTransform transformDecrypt = crypt.CreateDecryptor();
    CryptoStream csDecrypt = new CryptoStream(csDecode,
      transformDecrypt, CryptoStreamMode.Read);

    // Create a text reader.
    StreamReader r = new StreamReader(csDecrypt);
    string text = r.ReadToEnd();
    r.Close();

    MessageBox.Show("Retrieved: " + text);
    txt.Text = text;
}
```

Asymmetric Encryption

Asymmetric encryption, as we discussed in the previous chapter, uses a key pair that includes a private and a public key. The private key is carefully guarded, while the public key is made available to the entire world. These keys are mathematically linked, so that any data encrypted with one key can only be decrypted with the other. Thus, you could encrypt a message using the recipient's public key, ensuring that only the recipient could read it. In fact, even the sender will be unable to decrypt such a message once it is encrypted, because the sender won't have the recipient's private key.

Now, while it's possible to encipher data with either key, and then decipher it with the other, when data is enciphered with the private key, it is not really 'encrypted', in the sense of being hidden; it can be deciphered by anyone with the public key, which is by definition anybody. On the other hand, enciphering data with the public key does render the data hidden, so is conventionally termed 'encryption'. We don't usually call the operation of enciphering with the private key 'encryption', or deciphering with the public key 'decryption' – these operations are crucial to digital signatures and certificates, and are tied up in the processes we call 'signing' and 'verifying' This idea of message integrity and verification is developed in the next chapter.

So, in this section, when we talk about 'encryption', we mean enciphering with the public key, and when we talk about 'decryption', we mean deciphering with the private key.

Asymmetric key encryption has the following characteristics:

- ❏ As with symmetric key encryption, the strength of the encryption corresponds with the length of the key. However, key sizes in symmetric and asymmetric encryption are not directly comparable.

- ❏ Asymmetric encryption is mathematically complex. (The asymmetric algorithms we'll be using depend on the fact that that multiplying two prime numbers to generate a new number is computationally easy, but factoring the result to rediscover the original pair of prime numbers is difficult for large numbers.) For that reason it is roughly 1,000 times slower that symmetric encryption.

The particular problem with asymmetric encryption is that it performs slowly. It is much less practical for large amounts of data (for example, an encrypted image). It's common to combine the use of asymmetric encryption to negotiate a random secret value (known as a session key), which can then be used for faster symmetric encryption. This process is described in Chapter 5. It gets us the best of both worlds, because we use the slower, but secure, asymmetric process to agree the key at the beginning of a communication session, then conduct the majority of the session using fast block-based symmetric ciphers.

Asymmetric Algorithms

The following table lists the asymmetric algorithms provided by the .NET Framework. The default algorithm is RSA, as DSA is only suitable for creating and verifying digital signatures, not for encrypting data.

Algorithm	Abstract Algorithm Class	Default Implementation Class	Valid Key Size	Default Key Size
RSA	RSA	RSACryptoServiceProvider	364 -16,384 (in 8 bit inc)	1,024
DSA	DSA	DSACryptoServiceProvider	364 - 512 (in 64 bit increments)	1,024

Both RSA and DSA are implemented using the CryptoAPI, and thus need the high encryption pack on Windows 2000 or earlier, to use larger keys. You'll notice that asymmetric encryption has much larger key sizes. That is because the role of keys in asymmetric encryption is very different from their role in symmetric ciphers. In symmetric ciphers, any number up to the key size can be a key. In asymmetric cryptography, only numbers with certain mathematical properties will work as keys, and these numbers are only hard for attackers to find if they are very very large. So we need a lot of bits to store big numbers in. However, an attacker doesn't have to try every number to make a brute force attack, only those numbers that are possible keys. It's estimated that a 1024-bit RSA key (the default key size in .NET) is roughly equivalent, cryptanalytically, to a 75-bit symmetric key. You may want to consider using a larger key if possible, but consider the performance issues carefully. Larger keys take much longer to generate as well as to use.

The AsymmetricAlgorithm Class

The classes in the previous table are derived from AsymmetricAlgorithm, and thus support a few common properties, including KeySize and LegalKeySizes. In addition, you can use methods like the static Create() to generate the default asymmetric algorithm implementation class, and FromXmlString() and ToXmlString() to export and retrieve key information. However, you will not be able to generically perform encryption or signature verification through the methods of the AsymmetricAlgorithm class. Because not all algorithms may support this functionality, it is implemented in the abstract algorithm classes instead of the AsymmetricAlgorithm class. Unfortunately, .NET does not provide any interfaces or base classes that include this functionality, so programming with asymmetric algorithms requires us to write less generic code than programming with symmetric algorithms.

> **The .NET framework only provides one `AsymmetricAlgorithm` class that can be used for encryption and decryption: `RSA` and its implementation, `RSACryptoServiceProvider`. Thus, the following examples will focus on the members of these classes.**

Another difference is that the asymmetric algorithms do not support the `CryptoStream` model that's been discussed over the last few sections. This difference is partly because asymmetric algorithms are not designed to be used "on the fly" with other `Stream` instances, because they are far too slow. As a result, you will need to perform some of the heavy lifting yourself, converting strings to byte arrays, and subdividing byte arrays into the appropriate chunks before they are encoded or decoded. This makes asymmetric encryption more laborious to implement than symmetric encryption.

Encrypting Data

The base RSA class defines two methods, `EncryptValue()` and `DecryptValue()`, which all implementation classes must support. However, these methods are rarely called directly, because they use raw computations with no padding. Instead, you will use the `Encrypt()` and `Decrypt()` methods that are provided on the `RSACryptoServiceProvider` implementation class. These methods encrypt or decrypt data in a byte array.

The following code, converts a string of data into a byte array using UTF-8 encoding, encrypts the data, and then writes it to a file. Note that because the `Encrypt()` and `Decrypt()` methods are defined in the implementation class, it's easiest to begin your encryption code by directly creating an instance of the `RSACryptoServiceProvider` implementation class.

```
RSACryptoServiceProvider crypt = new RSACryptoServiceProvider();

// Convert text to a byte array.
System.Text.UTF8Encoding enc = new System.Text.UTF8Encoding();
byte[] bytes = enc.GetBytes("Secret string");

// Encrypt data.
bytes = crypt.Encrypt(bytes, false);

// Write it to a file.
FileStream fs = new FileStream("c:\\testfile.bin",
  FileMode.Create);
fs.Write(bytes, 0, bytes.Length);

fs.Flush();
fs.Close();
```

The `false` parameter passed to the `Encrypt()` method indicates that we will not use OAEP (Optimal Asymmetric Encryption Padding) padding. OAEP padding is only supported on Windows XP and later operating systems.

Retrieving the data is similarly straightforward, assuming you use the same `RSACryptoServiceProvider` instance:

```
// Read data from a file.
FileStream fs = new FileStream("c:\\testfile.bin",
  FileMode.Open);
byte[] bytes = new byte[fs.Length];
fs.Read(bytes, 0, bytes.Length);
fs.Close();

// Decrypt data.
bytes = crypt.Decrypt(bytes, false);

// Convert byte array to text.
System.Text.UTF8Encoding enc = new System.Text.UTF8Encoding();
Console.WriteLine(enc.GetString(bytes));
```

Note that if you are dealing with string data, it is extremely important to make sure you use the same encoding object to encode and decode the data. If you encode using the `UTF8Encoding` class and decode using `ASCIIEncoding`, for example, you will not be able to successfully retrieve the original information.

> **Remember, asymmetric encryption uses a key pair with both a public and private key. When you use the `Encrypt()` method, data is encrypted using the public key, and when you use `Decrypt()`, the private key is required.**

As an example, consider the encrypted file writer/reader test utility that was demonstrated earlier. To make this work with asymmetric encryption, you need to split the data into blocks before encrypting it. The allowed block size depends on the level of encryption – with the high encryption pack, you can encrypt 16 bytes at a time, but only 5 bytes at a time otherwise. Thus the first step this code performs is to check the key size. If the key size is 1,024 bits, high encryption is available, and 16 byte blocks can be used.

The file writing code is shown below. The most significant lines are highlighted.

```
private void cmdWriteFile_Click(object sender, System.EventArgs e)
{
  // Convert text to a byte array.
  System.Text.UTF8Encoding enc = new System.Text.UTF8Encoding();
  byte[] bytes = enc.GetBytes(txt.Text);
```

```
// Determine the optimum block size for encryption.
int blockSize = 0;
if (crypt.KeySize == 1024)
{
  // High encryption capabilities are in place.
  blockSize = 16;
}
else
{
  // High encryption capabilities are not in place.
  blockSize = 5;
}

// Create the file.
FileStream fs = new FileStream("c:\\testfile.bin",
  FileMode.Create);

// Move through the data one block at a time.
byte[] rawBlock, encryptedBlock;
for (int i = 0; i < bytes.Length; i += blockSize)
{
  if ((bytes.Length - i) > blockSize)
  {
    rawBlock = new byte[blockSize];
  }
  else
  {
    rawBlock = new byte[bytes.Length - i];
  }

  // Copy a block of data.
  Buffer.BlockCopy(bytes, i, rawBlock, 0, rawBlock.Length);

  // Encrypt the block of data.
  encryptedBlock = crypt.Encrypt(rawBlock, false);

  // Write the block of data.
  fs.Write(encryptedBlock, 0, encryptedBlock.Length);
}

// Clean up.
fs.Flush();
fs.Close();
}
```

The static `Buffer.BlockCopy()` method is used to copy each block from the source array into a new array called `rawBlock`. When the last block is encountered, the `rawBlock` array is shortened accordingly; this works because the `Encrypt()` method automatically performs the required padding.

When reading the file, you must take care to only decrypt one block at a time. In this case, the block size is determined by the key size of the algorithm used. The KeySize property provides this information, in bits, so dividing this number by 8 will give the result in bytes. For example, in this case the KeySize is 1,024 bits (or 128 bytes). Thus, data must be decrypted in 128-byte blocks.

After dividing the data into blocks to decrypt it, you need a way to reassemble it so you can convert it back to its original string format. The easiest way to handle this task is with another stream. In this example, the code writes the decrypted data to an in-memory stream, and then reads the complete information when converting it to a string.

```
private void cmdReadFile_Click(object sender, System.EventArgs e)
{
    // Read encrypted data from file.
    FileStream fs = new FileStream("c:\\testfile.bin", FileMode.Open);
    byte[] bytes = new byte[fs.Length];
    fs.Read(bytes, 0, (int)fs.Length);
    fs.Close();

    // Create the memory stream where the decrypted data
    // will be stored.
    MemoryStream ms = new MemoryStream();

    // Determine the block size for decrypting.
    int keySize = crypt.KeySize / 8;

    // Move through the data one block at a time.
    byte[] decryptedBlock, rawBlock;
    for (int i = 0; i < bytes.Length; i += keySize)
    {
        if ((bytes.Length - i) > keySize)
        {
            rawBlock = new byte[keySize];
        }
        else
        {
            rawBlock = new byte[bytes.Length - i];
        }

        // Copy a block of data.
        Buffer.BlockCopy(bytes, i, rawBlock, 0, rawBlock.Length);

        // Decrypt a block of data.
        decryptedBlock = crypt.Decrypt(rawBlock, false);

        // Write the decrypted data to the in-memory stream.
        ms.Write(decryptedBlock, 0, decryptedBlock.Length);
    }
```

```
// Read the in-memory information into a byte array.
ms.Position = 0;
byte[] decoded = new byte[ms.Length];
ms.Read(decoded, 0, (int)ms.Length);

// Convert byte array to text.
System.Text.UTF8Encoding enc = new System.Text.UTF8Encoding();
string text = enc.GetString(decoded, 0, decoded.Length);

// Display the result.
MessageBox.Show("Retrieved: " + text);
txt.Text = text;
}
```

Importing and Exporting Keys as XML

Unlike the symmetric algorithm classes, asymmetric algorithms do not provide any public Key property that you can use to retrieve key information. However, if you need to store the key pair for future use (ideally in some sort of secure store or a key management system), you can retrieve the key information as an XML document. Best of all, this XML document provides you with enough information to reconstruct an identical key later.

The following code outputs the full key information for a key pair using the ToXmlString() method.

```
RSACryptoServiceProvider crypt = new RSACryptoServiceProvider();

// Display XML source for this key.
Console.WriteLine(crypt.ToXmlString(true));
```

The generated information is shown below (in abbreviated form). Each of the values is a Base64 encoding of a binary number. By combining the numbers in one way, you can obtain the public key. By combining them in a different way, you obtain the private key. It's worth noting that this format matches that used for the XML Signatures standard introduced in the next chapter (as well as the XML Encryption and XKMS standards).

```
<RSAKeyValue>
  <Modulus>xTnyhC93bO...</Modulus>
  <Exponent>AQAB</Exponent>
  <P>7yoEyMvp5B63eud3...</P>
  <Q>0xwqy2Leud3GDUQ...</Q>
  <DP>dyzX/3rk421dbh...</DP>
  <DQ>MUdH7gX8O6K7Em...</DQ>
  <InverseQ>f+kt/KTGt...</InverseQ>
  <D>BU/DNUtELSgvqJkb...</D>
</RSAKeyValue>
```

You can create an identical key using this XML document:

```
RSACryptoServiceProvider crypt = new RSACryptoServiceProvider();

// Get XML source for this key.
string key = crypt.ToXmlString(true);

// Destroy the current key.
crypt.Clear();

// Reload the key.
crypt = new RSACryptoServiceProvider();
crypt.FromXmlString(key);
```

Remember, if you export the contents of your key pair, it is up to you to ensure that this XML document is kept secure at all times. If this document is obtained by a third party, your private key will be known, and your encryption system can be easily broken. Even such innocent tasks as storing the key in a string can be subject to an attack in the extreme situation where a malicious user can access your server, cause an error, and perform a memory dump.

> **This problem is impossible to defend against completely, but storing key information in string variables just compounds it, especially because the CLR has the freedom to reallocate memory at will, and may leave sensitive information floating in memory long after you think it has been disposed of or overwritten.**

In the previous example, the XML information was generated with a value of `true` for the `includePrivateParameters` parameter. This means that the full information for both the private and the public key is exported. If, however, you supplied `false`, you'd receive the shorter document shown here:

```
<RSAKeyValue>
  <Modulus>xTnyhC93bO...</Modulus>
  <Exponent>AQAB</Exponent>
</RSAKeyValue>
```

This document only has enough information to generate the public key portion of the key, and thus does not need to be secured. With this information, another user could create an `RSACryptoServiceProvider` object, and use it to encrypt data. Because they lack the private key, you will be the only person able to decrypt this information. They won't be able to use their `RSACryptoServiceProvider` to decrypt data, either, because it won't contain a private key.

Importing and Exporting Keys with Parameters

There's another way to manage key information. You can export information to a special parameter object using the ExportParameters() and ImportParameters() methods. In the case of the RSA algorithm, this parameter object is the RSAParameters class, while in the case of DSA, it's DSAParameters. These objects expose fields that correspond to the XML elements shown in the previous document (for example Modulus, Exponent, and so on). Each provider can define its own specific parameters object, and they don't implement a common interface or derive from a common base class.

Here's an example where the full key information is stored in an RSAParameters instance, and used to recreate the key:

```
RSACryptoServiceProvider crypt = new RSACryptoServiceProvider();

// Get the key information.
RSAParameters param = crypt.ExportParameters(true);

// Destroy the current key.
crypt.Clear();

// Reload the key.
crypt = new RSACryptoServiceProvider();
crypt.ImportParameters(param);
```

Here's an example where only the public key information is used:

```
RSACryptoServiceProvider crypt = new RSACryptoServiceProvider();

// Get the key information.
RSAParameters param = crypt.ExportParameters(false);

// Destroy the current key.
crypt.Clear();

// Reload the key.
crypt = new RSACryptoServiceProvider();
crypt.ImportParameters(param);
```

> **In the CryptoAPI library, it is possible to create key containers that don't allow key information to be exported. If you want to use this technique in .NET, you will need to make unmanaged P/Invoke calls to the CryptoAPI library.**

What if you want to retrieve parameter information from installed certificates? Unfortunately, the .NET Framework does not currently include this functionality. The System.Security.X509Certificates namespace includes the functionality necessary to create certificates, and load them from disk, but it does not allow you to access the computer-specific store. However, this functionality has been added with the WSE (Web Services Enhancements for .NET) in the Microsoft.Web.Services.SecurityX509 namespace.

With WSE, you can use the following code to retrieve information from the local certificate store and uses it to create an RSACryptoServiceProvider. It only works if you have a certificate with private keys in your Personal Certificate Store.

```
// Open the private certificate store of the current user.
X509CertificateStore store = X509CertificateStore.CurrentUserStore(
  X509CertificateStore.MyStore);
store.OpenRead();

// Read first certificates.
X509Certificate c = (X509Certificate)store.Certificates[0];

RSACryptoServiceProvider rsa = new RSACryptoServiceProvider();
rsa.ImportParameters(c1.Key.ExportParameters(true));
```

Storing CSP Keys with a Container

CryptoAPI stores key values in something called a *key container*. A key container is a part of the computer-specific key database where key pairs are stored. Key pairs can belong to a specific user, or just be a part of the shared computer store. When you use a class like RSACryptoServiceProvider, you don't usually worry about the key container, because it is acquired and destroyed automatically. However, in some cases, you might want to create a specific key container.

Using the CspParameter class, you can create a named CryptoAPI storage container. This way, you can generate a random key, and then reuse it by accessing the same key container at a later time.

```
// Set a name for the key container used to store the RSA key pair.
CspParameters cp = new CspParameters();
cp.KeyContainerName = "MyKeyContainerName";

// Create the key in this container.
RSACryptoServiceProvider crypt = new RSACryptoServiceProvider(cp);

// Display the key pair that is in use.
Console.WriteLine(crypt.ToXmlString(true));
```

If you run this application more than once, you will discover that the next time you create the RSACryptoServiceProvider using the same container, you will actually acquire the key created the first time. This is useful for long-term key usage, but it also makes the key potentially available to other applications on the same computer. This can constitute a security risk, depending on the environment.

To ensure that the key is not persisted in the container, add the following code statement:

```
crypt.PersistKeyInCsp = false;
```

Now, the key container will be destroyed along with the key information when you call Clear() or Dispose() on the algorithm implementation class.

Remember, this technique will not apply with an algorithm that is implemented in managed code (like Rijndael). It works because in the CryptoAPI system, every CSP has a key database in which it stores persistent cryptographic keys. The key database is divided into key containers, which contain key pairs for a specific client.

CryptoAPI stores key containers using the file system. They can be found in the Documents and settings directory on the drive where Windows is installed. Keys for interactive users are store in directories like <username>\Application Data\Microsoft\Crypto\RSA\<user SID>, while keys for non-interactive users (like an ASP.NET application) are stored under All Users\Application Data\Microsoft\Crypto\RSA\Machinekeys. If you are using Windows NT, they will be stored in the registry instead of the file system. As a result, users of your application may be able to determine the keys you use in your application if they have the appropriate rights. This is a basic fact of life in programming – a program acts on behalf of the user, and cannot use secret data that the user cannot determine somehow.

CSPs and ASP.NET

If you try to transplant the code examples presented so far into a web service or ASP.NET web page, you'll run into a little trouble. The problem is that when you are using the application from inside ASP.NET, you are not designated as interactive user. There is no current user profile, and thus the Windows operating system cannot retrieve a default key container. This is a problem if you are using an algorithm that relies on CryptoAPI, and you want to dynamically generate a new key.

To overcome this problem, you need to use the information stored in the local machine's keystore. To signal this change, you use the CspParameters object, and modify its Flags property. The Flags property can accept one of two values: UseDefaultKeyContainer (the default) or UseMachineKeyStore.

```
CspParameters cp = new CspParameters();
cp.Flags = CspProviderFlags.UseMachineKeyStore;
RSACryptoServiceProvider crypt = New RSACryptoServiceProvider(cp);
```

Below is an example of a private helper function that you might add to an ASP.NET web page or web service. It dynamically creates a key, and then stores it in application state. It also sets the CspParameters flag as needed.

```
private RSACryptoServiceProvider GetKeyFromState()
{
  RSACryptoServiceProvider crypt;

  // Check if the key has been created yet.
  // This ensures that the key is only created once.
  if (Application("Key") == null)
  {
    // Create a key for RSA encryption.
    CspParameters cp = new CspParameters();
    cp.Flags = CspProviderFlags.UseMachineKeyStore;
    crypt = new RSACryptoServiceProvider(cp);

    // Store the key in the server memory.
    Application("Key") = crypt;
  }
  else
  {
    crypt = (RSACryptoServiceProvider)Application("Key");
  }
  return crypt;
}
```

Remember, the CspParameters object is simply used to pass additional information to CryptoAPI. It should not be confused with the algorithm-specific parameter objects, which are used to export key information.

Encryption Strength

A commonly asked question is "how strong is my encryption"? The answer is often difficult to determine. The most critical weaknesses are errors using the encryption algorithm rather than limitations in the algorithm itself. For example, not storing the key securely (or having end users who talk too much), reusing the same key and initialization vector for all communication are obvious, yet often neglected security holes.

To decipher an encrypted message without the help of these mistakes, hackers typically resort to one of two methods. One method of attack is to look for patterns of repetition in the encrypted data. As discussed, you can defend against this by using CBC chaining and a varying, non-zero initialization vector. The other common form of attack is a brute force attempt to guess your key by trying every possible value. The only way to defend against this attack is to use the strongest possible algorithm (for example, TripleDES or Rijndael instead of DES) with the largest key size (for example, 256 or 192 bits instead of 128). However, experts differ on how long it would take to test every possible combination of key and initialization vector. With specialized hardware and a single expensive (six-figure) computer, it might only take hours to crack a DES-encrypted message. However, the performance cost of using a stronger algorithm is only warranted if you are sending sensitive information to which someone is likely to want to apply such specialized resources.

Summary

In this chapter, you learned how the .NET cryptographic model works with abstract classes, transforms, and streams. You also learned how to perform simple encryption and decryption tasks with symmetric and asymmetric algorithms.

Some of the key lessons we learned in this chapter include:

❑   Symmetric algorithms with key strengths of 128 bits or more are the workhorse of cryptography. The Rijndael algorithm represents the current state of the art in this field.

❑   Symmetric algorithms process data in blocks of a fixed size.

❑   Cipher Block Chaining (CBC) provides the most secure means to apply a symmetric algorithm on a sequence of data blocks.

❑   To add to the security of CBC, we must supply an initialization vector (IV).

❑   .NET CryptoStreams provide a simple interface for reading and writing binary data through a symmetric cryptographic processor, and provide buffering so we don't need to worry about block sizes and padding.

❑   Cryptographic operations work on binary data in the form of byte arrays. We can convert data to byte arrays and back using the BitConverter and System.Text.Encoding classes.

❑   Encrypted binary data can be represented as printable text characters using Base64 encoding.

- Asymmetric ciphers use much larger keys than symmetric ciphers because of the kind of mathematics on which they rely. The default algorithm is RSA, and default keysize is 1,024 bits.

- .NET Asymmetric ciphers don't work with `CryptoStreams`. We must break our own data into blocks, and reconstruct it from blocks. For encryption, we must use blocks of 5 bytes, or 16 bytes if the high encryption support is available. For decryption, we use blocks of the same size as the key (128 bytes for a 1,024 bit key).

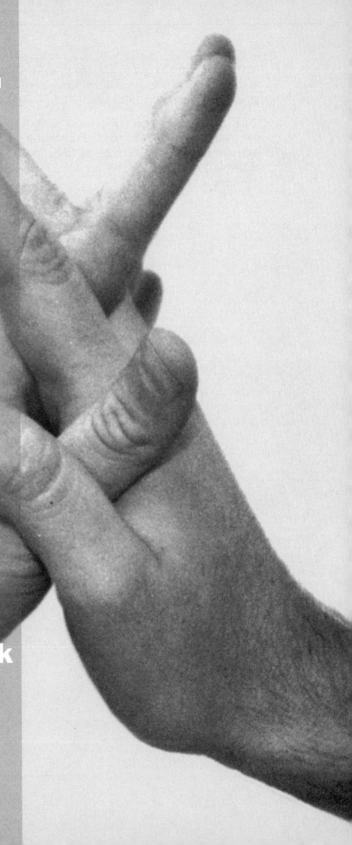

C#

Data Security

Handbook

3

3

Data Integrity – Hash Codes and Signatures

Data encryption may protect your information from prying eyes, but it doesn't stop a malicious user from tampering with it. For example, consider a scenario where you are sending a message over the Internet. If you use encryption, the recipient of this message can be relatively sure that no one else has read the message, but you cannot be as sure that it is the same message the sender originally sent. It may have been altered along the way. Often, such an alteration would lead to obviously garbled data when the message is decrypted. Sometimes the consequences could be more serious, particularly if you are expecting raw binary data or if an entire new message is substituted. To combat this we need an easy, efficient way to verify the integrity (and sometimes authenticity) of a message.

This is the role played by hash codes in cryptography. Hash codes are, in essence, a cryptographically strong checksum. By cryptographically strong we mean that it is practically impossible to find two documents that have the same hash code. In a message exchange scenario, the sender calculates a hash, and appends it to the message. The recipient recalculates the hash code based on the received document, and verifies that it matches the sender's hash code. Of course, hash codes also have a variety of non-cryptography applications, like identifying objects uniquely – but in this case, you don't need a cryptographically strong hash algorithm.

Depending on the hash algorithm, the process can become a little more complicated. You may need to mix hashing with a separate form of encryption to ensure that if a third party intercepts the message, they won't be able to create a new message *and* generate a matching hash code for it. However, the basic principle remains unchanged: hash codes allow you to verify that data remains unaltered, while encryption makes the data opaque to any eavesdroppers.

Of course, safeguarding communication is only one example where hash codes can come into play. Hash codes are also used for all of the following tasks:

❑ To verify that data you are storing on disk hasn't been changed outside your application

❑ To verify that an executable was created by a trusted party (using .NET's ingrained support for public key signing and strong names)

❑ To verify that an executable hasn't changed *at all* since it's been deployed

❑ To verify that all or part of an XML document hasn't been changed

❑ To validate passwords without storing the original password data (all you need to do is verify the hash)

❑ To create a short, unique identifier for a document or application file

In this chapter, you'll learn how to apply these hashing techniques. We'll explore basic hashing, keyed hashes, digital signatures, and the XML Signatures standard.

Hash Algorithms

A hash algorithm takes an arbitrary amount of data (as a large block of binary information), and uses it to generate a small hash code that is effectively unique to that information. The following pseudo code represents this process.

```
Hash = HashAlgorithmFunction(Data)
```

All cryptographic hash algorithms must be:

❑ **One-way** – as you might expect, it should completely impossible to recreate the document from the hash, because the hash will not include all the information that was in the document. However, it is also computationally unfeasible to determine *anything* about the information just by examining the hash.

❑ **Collision resistant** – meaning that it is computationally unfeasible to create another document that generates an identical hash. There are more possible documents to hash than there are 20-byte hashes – a typical size for a hash code. But the number of possible 20 byte hashes is actually vastly larger than the number of documents the human race will ever manage to produce. If you assign the hash value to the document in the right way you can statistically guarantee that there will never be a collision because the number of possible hashes is so big.

This behavior is important in a wide variety of circumstances. For example, you wouldn't want a client to create an altered version of a contract that still has the same hash code.

It's for these reasons that hashes are sometimes referred to as cryptographically strong checksums. With a typical checksum (like the Cyclical Redundancy Check (CRC) commonly used in filesystems), it is relatively easy to create another document that generates an identical checksum. In the case of a hash code, this is all but impossible.

.NET Hash Classes

Hash algorithm classes use the same three-layer inheritance model introduced in Chapter 2. All hash algorithms supported in by the .NET Framework inherit from the HashAlgorithm abstract class. The following table lists all the supported algorithms (except keyed hash algorithms, which are covered later in the chapter).

Algorithm	Abstract Hash Algorithm Class	Implementation Classes	Hash Size (in bits)
MD5	MD5	MD5CryptoServiceProvider	128
SHA-1	SHA1	SHA1CryptoServiceProvider	160
		SHA1Managed	160
SHA-256	SHA256	SHA256Managed	256
SHA-384	SHA384	SHA384Managed	384
SHA-512	SHA512	SHA512Managed	512

> *The SHA-1 algorithm is currently the only algorithm in the .NET Framework that has both a managed and a CryptoAPI implementation. The CryptoAPI implementation (SHA1CryptoServiceProvider) is the default, but you can use the managed implementation (SHA1Managed) manually if desired.*

All hash algorithms use either SHA (Secure Hash Algorithm) or MD5 (Message Digest 5). For the most part, the larger the hash size, the more resistant the hash code will be against brute force attacks (the harder it would be to find a document that satisfies the same hash). Generally, hash strengths map to encryption strength with a key size that is half the size of the hash algorithm. In other words, SHA-256 provides approximately the same resistance to brute force attacks as Rijndael with 128-bit key, SHA-384 maps to a 192-bit key, and SHA-512 maps to a 256-bit key.

The likelihood of a duplicate hash value being created is inversely related to the size of the hash. If a hash is 256-bits, there are 2^{256} different possible hash codes. By pure chance, you wouldn't expect to find a duplicate until you looked at about 10^{76} documents. Keep in mind as a comparison, there are only an estimated 10^{66} atoms in the universe!

The HashAlgorithm Class

The abstract `HashAlgorithm` class defines the members supported by concrete algorithm implementation classes. The abstract `KeyedHashAlgorithm` class, derives from `HashAlgorithm` and adds a `Key` property, which we'll consider later on.

The `HashAlgorithm` provides a `Create()` method that generates the default implementation class. As with symmetric encryption, you should use this method, and leave your code more generic. For example, the following code statement creates the default MD5 implementation class (which is `MD5CryptoServiceProvider`).

```
HashAlgorithm hash = MD5.Create();
```

Moreover, this code creates an instance of the default implementation for the default hashing algorithm, `SHA1CryptoServiceProvider`:

```
HashAlgorithm hash = HashAlgorithm.Create();
```

The `HashAlgorithm` class also defines a `Clear()` method, which erases the last generated hash from memory, (which can also be called indirectly through the `Dispose()` method) and a `ComputeHash()` method, which creates the hash for a given buffer of data. Finally, `HashAlgorithm` also implements the `ICryptoTransform` interface, which means it can be used as part of a `CryptoStream` to wrap another `Stream`-derived object.

Computing a Hash

Calculating a hash value is as simple as calling the `ComputeHash()` method. The `ComputeHash()` method is overloaded in two useful ways, which allows you to calculate a hash for just a portion of a byte array by specifying an offset, or for a stream. The example below is a simple console application that creates a hash algorithm instance and displays the size of the hash. Then it creates a hash value for a small array of binary data (`data`) and prints out the resulting hash value

```
// HashTest.cs

using System;
using System.Security.Cryptography;

public class HashTest
  {
    static void Main(string[] args)
    {
    HashAlgorithm hash = HashAlgorithm.Create();
```

```
    // Display hash algorithm information.
    Console.Write("Hash size: ");
    Console.WriteLine(hash.HashSize.ToString() + " bits");
    Console.Write("Hash size: ");
    Console.WriteLine((hash.HashSize/8).ToString() + " bytes");
    Console.WriteLine();

    // Data to be hashed
    byte[] data = {200, 34, 12, 14, 210, 199, 172, 77};
    // Create hash
    byte[] hashBytes = hash.ComputeHash(data);

    // Display the hash.
    Console.Write("Hash: " + BitConverter.ToString(hashBytes));
    Console.Read();
  }
}
```

The output looks like this:

```
Hash size: 160 bits
Hash size: 20 bytes

Hash: 6F-F3-AD-EC-31-4A-63-C6-80-95-62-B9-C6-16-22-64-F4-03-91-26
```

You'll notice that the hash size is fixed. For example, when using the SHA-1 algorithm (as we are in this example), the resulting hash will always be 20 bytes, no matter how small or large the source data is.

> *(However, it's recommended for best security that your source data be at least equal to the hash size. This prevents attacks that work by computing the hash codes of all possible short messages.)*

Interestingly, the last computed hash is always available in the Hash property of the implementation class. Thus, you could iterate through the hash in the previous example with the following equivalent code:

```
foreach (byte hashByte in hash.Hash)
{
    ...
}
```

If you run this test application multiple times, you will receive the same hash, unless you alter the source data. To drive this point home, consider the next example, which uses a test to verify two identical strings. We create the hashes independently, using separate instances of the SHA1CryptoServiceProvider. Then, the code iterates through the hash data, testing for each byte for value equality. Because the hashes are identical, this will produce a match.

Note that you *cannot* use the `Equals()` method to compare the two arrays. This method tests for reference equality. It will only return `true` if both objects are stored in the same location in memory – in other words, if both variables are actually pointing at the same array.

```
// HashTest2.cs

using System;
using System.Security.Cryptography;

class HashTest2
{
  static void Main(string[] args)
  {
    HashAlgorithm hashA = HashAlgorithm.Create();
    HashAlgorithm hashB = HashAlgorithm.Create();

    // Create two identical strings
    string sourceString = "This is a test string";
    string matchString = "This is a test string";

    System.Text.UTF8Encoding enc = new System.Text.UTF8Encoding();

    // Create a hash for the first string
    byte[] sourceBytes = enc.GetBytes(sourceString);
    byte[] sourceHash = hashA.ComputeHash(sourceBytes);

    // Create a hash for the second string
    byte[] matchBytes = enc.GetBytes(matchString);
    byte[] matchHash = hashB.ComputeHash(matchBytes);

    // Test for value equality.
    bool match = true;
    for (int i = 0; i < sourceHash.Length; i++)
    {
      if (sourceHash[i] != matchHash[i])
      {
        match = false;
      }
    }

    if (match)
    {
      Console.WriteLine("The hashes are identical");
    }
    else
    {
      Console.WriteLine("The hashes do not match");
    }
```

```
      Console.ReadLine();
   }
}
```

The output for this demonstration is as follows:

```
The hashes are identical
```

You could also test for matching hashes by converting them to a common representation (like a string), and then comparing the two strings. However, the approach shown above is commonly used.

> **Note that in order for this to work; you must be sure that you use the same encoding when to converting the string to bytes. There is no easy way to enforce this, or detect a hash discrepancy that is caused by a different type of text encoding.**

What you actually do with a hash code once you create it depends on the application itself. We'll look at these issues latter on in the section *Storing Hashes and Signatures*.

Hashing Data in a Stream

The ComputeHash() method also provides an overloaded version that accepts a stream. In this case, the ComputeHash() method reads the entire stream from the current position, and calculates a hash on all the data it reads.

```
// HashStream.cs

using System;
using System.IO;
using System.Security.Cryptography;

class HashStream
{
   static void Main(string[] args)
   {
      Console.WriteLine("Enter A File Name:");
      String fileName = Console.ReadLine();
      FileStream fs = new FileStream(fileName, FileMode.Open);
      // Calculate the hash.
      HashAlgorithm hash = HashAlgorithm.Create();
      Byte[] hashBytes = hash.ComputeHash(fs);
      fs.Close();
```

```
        // Display the hash data
        Console.Write("Hash: ");
        Console.Write(BitConverter.ToString(hashBytes));
        Console.Read();
    }
}
```

If you want to use the stream after this operation, you will need to reset the position of the stream back to the beginning (and in this example, you would need to leave the file open).

Hashing Data in a CryptoStream

Because HashAlgorithm class implements the ICryptoTransform interface, you can also use it with a CryptoStream instance. This is primarily useful when you are performing another cryptography operation at the same time – for example, if you are encrypting a document along with its hash code. The HashAlgorithm acts as a pass-through transform; it doesn't actually alter the data. However, once you call FlushFinalBlock() on the CryptoStream, you can retrieve the computed hash for all the data that went through the stream. Note that the CryptoStream used for hashing must be in write mode, or it will not compute the hash correctly. This makes some tasks a little more awkward. If you want to compute a hash value on a read-only stream, you must read this information into an in-memory buffer. This is obviously less suitable if you need to create a hash code for a large amount of data.

> When using the HashAlgorithm in a CryptoStream, the CryptoStream must be in write mode. If you try to use read mode (for example, calculate a hash while retrieving file information) an exception will not be thrown – but the hash value will be invalid. In fact, it may contain hash data corresponding to a random location in memory.

The following code shows a console application that uses a CryptoStream to perform hashing while reading a file.

```
// HashStream2.cs

using System;
using System.IO;
using System.Security.Cryptography;

class HashStream2
{
    static void Main(string[] args)
```

```csharp
{
    // Open the file
    Console.Write("Enter A File Name: ");
    string fileName = Console.ReadLine();
    FileStream fs = new FileStream(fileName, FileMode.Open);

    /*
       Create the hashing stream (must map to a writable stream,
       like a memory stream)
    */
    HashAlgorithm hash = HashAlgorithm.Create();
    MemoryStream ms = new MemoryStream();
    CryptoStream cs = new CryptoStream(ms, hash,
                                       CryptoStreamMode.Write);

    // Display the data
    Console.Write("Data: ");
    byte fileByte;
    do
    {
        fileByte = (byte)fs.ReadByte();
        cs.WriteByte(fileByte);
        Console.Write(fileByte.ToString() + " ");
    } while (fs.Position != fs.Length);
    cs.FlushFinalBlock();
    fs.Close();

    // Display the hash data (note that ComputeHash() is not used)
    byte[] hashBytes = hash.Hash;
    Console.WriteLine();
    Console.Write("Hash: ");
    Console.Write(BitConverter.ToString(hashBytes));
    Console.Read();
}
}
```

Salted Hashes

We mentioned earlier that if the data hashed is short and very predictable, it is feasible for someone to hash every string in a dictionary of possible values and use this as a lookup table to find the secret value. Even if it takes a very long time to compute this lookup table that's not such a big problem as you only have to do it once.

It is common in many systems to store passwords in hashed form so that if someone manages to break into the system and steal the password file you don't give up all your users' passwords. Unfortunately, this file will be vulnerable to someone who has created a list of the hash values of likely passwords.

One way to defeat precompiled dictionary attacks is to use a salted hash. This is the approach taken by many operating systems (including Unix) when storing passwords. One approach to hashing and salting is shown below. Essentially, it works as follows. When a hash is created, these steps are taken:

1. Convert the data (say a password) to a byte array

2. Add the random salt to the password, and hash everything

3. Store the hashed value and the original salt together.

It is important to use an unguessable, cryptographically strong, random number as the salt value; see Appendix B for more information on this. The basic principle is that the hash value is generated using a random series of bytes (the "salt"). In a table of passwords, each password would have a different salt value. This means that the attacker will have to run a dictionary attack against each hash in the file rather than use a precompiled lookup table as the data has a random component. An example of storing passwords using this technique is given in Chapter 4.

This technique does offer extra security but given the speed of modern processors not very much. At best it will slow an attacker down and give you time to warn users that their passwords have been compromised.

Hash Codes with Encryption

Hash codes allow you to verify that data hasn't been altered. However, hash codes have an obvious limitation, which is particularly prominent in distributed communication scenarios. The problem is that a malicious individual could substitute a false message and generate a corresponding hash code for it. The receiving application would then test the message, see that the hash code is accurate, and have no way of knowing that this wasn't the original message. This is the man-in-the-middle attack, which we introduced in Chapter 1.

There are three approaches to solve this problem, and all of them blend hashing with encryption:

❑ **Encrypt the entire message**, including the message body and its hash. You could use either symmetric or asymmetric encryption, depending on the scenario. Alternatively, you could encrypt just the hash, using one of the following techniques.

❑ **Use a keyed hash function**, which combines hashing with symmetric encryption. *Keyed hash* functions use a secret key along with the message when creating the hash. A malicious user cannot generate a hash for a new message, because they won't have the secret key.

❑ **Use a digital signature,** which combines hashing with asymmetric encryption. Essentially, you compute the hash, and then encrypt it using a private key. A malicious user can't generate a false hash, because they lack the private key.

Use the first option when you need to protect your message from eavesdropping and from tampering. If you only need to protect the message from tampering, but not from eavesdropping, you can either of the other options. Your choice of a keyed hash function or a digital signature depends on the scenario. If there is a suitable value to use as a shared secret key, you might use a keyed hash function, while a digital signature would ensure that anyone could verify your message by using your public key.

Hashing and Encrypting a File

The easiest way to hash and encrypt at the same time is to use a single CryptoStream object for encrypting, and calculate the hash directly with the HashAlgorithm class. The important detail to remember is that you must encrypt the hash. The easiest way to do this is to perform the hashing first, and then encrypt the entire resulting document. If you encrypt the document, and then generate a hash, your hash code is not protected, and an attacker would still be able to substitute a false message (even if that message would not be decipherable at the other end).

The basic process is to read the file, write the encrypted file data to a new stream, and append a hash code, the code for this section can be found in the file EncryptHash.cs. We begin by creating two file streams, one for reading, and one for writing:

```
// EncryptHash.cs
// ...
// Open the input file.
FileStream fsInput = new FileStream("c:\\customers.xml",
  FileMode.Open);

// Open the output file.
FileStream fsOutput = new FileStream("c:\\customers.enc",
  FileMode.Create);
```

Next, you must create two CryptoStream objects. The first wraps the output file, and performs the encryption. The second wraps the encrypting stream, and calculates the hash.

```
// Create the encrypting stream (in write mode).
Rijndael crypt = Rijndael.Create();
CryptoStream csEncrypt = new CryptoStream(fsOutput,
  crypt.CreateEncryptor(), CryptoStreamMode.Write);
```

```
// Create the hash stream (in write mode).
HashAlgorithm hash = HashAlgorithm.Create();
CryptoStream csHash = new CryptoStream(csEncrypt, hash,
  CryptoStreamMode.Write);
```

With these streams in place, you can now write the data. In this case, we transfer data one block at a time. This offers good performance, and would give you the chance to update some sort of progress counter if needed.

```
byte[] bytes = new byte[1024];
int bytesRead = 0;
do
{
  // Read a block of 1K.
  bytesRead = fsInput.Read(bytes, 0, 1024);

  // Write the block (encrypted).
  csEncrypt.Write(bytes, 0, bytesRead);
} while (bytesRead > 0);
```

After writing the data we calculate the hash and added it to the file.

```
fsInput.Position = 0;
hash.ComputeHash(fsInput);
fsInput.Close();
csEncrypt.Write(hash.Hash, 0, hash.Hash.Length);

csEncrypt.FlushFinalBlock();
fsOutput.Close();
```

The reverse is slightly more awkward, because you need to manually calculate the byte offsets, strip out the hash, and verify it. If you aren't careful, you'll end up with a great deal of byte copying logic, which is bound to be inefficient and difficult to maintain. Unfortunately, the .NET Framework does not provide any higher-level abstractions for these tasks.

To make life a little easier, the code below uses a MemoryStream to piece together the chunks read from the file. The other alternative would be to create a byte array with the correct size by examining the length of the encrypted file, calculating the length of the corresponding decrypted data using the block size of the encryption algorithm, and then subtracting the size of the hash. Not only would this code be more subject to error, but also it would probably need updating if you wanted to modify your encryption logic to use a different hash size. To get around this, you might want to store some information about the hash algorithm with the hash, much as digital signatures do.

```csharp
// Open the input file
FileStream fsInput2 = new FileStream("c:\\customers.enc",
                                     FileMode.Open);

// Create the decrypting stream (in read mode).
CryptoStream csInput = new CryptoStream(fsInput2,
  crypt.CreateDecryptor(), CryptoStreamMode.Read);

// A memory stream makes it easy to piece together the data
MemoryStream ms = new MemoryStream();

do
{
  // Read a block of 1K.
  bytesRead = csInput.Read(bytes, 0, 1024);

  // Write the block (decrypted), into memory.
  ms.Write(bytes, 0, bytesRead);
} while (bytesRead > 0);
fsInput2.Close();

// Copy the file data into a byte array
byte[] fileBytes = new byte[ms.Length - hash.HashSize/8];
ms.Position = 0;
ms.Read(fileBytes, 0, fileBytes.Length);

// Copy the hash data into a byte array
byte[] hashBytes = new byte[hash.HashSize/8];
ms.Read(hashBytes, 0, hash.HashSize/8);

// Calculate the hash of the decrypted data
hash.ComputeHash(fileBytes, 0, fileBytes.Length);

// Check if the hashes check out
if (CompareHash(hashBytes, hash.Hash))
{
  System.Text.UTF8Encoding enc = new System.Text.UTF8Encoding();
  Console.WriteLine(enc.GetString(fileBytes));
}
else
{
  Console.WriteLine("The file has been tampered with");
}
Console.Read();
```

In this case, we also make use of a private helper function called `CompareHash()`:

```
// Tests two byte arrays for value equality.
private static bool CompareHash(byte[] hashA, byte[] hashB)
{
  // Verify the array sizes match.
  if (hashA.Length != hashB.Length)
  {
    throw new ArgumentException("Hashes must be same length");
  }

  // Verify that each individual byte matches.
  bool match = true;
  for (int i = 0; i < hashA.Length; i++)
  {
    if (hashA[i] != hashB[i])
    {
      match = false;
    }
  }
  return match;
}
```

This works well enough as an example, but you might think twice before implementing this hashing approach in a production system. A good rule of thumb is to write as little encryption code as possible, and always have a cryptography expert review it. Quite simply, it's far too easy to make a low-level error that will be time-consuming to discover. Common problems include:

❑ Errors caused by calculating byte lengths using the encrypted data instead of the source data, and vice versa.

❑ Trying to perform hashing on a read-only stream, or incorrectly layering more than one `CryptoStream`. This can lead to problems where you inadvertently write an unencrypted hash value at the end of an encrypted file.

❑ Calculating the hash size incorrectly or using different hash sizes when creating the hash and when verifying it.

❑ Expecting the hashed data at the beginning of the file, when it is at the end. (Ideally, you will sidestep this problem by using a secure catalog like a database to record hashes, but this is not always possible.)

All these trivial problems have big consequences. If you change even one byte in your source, the hash will be completely different (technically, every bit has a 50/50 chance of changing). This could have a serious implication if you change the data you hash. For example, consider an application that use hash codes to verify some portions of serialized data. If you change this application to hash additional information, you'll break backward compatibility with all existing documents.

If you need to hash and encrypt information in the same file, consider developing your own helper methods similar to CompareHash() to automate some of the low-level work needed to work with raw bytes. Ideally, these helper functions could be included in a dedicated component, which would encapsulate all details about string to binary conversion, hash size, and verification, and the functionality required to split a hash from its data when they are lumped together in one stream.

Keyed Hash Algorithms

The .NET Framework provides two keyed hash algorithms. Both of these derive from the KeyedHashAlgorithm class, which adds a Key property to store the secret value that will be used to create the hash.

Algorithm	Abstract Class	Default Implementation Class	Hash Size (bits)	Key Size
HMAC-SHA1	KeyedHashAlgorithm	HMACSHA1	160	64 (recommended)
MAC-3DES-CBC	KeyedHashAlgorithm	MACTripleDES	64	24

HMAC-SHA1 combines the HMAC (Hash-based Message Authentication Code) hash encryption standard with SHA1 hashing. MAC-3DES-CBC encrypts the entire message with TripleDES, using Cipher Block Chaining (CBC) mode so that each block influences the encryption of the next block, and then retains just the last block. It automatically pads with zeroes and sets the initialization vector to all zeroes. HMAC-SHA1 is the default keyed hash algorithm, and so an instance of the HMACSHA1 class will be created when invoking KeyedHashAlgorithm.Create(). It provides greater security through a larger size, and is preferred unless message size is a concern.

The easiest way to understand keyed hashed algorithms is to consider our earlier example that independently hashed two strings. If you substitute a KeyedHashAlgorithm in the place of the HashAlgorithm, the hashes will not be equal, because the automatically generated key will differ:

```
// HashTest3.cs

...

KeyedHashAlgorithm hashA = KeyedHashAlgorithm.Create();
KeyedHashAlgorithm hashB = KeyedHashAlgorithm.Create();
```

```
// Create two identical strings.
string sourceString = "This is a test string";
string matchString = "This is a test string";

System.Text.UTF8Encoding enc = new System.Text.UTF8Encoding();

// Create a hash for the first string.
byte[] sourceBytes = enc.GetBytes(sourceString);
byte[] sourceHash = hashA.ComputeHash(sourceBytes);

// Create a hash for the second string.
byte[] matchBytes = enc.GetBytes(matchString);
byte[] matchHash = hashB.ComputeHash(matchBytes);

// Test for value equality.
bool match = true;
for (int i = 0; i < sourceHash.Length; i++)
{
  if (sourceHash[i] != matchHash[i])
  {
    match = false;
  }
}
```

To make this sample work, all you need to do is make sure that each
KeyedHashAlgorithm instance is using the same key. In this case you can just add
the following code after both instances are created:

```
hashA.Key = hashB.Key;
```

Of course, in a real-world scenario, this key would be retrieved from some sort of
secure key storage, possibly a database.

Digital Signatures

Digital signatures are hash codes that have been encrypted using an asymmetric
algorithm. The benefit is that you can verify digital signatures without requiring a secret
key exchange, because only the public key is required. If desired, the public key can
even be added to the end of the signed message, although the recipient must take care
to check that the public key matches that of the expected sender!

There is more than one way to create a digital signature, but both rely on either the
DSACryptoServiceProvider or the RSACryptoServiceProvider class, which
were introduced in the last chapter. You may remember from the last chapter that it's
easiest to create the concrete implementation classes directly, because they expose
useful methods for encryption and decryption that are not available in the abstract DSA
and RSA classes. The same is true of the digital signatures.

The first example uses the DSACryptoServiceProvider, which exposes a SignData() and a VerifyData() method. The code begins by creating two instances of DSACryptoServiceProvider, each with different key information. The first instance signs a byte array, and the second is used to attempt to authenticate it.

```
// DigitalSig.cs
// ...
// Create two signature objects
DSACryptoServiceProvider dsaA = new DSACryptoServiceProvider();
DSACryptoServiceProvider dsaB = new DSACryptoServiceProvider();

// Create some data.
string sourceString = "This is a test string";
System.Text.UTF8Encoding enc = new System.Text.UTF8Encoding();
byte[] sourceBytes = enc.GetBytes(sourceString);

// Create a hash for the data, and sign it
byte[] signedHash = dsaA.SignData(sourceBytes, 0,
  sourceBytes.Length);

// Export the public key data from the signer
string publicKey = dsaA.ToXmlString(false);
//Import public key data
dsaB.FromXmlString(publicKey);

if (dsaB.VerifyData(sourceBytes, signedHash))
{
  Console.WriteLine("Signature authenticated");
}
else
{
  Console.WriteLine("Invalid signature.");
}
Console.Read();
```

Note that the dsaB object is created using the public key of dsA. The ToXmlString() method is used to export the key information from the signing object, and the FromXmlString() method imports it into the verifying object. Note that the false parameter is used to ensure that only the public key is exported. However, this is all that is needed to verify the signature.

Of course, you could perform both steps with the same DSACryptoServiceProvider object, but this is not very likely in a real-world scenario. Normally the signature verification will take place some period after the actual signing, and possibly on another computer or in another application. In that case you would create the DSACryptoServiceProvider by retrieving the public key, proably from a digital certificate; for more information on managing keys see Chapter 6.

The `DSACryptoServiceProvider` relies on the SHA1 algorithm. When you call `SignData()` it generates an SHA1 hash, and then encrypts it using DSA. You could perform this task manually by using the `SHA1CryptoServiceProvider` class to create the hash code, and then using this hash code with the `SignHash()` and `VerifyHash()` methods of the `DSACryptoServiceProvider`. However, using the `VerifyData()` method is much easier and more conventional. It also performs the tedious work of comparing hash bytes.

The `SignData()` method also provides two overloads, which allow you to create a signature for a portion of a byte array, or a stream (starting at the current position and reading to the end).

> **Remember digital signatures are nothing more than encrypted hash codes. You will still need to send the data along with the signature. The recipient will also need to separate the signature from the data (based on the signature size) before validating it.**

Specifying the Hash Algorithm

The `RSACryptoServiceProvider` includes slightly different versions of the `SignData()` and `VerifyData()` methods. These methods accept an additional parameter, which specifies what hashing algorithm should be used. However, you can only use algorithms that are supported by CryptoAPI. For example, here is the rewritten code, which uses MD5 hashing.

```
// DigitalSig2.cs
// ...
// Create two signature objects
RSACryptoServiceProvider dsaA = new RSACryptoServiceProvider();
RSACryptoServiceProvider dsaB = new RSACryptoServiceProvider();

// Create some data
string sourceString = "This is a test string";
System.Text.UTF8Encoding enc = new System.Text.UTF8Encoding();
byte[] sourceBytes = enc.GetBytes(sourceString);

// Create a hash for the data, and sign it
byte[] sourceHash = dsaA.SignData(sourceBytes, 0, sourceBytes.Length,
  MD5.Create());

// Copy the public key
string signature = dsaA.ToXmlString(false);
dsaB.FromXmlString(signature);

// Verify hash
Console.WriteLine(dsaB.VerifyData(sourceBytes, MD5.Create(),
  sourceHash));
```

Signing after Hashing

There is another, equivalent way to use digital signatures: by using
CreateSignature() and VerifySignature() methods of an
AsymmetricSignatureFormatter class. These methods sign a hash value, so you
need to perform the hashing yourself first, using your preferred algorithm. The
example below explicitly calls ComputeHash() using the
SHA1CryptoServiceProvider class.

```
// DigitalSig3.cs
// ...
// Create some data.
string sourceString = "This is a test string";
System.Text.UTF8Encoding enc = new System.Text.UTF8Encoding();
byte[] sourceBytes = enc.GetBytes(sourceString);

// Create asymmetric algorithm class and linked signature formatter.
DSACryptoServiceProvider dsaA = new DSACryptoServiceProvider();
DSASignatureFormatter formatter = new DSASignatureFormatter(dsaA);

// Create a hash algorithm class.
SHA1 sha = SHA1.Create();

// Create a signature.
byte[] signedHash = formatter.CreateSignature(
   sha.ComputeHash(sourceBytes));
```

The process works more or less the same in reverse with the
DSASignatureDeformatter, the main difference being you need to import the
signature. In this case

```
DSACryptoServiceProvider dsaB = new DSACryptoServiceProvider();
string signature = dsaA.ToXmlString(false);
dsaB.FromXmlString(signature);
DSASignatureDeformatter deformatter =
   new DSASignatureDeformatter(dsaB);

// Verify the signature.
Console.WriteLine(deformatter.VerifySignature(
   sha.ComputeHash(sourceBytes), signedHash));
Console.Read();
```

Currently, there isn't much benefit to this alternative approach, but it does allow
developers to create additional formatters (or use those that third-party vendors or
future versions of the .NET Framework may provide).

> **The DSA algorithm generates and uses a random number, which means that signatures of the same data with the same key will not be the same. Also note the DSA is more computationally intensive than the equivalent use of RSA (some 10-40 times).**

Storing Hashes and Signatures

What you actually do with a hash code once you've create it depends on the application itself, but there are only two basic options:

❑   **Store it in a separate (secure) location** – This option is useful if you want to use plain unencrypted hash values but need to be sure that the file-hash pair cannot be substituted. The other place where this option might be useful is as part of a logging system.

   In many circumstances using a keyed hash or digital signature might be better.

❑   **Store it with the data** – this option is not suitable for plain hashes if any level of security is required. However with keyed hashes and signature it is the preferred option.

   •   Prepend/Append the hash to the message or file. This is very simple to do but not very flexible. When extracting the hash at a later point you need to know the size of the hash and which end of the file it is at.

   •   Normally when you are extracting the hash you will just take the first/last x many bytes. So this approach assumes you know how big the hash is and the file is encoded in the same way as it was when the hash was appended.

   •   Envelope the hash within the file. This is a bit more complex, but it a bit more flexible as it would make it simple to add information about the type of hashing used to the file, enabling the application to support more than one type of algorithm. PGP use this sort of encapsulation placing the signature of a signed message inside delimiters:

```
To: <someone@wrox.com>
From: <someoneelse@somewhere.com>
-----BEGIN PGP SIGNED MESSAGE-----
Hash: SHA1

This is a PGP signed message

-----BEGIN PGP SIGNATURE-----
Version: PGPfreeware 6.5.3 for non-commercial use
<http://www.pgp.com>
```

iQA/AwUBPey8XgvjnxKFgR95EQKWfQCgnmPWjTQtiHeyUior3OLIgWvfZs8An
3mCZiYUqtAsVMkhq2lwkzrOAwOG=6Iy7
```
-----END PGP SIGNATURE-----
```

- Store it in a separate file
  If you are hashing a file/message used by other applications altering
  the file format probably isn't an option. For instance if you want to
  sign an executable file `MyProgramme.exe` you could not append a
  signature to the file as it wouldn't run. However you could store the
  signature in a file `MyPrograme.sig`.

- If you were hashing a serializable object you could store the hash
  value in a custom field and verify it when you deserialize the object.

All these approaches limit interoperability and are non-standard. To address these
problems a standard XML-based format for working with signatures has been defined.

XML Signatures

You can apply all the techniques you've learned so far to encrypt an XML document
(just like any other data), and generate a hash code for it. This is suitable if you want
to encrypt an entire XML document at once. The resulting format will no longer be
XML, and you are free to use your own proprietary system to decide whether to
prepend or append a hash code or digital signature.

The situation becomes a little less clear if you want to deal with XML data in a way that
is standardized and platform independent. The problems you might face include:

- How do you encode just part of an XML document, and in such a way that
  the resulting document is still valid XML?

- How do you determine a consistent way of representing XML so that hash
  code verification will succeed on multiple platforms and with multiple
  XML parsers?

- How do you apply different digital signatures to different parts of an
  unencrypted XML document? Moreover, where in the XML document can
  you store the digital signatures or hash values in a way that is consistent,
  flexible, and easy to retrieve?

- Should you perform encryption or signing first? Remember, because signing
  involves a private key, the signature does not need to be manually encrypted.

Unfortunately, these answers are not all available today. Answering these questions takes a far more fine-grained approach to encryption and digital signing than is currently the norm. There are a number of recommendations or draft specifications from the World Wide Web Consortium, including XML Encryption Syntax and Processing (http://www.w3.org/TR/xmlenc-core), XML Signatures (http://www.w3.org/TR/xmldsig-core), and XML Decryption Transform for XML Signatures (http://www.w3.org/2001/04/decrypt#). Out of these three, the only one that is incorporated in the .NET Framework in any way is XML Signatures, through the `System.Security.Cryptography.Xml` namespace. These types are the focus of the remainder of this chapter.

XML Canonicalization

One critical issue with XML signing is determining the appropriate form that the XML should be placed in before the signature is computed. As you'll remember from earlier in this chapter, changing a single value in a source document will dramatically alter a hash or signature for that data. That means that the flexibility of XML can actually become a serious problem. For example, consider these two documents:

```
<parentNode>
  <childNode></childNode>
</parentNode>
```

```
<parentNode>
  <childNode />
</parentNode>
```

The two XML InfoSets are equivalent, but the markup is different. Thus, the digital signatures for these two documents will not agree. This could lead to a problem if the first document is converted into the second document by a different XML parser (perhaps one used on a different platform). The recipient will no longer be able to verify the original signature. Even more frustrating, the same problem can occur just by the addition of insignificant whitespace.

To overcome this sort of problem, it's necessary to use a canonicalization algorithm. Canonicalization is the process of resolving various equivalent forms of something to a single, standard form. In this case, we are converting an XML document into a standardized format. One such standard is the Canonical XML specification (http://www.w3.org/TR/xml-c14n), which is also used in conjunction with XML Signatures. If you applied the canonicalization algorithm to both of the documents in the previous example, they would both be formatted to use the extra `</childNode>` tag. The .NET Framework provides an implementation of the Canonical XML specification, which is applied automatically when you use the types in the `System.Security.Cryptography.Xml` namespace.

The XML Signature Specification

The XML Signatures specification defines a `<Signature>` element that includes the signature data, and other information about the signature. This information includes details like the type of signature used, a reference to the signed data, and optionally the public key information required to verify the signature. The basic skeleton of the `<Signature>` element is shown here:

```
<Signature>
  <SignedInfo>
    <CanonicalizationMethod>
      <SignatureMethod>
        (<Reference URI="">
          (<Transforms>)?
          <DigestMethod>
          <DigestValue>
        </Reference>)+
  </SignedInfo>
  <SignatureValue>
  (<KeyInfo>)?
  (<Object>)*
</Signature>
```

In this case, ? means zero or one occurrence, + means one or more occurrences, and * means zero or more occurrences. The parentheses indicate to what elements these special characters apply.

Element	Description
SignedInfo	Includes the signature, and information about how it is computed and what data it was computed for.
CanonicalizationMethod	Specifies the algorithm used to canonicalize the XML so that logically equivalent XML is physically identical. This will be the Canonical XML algorithm.
SignatureMethod	Specifies the algorithm used to sign the XML. The XML Signatures specification defines two algorithms: DSA, and RSA with SHA-1 hashing (known as PKCS1).
Reference	Identifies the data that is signed. This can be a reference to data embedded inside the `<Signature>` element, information in the same document but separate from the `<Signature>` element, or information in a separate file.

Table continued on following page

Element	Description
Transforms	Specifies transforms (like a Base64 conversion) that are applied before hashing, and information about the type of signature (enveloped, detached, or embedded). The order of multiple transform elements is significant – it determines the order that transforms are applied.
DigestMethod	Specifies the algorithm used to hash the XML before signing it. (Digest is a synonym for hash.)
DigestValue	Specifies the computed hash. This hash is encrypted to create the signature.
KeyInfo	Specifies information about the public key that can be used to verify the signature, such as the algorithm and possibly even including the public portion of the key. This element is optional.
Object	If you are using an embedded signature, this contains the signed data.

There is a security risk involved with specifying the public key information in the XML file. A user could theoretically substitute a new signature and a new public key, and the document would be successfully validated. This is a classic man-in-the-middle attack; the only defense is to verify that the public key is from the expected sender.

You can use a signature to sign a single element in an XML document, or an entire document. The <Reference> element identifies the data that is signed. This could be a URI pointing to another file, or a reference pointing to a portion of the current document. If the signed data is embedded in the signature, it will be found inside an <Object> element). You can also use multiple signatures in a single document.

When the XML Signatures specification was first created, there was significant discussion about the best way to attach a signature to a document. However, because different applications may require different approaches, the XML Signature specification supports three different possibilities:

❑ **Detached signatures** – in this case, the <Signature> element is stored in a different file, and the <Reference> element uses a URI to refer to the signed document.

❑ **Enveloping signatures** – in this case, the signed data is embedded inside an `<Object>` element in the `<Signature>` element.

❑ **Enveloped signatures** – in this case, the `<Signature>` element is inserted into the XML document that contains the information it is signing. The `<Reference>` element uses an XPath expression to indicate the element that has been signed. There is no direct support for enveloped signatures in .NET, but they can still be created with a few additional steps.

Figure 1

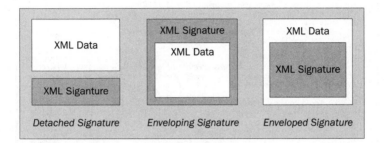

Detached Signature *Enveloping Signature* *Enveloped Signature*

.NET Support for Signed XML

The .NET Framework provides everything you need to sign XML in the `System.Security.Cryptography.Xml` namespace. Disregard the .NET class library reference, which warns, "This XML model should not be used for general purposes." In other documentation, Microsoft encourages the use of this namespace. The warning can probably be attributed to the possibility of changes in future releases.

The `System.Security.Cryptography.Xml` namespace includes:

❑ A set of objects that wrap the XML elements in the `<Signature>` element. They include `Signature`, `SignedInfo`, `Reference`, `KeyInfo`, and `DataObject`. Although you could create these elements using the types in the `System.Xml` namespace, you would need to take extra steps to specify the correct namespaces, and extraneous details like the encryption, hashing, and canonicalization algorithms you use. The `System.Security.Cryptography.Xml` types automate this task.

❑ The `SignedXml` class, which provides the functionality for signing XML data, and verifying XML signatures, through its `ComputeSignature()` and `CheckSignature()` methods.

There are also other classes included to represent various types of transforms, which we won't describe in this book.

To test XML signing, we'll create a simple Windows Form application that allows you to create a detached, enveloped, or enveloping signature. The signed XML document is written to disk, and displayed on screen in a textbox. The application also allows the signature to be verified using the key data in the document. Best of all, the verification code works equally well for all types of signatures – no changes or conditional logic are required.

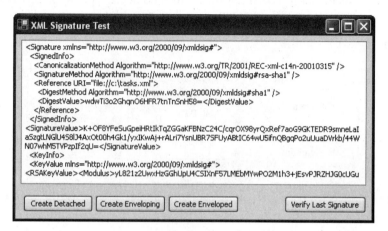

The XML data for signing is found in the extremely simple document below (`tasks.xml`). It defines a list of task requests from a user to some sort of server-side application. In an application scenario, the server-side component would only perform the task if the digital signature was successfully verified (and the requesting user has the required privileges for the requested task). Of course, digital signatures are also useful for non-repudiation – in other words, the signed document proves that a specific user made the given request.

```
<Requests>
 <Request>
  <TaskCode>130</TaskCode>
  <User>23</User>
  <ConfirmCode>A</ConfirmCode>
 </Request>
</Requests>
```

Before continuing, you should import the following three namespaces:

```
using System.Xml;
using System.Security.Cryptography;
using System.Security.Cryptography.Xml;
```

You will also need to add a reference to the `System.Security.dll` and `System.Xml.dll` assemblies, if they are not already referenced by default in your project.

Creating a Detached Signature

A detached signature is the simplest type of signature to generate, because it doesn't require you to deal with the XML document that contains the data. You simply set the URI attribute of the <Reference> element with a URI that references the file. For example, both of the following URIs are valid:

http://MyWeb/MyXmlDocuments/MyDoc.xml
file://S:\MyServer\MyXmlDocuments\MyDoc.xml

When .NET calculates the signature, it will automatically examine the document specified in the URI. If it can't find this document, or it can't understand the format of the URI, then it will generate an XmlException.

```csharp
private void cmdDetached_Click(object sender, System.EventArgs e)
{
  // Create the XML signature.
  SignedXml signedXml = new SignedXml();

  // Add a reference to an external file.
  Reference reference = new Reference();
  reference.Uri = @"file://" + Application.StartupPath +
   @"\tasks.xml";
  signedXml.AddReference(reference);

  // Use the RSA algorithm for encryption.
  RSA crypt = RSA.Create();

  // Add the key details to the signature.
  signedXml.SigningKey = crypt;
  KeyInfo keyInfo = new KeyInfo();
  RSAKeyValue rsaKey = new RSAKeyValue(crypt)
  keyInfo.AddClause(rsaKey);
  signedXml.KeyInfo = keyInfo;

  // Calculate the signature.
  signedXml.ComputeSignature();

  // Transfer the signature into an empty XML document.
  XmlElement xmlSignature = signedXml.GetXml();
  XmlDocument doc = new XmlDocument();

  // The signature must be imported to ensure the namespace is
  // preserved correctly.
  XmlNode node = doc.ImportNode(xmlSignature, true);
  doc.AppendChild(node);

  // Save the signature document.
  doc.Save(Application.StartupPath + "\\tasks_sign.xml");
```

```
        // Display the signature.
        txtSig.Text = xmlSignature.OuterXml;
}
```

In this case, the generated signature document (stored as `tasks_sign.xml`) looks like this, in somewhat abbreviated form:

```
<Signature xmlns="http://www.w3.org/2000/09/xmldsig#">

  <SignedInfo>
   <CanonicalizationMethod
    Algorithm="http://www.w3.org/TR/2001/REC-xml-c14n-20010315" />
   <SignatureMethod
    Algorithm="http://www.w3.org/2000/09/xmldsig#rsa-sha1" />
    <Reference URI="file://c:\DataSecurity\Chapter03\tasks.xml">
     <DigestMethod
      Algorithm="http://www.w3.org/2000/09/xmldsig#sha1" />
     <DigestValue>wdwTi3o2GhqnO6HFR7tnTnSnH58=</DigestValue>
    </Reference>
  </SignedInfo>

  <SignatureValue>FZPhN40aE49pfayPFz...</SignatureValue>

  <KeyInfo>
   <KeyValue xmlns="http://www.w3.org/2000/09/xmldsig#">
    <RSAKeyValue>
     <Modulus>021jHOZcGm0+E3J3...</Modulus>
     <Exponent>AQAB</Exponent>
    </RSAKeyValue>
   </KeyValue>
  </KeyInfo>

</Signature>
```

Note that the XML format used to store public key information is the same as the XML format used when you invoke the `RSA.ToXmlString(false)` method.

Creating an Enveloping Signature

An enveloping signature is one where the signed data is stored directly in the signature. This type of signature is relatively easy to implement with the `SignedXml` class. You simply need to follow three additional steps:

1. Create a separate `XmlDocument` instance to hold the source XML document.

2. Create a `DataObject`, and use it to package up the data from the source document that you want to sign.

3. Use the `SignedXml.AddObject()` method to insert the `DataObject` into the signature.

In addition, you need to identify the data using the `Reference.Uri` property. In this case, you use the # operator to specify that the element is found inside the signature itself, followed by the element ID. You use this value to set the `Reference.Uri` property and the `DataObject.ID` property. In fact, the element name that you use doesn't really matter, as long as you are consistent in both places. In the following example, we use the element name `TaskData`.

```
private void cmdEnveloping_Click(object sender, System.EventArgs e)
{
  // Load the XML data that must be signed
  XmlDocument doc = new XmlDocument();
  doc.Load(Application.StartupPath + "\\tasks.xml");

  // Create a data object to hold the data to sign
  System.Security.Cryptography.Xml.DataObject dataObject =
   new System.Security.Cryptography.Xml.DataObject();
  dataObject.Data = doc.ChildNodes;
  dataObject.Id = "#TaskData";

  // Create the XML signature
  SignedXml signedXml = new SignedXml();

  // Add the data object to the signature
  signedXml.AddObject(dataObject);

  // Create a reference that identifies the part of the document
  // you want to sign
  Reference reference = new Reference();
  reference.Uri = "#TaskData";
  signedXml.AddReference(reference);

  // Use the RSA algorithm for encryption
  RSA crypt = RSA.Create();

  // Add the key details to the signature
  signedXml.SigningKey = crypt;
  KeyInfo keyInfo = new KeyInfo();
  keyInfo.AddClause(new RSAKeyValue(crypt));
  signedXml.KeyInfo = keyInfo;

  // Calculate the signature.
  signedXml.ComputeSignature();

  // Insert the XML signature into the document
  XmlElement xmlSignature = signedXml.GetXml();
  doc = new XmlDocument();
  XmlNode node = doc.ImportNode(xmlSignature, true);
  doc.AppendChild(node);

  // Save the XML document with the enveloping signature
  doc.Save(Application.StartupPath + "\\tasks_sign.xml");
```

```
    // Display the full document, with signature
    txtSig.Text = doc.OuterXml;
}
```

Note that the `DataObject` class name must be fully qualified with the `System.Security.Cryptography.Xml` namespace, because there is another class named `DataObject` in the `System.Windows.Forms` namespace.

The generated signature document is shown here:

```
<Signature xmlns="http://www.w3.org/2000/09/xmldsig#">

 <SignedInfo>
  <CanonicalizationMethod
   Algorithm="http://www.w3.org/TR/2001/REC-xml-c14n-20010315" />
  <SignatureMethod
   Algorithm="http://www.w3.org/2000/09/xmldsig#rsa-sha1" />
  <Reference URI="#TaskData">
   <DigestMethod
    Algorithm="http://www.w3.org/2000/09/xmldsig#sha1" />
   <DigestValue>wdwTi3o2GhqnO6HFR7tnTnSnH58=</DigestValue>
  </Reference>
 </SignedInfo>

 <SignatureValue>FZPhN40aE49pfayPFz...</SignatureValue>

 <KeyInfo>
  <KeyValue xmlns="http://www.w3.org/2000/09/xmldsig#">
   <RSAKeyValue>
    <Modulus>021jHOZcGm0+E3J3...</Modulus>
    <Exponent>AQAB</Exponent>
   </RSAKeyValue>
  </KeyValue>
 </KeyInfo>

 <Object Id="#TaskData">
  <Requests xmlns="">
   <Request>
    <TaskCode>130</TaskCode>
    <User>23</User>
    <ConfirmCode>A</ConfirmCode>
   </Request>
  </Requests>
 </Object>

</Signature>
```

Note that in this example, the entire XML document is signed. You could sign just part of the document by changing the DataObject.Data property. For example, instead of using XmlDocument.ChildNodes (which represents the entire document), you could use the following XPath expression. In selects all instances of the <ConfirmCode> element that are nested inside <Request> elements (which are, in turn, nested inside the <Requests> element):

```
dataObject.Data = doc.SelectNodes("Requests/Request/ConfirmCode")
```

When you create or verify the XML signature, it will be calculated on just this portion of the document.

Creating an Enveloped Signature

With an enveloped signature, the <Signature> element becomes a part of the original document. The code is similar to the previous example, although it needs one additional ingredient: an instance of the XmlDsigEnvelopedSignatureTransform, which can be added directly through the Reference object. This represents the transformation responsible for mapping the XML digital signature to the enveloped <Signature> element.

```
private void cmdEnveloped_Click(object sender, System.EventArgs e)
{
    // Load the XML data that must be signed.
    XmlDocument doc = new XmlDocument();
    doc.Load(Application.StartupPath + "\\tasks.xml");

    // Create XML signature.
    SignedXml signedXml = new SignedXml(doc);

    // Create a reference that refers to the entire document.
    Reference reference = new Reference();
    reference.Uri = "#xpointer(/)";

    // Use a transform required for enveloped signatures.
    reference.AddTransform(new XmlDsigEnvelopedSignatureTransform());

    signedXml.AddReference(reference);

    // Use the RSA algorithm for encryption.
    RSA crypt = RSA.Create();

    // Add the key details to the signature.
    signedXml.SigningKey = crypt;
    KeyInfo keyInfo = new KeyInfo();
    keyInfo.AddClause(new RSAKeyValue(crypt));
    signedXml.KeyInfo = keyInfo;
```

```
    // Calculate the signature.
    signedXml.ComputeSignature();

    // Get the XML representation of the signature.
    XmlElement xmlSignature = signedXml.GetXml();

    // Insert the XML signature into the document.
    XmlNode node = doc.ImportNode(xmlSignature, true);
    XmlNode root = doc.DocumentElement;
    root.InsertAfter(node, root.FirstChild);

    // Save the XML document with the enveloping signature.
    doc.Save(Application.StartupPath + "\\tasks_sign.xml");

    // Display the full document, with signature.
    txtSig.Text = doc.OuterXml;
}
```

The generated signature document is shown below. The first portion of the document is identical to the original unsigned XML document. The `<Signature>` element follows immediately after. Note that it adds a `<Transform>` element, which wasn't in the previous examples.

```
<Requests>
  <Request>
    <TaskCode>130</TaskCode>
    <User>23</User>
    <ConfirmCode>A</ConfirmCode>
  </Request>
</Requests>
```

```
<Signature xmlns="http://www.w3.org/2000/09/xmldsig#">
  <SignedInfo>
    <CanonicalizationMethod
      Algorithm="http://www.w3.org/TR/2001/REC-xml-c14n-20010315"
    />
    <SignatureMethod
      Algorithm="http://www.w3.org/2000/09/xmldsig#rsa-sha1"
    />
    <Reference URI="#xpointer(/)">
      <Transforms>
        <Transform
          Algorithm=
            "http://www.w3.org/2000/09/xmldsig#enveloped-signature"
        />
      </Transforms>
      <DigestMethod
        Algorithm="http://www.w3.org/2000/09/xmldsig#sha1"
      />
      <DigestValue>wdwTi3o2GhqnO6HFR7tnTnSnH58=</DigestValue>
```

```
      </Reference>
    </SignedInfo>

  <SignatureValue>FZPhN40aE49pfayPFz...</SignatureValue>

  <KeyInfo>
    <KeyValue xmlns="http://www.w3.org/2000/09/xmldsig#">
      <RSAKeyValue>
        <Modulus>021jHOZcGm0+E3J3...</Modulus>
        <Exponent>AQAB</Exponent>
      </RSAKeyValue>
    </KeyValue>
  </KeyInfo>
</Signature>
```

Verifying a Signature

One of the nicest details about XML signatures with .NET is the fact that the verification code is the same, regardless what type of signature you use. .NET uses the details specified in the <Signature> element to find the signed data, and verify it using the defined public key. However, if you are using a detached signature and the reference XML document cannot be found, an exception will be thrown. This makes the signature more fragile, especially if you need to send it to another computer or platform.

To verify an XML signature, you simply load the signed document (or detached signature) into an ordinary XmlDocument class, and then create a new SignedXml instance that wraps it. You then retrieve the <Signature> element by name from the source document, and submit it to the SignedXml.LoadXml() method. The final step is calling CheckSignature() to verify that the signature is valid.

```
private void cmdVerify_Click(object sender, System.EventArgs e)
{
  // Load the XML signature (which may contain the data).
  XmlDocument xmlDocument = new XmlDocument();
  xmlDocument.Load(Application.StartupPath + "\\tasks_sign.xml");

  // Create a SignedXml object for verification
  SignedXml signedXml = new SignedXml(xmlDocument);

  // Find the first signature.
  XmlNodeList nodeList =
   xmlDocument.GetElementsByTagName("Signature",
   "http://www.w3.org/2000/09/xmldsig#");
  signedXml.LoadXml((XmlElement)nodeList[0]);
```

```
// Verify the signature.
if (signedXml.CheckSignature())
{
  MessageBox.Show("Signature authenticated.");
}
else
{
  MessageBox.Show("Invalid signature.");
}
}
```

If there are multiple signatures in the document, you can step through them one at a time, verifying each in turn. This is commonly the case in transaction processing, where a single document may be altered, verified, or accepted by multiple different parties.

```
XmlNodeList nodeList =
  xmlDocument.GetElementsByTagName("Signature",
  "http://www.w3.org/2000/09/xmldsig#");

foreach (XmlNode node in XmlNodeList)
{
  // (Load signature from node and verify it here.)
}
```

Note that if the key information is not found in the XML document, you will need to submit an AsymmetricAlgorithm that contains the public key information as an addition argument to the CheckSignature() method.

> If you are using encryption with signatures in the XML
> document, it's easiest to encrypt data first, and then sign it.
> This allows an application to verify the signature without
> needing to be able to decrypt the information. However, this
> ordering is not governed by the XML Signature standard – it
> is just an additional piece of application logic. In the future,
> as the XML security standards become more widely adopted,
> there will be standard libraries for creating encrypted and
> signed XML data.

Summary

This chapter focused in detail on the role encryption plays in verifying data and ensuring its integrity. It considered hash functions in detail, along with keyed hash algorithms, digital signatures, and ways that you could combine these technologies with other cryptographic services like encryption.

Finally, we ended the chapter by looking in detail at how to create XML signatures. The XML Signatures specification allows you to easily sign portions of an XML document instead of an entire file. This will become more important as B2B transactions become the norm, and XML is used to route business information that may be aggregated from or sent to multiple sources. Products like BizTalk Server, which uses XML exclusively as its messaging format, continue to grow in the enterprise world. In future versions of the .NET Framework, Microsoft is certain to add increasing support for other developing XML standards. In fact, it may provide technology previews or add-ons long before new framework versions are releases. If you plan to do a significant amount of work with XML, keep a careful watch on Microsoft's XML portal site at http://msdn.microsoft.com/xml/, which contains the latest news about XML and .NET integration.

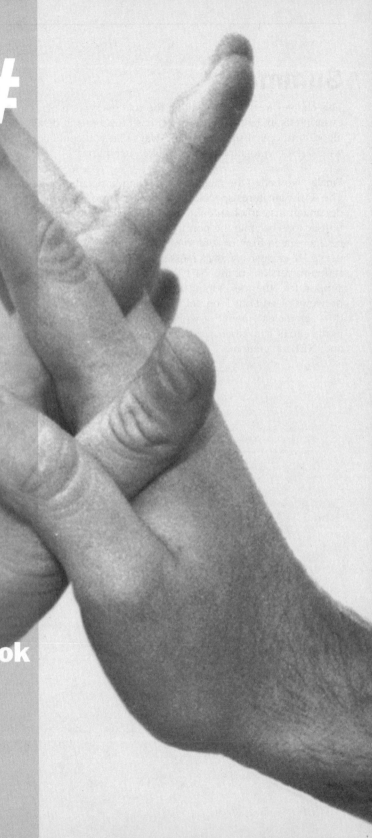

4

Securing Persisted Data

The previous chapters have explained everything you need to know to start encrypting
and signing data. In this chapter, we'll build on those basics with some practical
considerations that come into play when securing persisted data – data that is stored
for long periods in some sort of semi-permanent storage. Along the way, you'll see a
few new examples that store encrypted data in files, XML documents, and databases.
We'll also look at support for operating system features like encrypting file system
(EFS), and what role these technologies can play in a secure application.

Securing persisted data raises some hard practical considerations. There are at least five
questions you need to ask when shaping your data security policy. These questions are
often considered when deciding the authentication and authorization logic for an
application (how the application confirms user identities and assigns permissions), but
they are just as relevant to keep in mind when thinking about back-end data encryption.

❑ **Who will have access to the data and who should not?** This question
will help you determine the rules for how your encrypt data and what
secret keys you use. For example, an e-commerce system might need to
protect credit card numbers so that only the server-side application can
access them. Another type of document storage application might need to
ensure that no one can access a file except the user who created it.

❑ **What is the value of the secured data?** In other words, how much
expense are you willing to pay (in increased hardware or performance
tradeoffs) in order to protect the data. All encryption has an overhead, and
it makes no sense to spend a $1000 to protect something worth $10. Often
it is difficult to put a monetary value on your data but it is still worth trying
to make an estimate.

❑ **Who wants the data?** Security is about mitigating *threats*, and thus every security design should begin by determining possible threats and how they can be reduced. The techniques you'd use to hide data from the NSA are very different from the techniques you use to hide data from bored teenagers, which are very different from the techniques you'd use to hide data from nosy coworkers.

❑ **What other factors can compromise this security?** If you store key information in an unsecured database, or use a password that is known to many users and carelessly discussed, it makes no difference how well you apply encryption or what key size you use. The entire chain of trust is broken.

❑ **Is hashing or digital signatures an alternative?** If you need to protect data against tampering, but you don't need to hide it, hash codes and digital signatures will provide you with a better performing solution.

The single best piece of advice is to think in layers. Attackers should be forced to do ten "impossible" things, so that even if they manage to do one "impossible" thing, your security isn't completely compromised.

Defending the server environment is the most important consideration. However, you should also include additional layers of security that can limit the damage of a security breach. These include storing information like credit card data and user passwords in encrypted form in the database. This way, an attacker who gains access to your server will not find easy access to important secrets. Similarly, you should apply different security measures to your server and your publishing point (the computer where code is signed and deployed to the server). That way, if an attacker manages to steal the key pair used to sign code, there still will be some obstacles preventing them from running malicious code on your server. We'll look at some of these considerations in this chapter.

Storing Data to Disk

Chapter 2 introduced several examples of how to encrypt data and store the result in a file. The basic principles are:

❑ Use symmetric encryption when encrypting large amounts of information, because asymmetric encryption is much, much slower.

❑ Symmetric encryption can use a stream-based model, which allows you to wrap write or read operations to another stream (like a `FileStream`). Asymmetric encryption requires more work, by calling encryption methods that work with a block of data at a time.

❑ With symmetric encryption, you don't just need a shared key, but also a known initialization vector (IV). If there is no other secret information that you can use, consider using `PasswordDeriveBytes` to create an IV from the user's name, randomly generating an IV and writing it to the beginning of the encrypted file, or using a zero-value IV. Of course, all of these approaches will lessen the strength of your security against dictionary attacks, particularly if a malicious user has access to the client code and can discover what IV values you are using.

❑ Encryption works with data in binary format. In order to convert text to binary input data, you will need to use a class like the `StreamWriter`, or an encoding class from the `System.Text` namespace (like `System.Text.ASCIIEncoding` or `System.Text.UTF8Encoding`). If binary output data is not allowable in your given storage format, you can use an additional step (like a Base64 transform) after encryption.

> **If you must use asymmetric encryption, consider storing a randomly generated symmetric key using asymmetric encryption, and using this random symmetric key to encrypt the bulk of your data. This allows the encryption to be much quicker, and it's the method used intrinsically by Windows Encrypting File System.**

The following code shows how a file can be easily encrypted and decrypted using symmetric encryption and the `CryptoStream`. The `StreamWriter` and `StreamReader` classes perform the conversion between text and binary data.

```
Rijndael crypt = Rijndael.Create();

// Create the encryption transform for this algorithm.
ICryptoTransform transform = crypt.CreateEncryptor();

// Open a file for writing to.
FileStream fs = new FileStream("c:\\testfile.bin",
  FileMode.Create);

// Create a cryptographic stream.
CryptoStream cs = new CryptoStream(fs, transform,
  CryptoStreamMode.Write);

// Create a text writer.
StreamWriter w = new StreamWriter(cs);
w.Write("Secret data!");

w.Flush();
cs.FlushFinalBlock();
```

```
w.Close();

// Create the decryption transform for this algorithm.
transform = crypt.CreateDecryptor();

// Open a file for reading from.
fs = new FileStream("c:\\testfile.bin", FileMode.Open);

// Create a cryptographic stream.
cs = new CryptoStream(fs, transform, CryptoStreamMode.Read);

// Create a text reader.
StreamReader r = new StreamReader(cs);
string text = r.ReadToEnd();
r.Close();

MessageBox.Show("Retrieved: " + text);
```

In a real-world application, this simple approach is not always enough. For example, it's often necessary to encrypt only a portion of the data. This allows you to hide sensitive data and optimize performance. Another common requirement is to integrate encryption into an application in such a way that the business objects perform the required encryption almost automatically. In the following sections, we'll consider both of these requirements.

Selective Encryption with XML

When performing selective encryption, you have two choices. You can use application logic to determine when encryption is needed. For example, your code could be hardwired with knowledge that credit card numbers are always encrypted, and it could automatically decrypt them when retrieving data from a file. A more flexible approach would be to store some metadata in your output file that indicates whether a given value is encrypted or not (and optionally adds information about the key that was used). This approach is more flexible, and particularly easy to implement using a standard markup format like XML.

For example, consider the example document shown below. It encrypts the data in a single node. The fact that this node contains encrypted text is denoted by an encrypted attribute.

```
<DocNode>
   <Node>Text</Node>
   <Node>Text</Node>
   <Node encrypted="true">zCHHw4Td76SLCWsHO0KnVQ==</Node>
   <Node>Text</Node>
</DocNode>
```

To work with this format, you can create a special subclass that derives from XmlDocument (we'll call it XmlEncryptedDocument), and automatically performs the encryption and decryption when saving and loading a document, depending on which nodes have the encrypted attribute set to true.

```
public class XmlEncryptedDocument : XmlDocument
{ ... }
```

First of all, consider the steps required to load a document. The XmlDocument provides four overloaded versions of the Load() method, which accept a filename, Stream, XmlReader, and TextReader, respectively. These methods work identically in the XmlEncryptedDocument, but they will retrieve the raw encrypted data, as shown above. In addition, the XmlEncryptedDocument adds four new overloads for the Load() method, which accept a SymmetricAlgorithm object that will automatically be used to perform any required decryption.

```
public void Load(string fileName, SymmetricAlgorithm key)
{
  this.Load(fileName);
  this.ProcessLoad(key, this.DocumentElement);
}

public void Load(Stream stream, SymmetricAlgorithm key)
{
  this.Load(stream);
  this.ProcessLoad(key, this.DocumentElement);
}

public void Load(TextReader reader, SymmetricAlgorithm key)
{
  this.Load(reader);
  this.ProcessLoad(key, this.DocumentElement);
}

public void Load(XmlReader reader, SymmetricAlgorithm key)
{
  this.Load(reader);
  this.ProcessLoad(key, this.DocumentElement);
}
```

The new Load() method overloads call the base XmlDocument.Load() method to read the document, and then use a private subroutine called ProcessLoad() to perform the decryption.

Note that the SymmetricAlgorithm is not stored in an XmlEncryptedDocument class member. There is no need to retain this information in memory, and not doing so tightens security another degree, especially if you might use the class in conjunction with another third-party component.

127

The `ProcessLoad()` procedure simply iterates through the collection of nodes, looking for the `encrypted` attribute. When it is found, the text inside the node is decrypted using the user-supplied key. Other values are simply left as is.

```
private void ProcessLoad(SymmetricAlgorithm key, XmlNode node)
{
    foreach (XmlNode child in node.ChildNodes)
    {
        for (int i = 0; i < node.Attributes.Count; i++)
        {
            if (child.Attributes[i].Name == "encrypted" &&
                child.Attributes[i].Value == "true" &&
                child.InnerText != "")
            {
                child.InnerText = this.Decrypt(child.InnerText, key);
            }
        }
        // Use a recursive call to get all inner nodes.
        if (child.HasChildNodes)
        {
            ProcessLoad(key, child);
        }
    }
}
```

The actual decryption is performed through a separate private function called `Decrypt()`.

There is a significant value in separating the decryption logic from the node-iteration logic. For example, you could alter the `XmlEncryptedDocument` class so that instead of a `SymmetricAlgorithm`, it accepted a class that would itself perform the node text decryption. This class would have to implement a common interface (perhaps called `IXmlCryptDecrypt`). The `ProcessLoad()` procedure would then call a method in that interface (perhaps called `DecryptNode`) to perform the work every time it discovered an encrypted node. This way, you could use the `XmlEncryptedDocument` with asymmetric encryption or additional transformations. Alternately, you could embed metadata about the encryption algorithm and key recovery in the encrypted node's attributes.

The `Decrypt()` function creates an in-memory stream to perform the decryption. It applies two `CryptoStream` transformations: a conversion form Base64 encoding (which must be performed first), and a decryption.

```
private string Decrypt(string text, SymmetricAlgorithm key)
{
    // Create an in-memory stream.
    MemoryStream ms = new MemoryStream();
```

```
// Convert the string data to binary.
System.Text.UTF8Encoding enc = new System.Text.UTF8Encoding();
byte[] rawData = enc.GetBytes(text);

// Create a cryptographic stream for decryption.
CryptoStream csDecrypt = new CryptoStream(ms,
key.CreateDecryptor(), CryptoStreamMode.Write);

// Create a cryptographic stream for a Base64 transform.
ICryptoTransform transformDecode = new FromBase64Transform();
CryptoStream csDecode = new CryptoStream(csDecrypt,
  transformDecode, CryptoStreamMode.Write);

// Write the data to the memory stream
// (which will then be decoded and decrypted).
csDecode.Write(rawData, 0, rawData.Length);
csDecode.FlushFinalBlock();

// Now move the information out of the stream,
// and into an array of bytes.
byte[] bytes = new Byte[ms.Length];
ms.Position = 0;
ms.Read(bytes, 0, (int)ms.Length);

return (enc.GetString(bytes));
}
```

These transformations are applied to the memory stream in write mode, so they take effect as data is copied into memory. They could also be used when reading the data *from* the memory stream, but this would make it more difficult to calculate the number of bytes required to store the decrypted and decoded data. You could not simply use the MemoryStream.Length property, as is used in this example, because the length would correspond to the size of the encrypted, Base64-encoded data.

Next, consider the steps required to save a document. The XmlDocument provides four overloaded versions of the Save() method, which accept a filename, Stream, XmlWriter, and TextWriter, respectively. XmlEncryptedDocument adds four new overloads for the Save() method, which accept a SymmetricAlgorithm object that will automatically be used to perform any required encryption.

```
public void Save(string fileName, SymmetricAlgorithm key)
{
   this.ProcessSave(key, this.DocumentElement);
   this.Save(fileName);
}

public void Save(Stream stream, SymmetricAlgorithm key)
{
   this.ProcessSave(key, this.DocumentElement);
```

```
    this.Save(stream);
}

public void Save(TextWriter writer, SymmetricAlgorithm key)
{
  this.ProcessSave(key, this.DocumentElement);
  this.Save(writer);
}

public void Save(XmlWriter writer, SymmetricAlgorithm key)
{
  this.ProcessSave(key, this.DocumentElement);
  this.Save(writer);
}
```

The ProcessSave() subroutine searches for data that needs to be encrypted before the document is saved.

```
private void ProcessSave(SymmetricAlgorithm key, XmlNode node)
{
  foreach (XmlNode child in node.ChildNodes)
  {
    for (int i = 0; i < child.Attributes.Count; i++)
    {
      if (child.Attributes[i].Name == "encrypted" &&
        child.Attributes[i].Value == "true" &&
        child.InnerText != "")
      {
        child.InnerText = this.Encrypt(child.InnerText, key);
      }
    }

    // Use a recursive call to get all inner nodes.
    if (child.HasChildNodes)
    {
      ProcessSave(key, child);
    }
  }
}
```

Finally, the Encrypt() method performs the same work as Decrypt(), in reverse:

```
private string Encrypt(string text, SymmetricAlgorithm key)
{
  // Create an in-memory stream.
  MemoryStream ms = new MemoryStream();

  // Create a cryptographic stream for a Base64 transform.
  ICryptoTransform transformEncode = new ToBase64Transform();
```

```
    CryptoStream csEncode = new CryptoStream(ms, transformEncode,
      CryptoStreamMode.Write);

    // Create a cryptographic stream for encryption.
    CryptoStream csEncrypt = new CryptoStream(csEncode,
      key.CreateEncryptor(), CryptoStreamMode.Write);

    // Convert the string data to binary.
    System.Text.UTF8Encoding enc = new System.Text.UTF8Encoding();
    byte[] rawData = enc.GetBytes(text);

    // Write the data to the stream (which will then be encrypted
    // and encoded).
    csEncrypt.Write(rawData, 0, rawData.Length);

    // Make sure the CryptoStream has everything.
    csEncrypt.FlushFinalBlock();

    // Now move the information out of the stream,
    // and into an array of bytes.
    byte[] encryptedData = new Byte[ms.Length];
    ms.Position = 0;
    ms.Read(encryptedData, 0, (int)ms.Length);

    return (enc.GetString(encryptedData));
}
```

To test the XmlEncryptedDocument, you can create a simple test program that allows you to load and edit an encrypted XML document.

The Read File button creates an XmlEncryptedDocument instance, loads it with data (at which point all data will be decrypted), and displays the results.

```
private void cmdReadFile_Click(object sender, System.EventArgs e)
{
   XmlEncryptedDocument doc = new XmlEncryptedDocument();
   doc.Load(Application.StartupPath + "\\test.xml", crypt);
   txtXml.Text = doc.InnerXml;
   MessageBox.Show("Successfully read file.");
}
```

The Write File button creates an XmlEncryptedDocument, fills it with the data in the textbox, and writes it to disk (at which point all values with the encrypted attribute will be encrypted).

```
private void cmdWriteFile_Click(object sender, System.EventArgs e)
{
   XmlEncryptedDocument doc = new XmlEncryptedDocument();
   doc.InnerXml = txtXml.Text;
   doc.Save(Application.StartupPath + "\\test.xml", crypt);
   MessageBox.Show("Successfully wrote file.");
}
```

The current XmlEncryptedDocument assumes that only one key is used to encrypt the entire document. If you need to encrypt different data with different algorithms or secret keys, you could add additional attribute information. One example is shown below, with named keys:

```
<DocNode>
   <Node>Text</Node>
   <Node>Text</Node>
   <Node encrypted="true" keyName="CorpKey02">zCH476SLCWs0KnVQ==</Node>
   <Node>Text</Node>
</DocNode>
```

Presumably, the keys would be identified by name in some sort of permanent storage (like a database). They could be passed to the Save() and Load() method using a Hashtable of SymmetricAlgorithm instances. The XmlEncryptedDocument could then look up the required SymmetricAlgorithm in the Hashtable by name.

If you want to use selective encryption with XML in a cross-platform programming project, you might want to consider a more standardized approach. One possibility is to use the XML Encryption specification, which suggests a standard way to identify encrypted elements and related key information (see http://www.w3.org/TR/xmlenc-core). XML Encryption was only a candidate recommendation when .NET was first designed, and it is almost certain that future versions of the .NET Framework will include some sort of XML Encryption support (although none is included in version 1.0 or 1.1).

This example also assumes that the entire object is decrypted at the time that it is opened, which is the most efficient approach. However, this may not be the best approach in a distributed application where the data has to cross trust boundaries. In this case, a file might actually include information that's encrypted with different keys. A given component in the application will only need to access some of the information, and will take care of decrypting whatever data it needs. This way, every part of the application is forced to supply a secret key before it can access sensitive data. To implement this design, you probably won't use a helper class like the one shown above. Instead, you'll probably want to create a special "information package" object, like the one described in the next section.

Encrypting Objects

In an application, developers are often faced with the task of persisting the state of an object. You are probably already familiar with .NET's support for serialization, which provides a standardized way to convert objects into an XML or binary stream that can be saved to disk or sent as a message in a distributed system. It might occur to you that you could customize the serialization process of an object (by implementing ISerializable) to ensure that this serialization uses encryption. Unfortunately, reality is not quite as simple.

The central problem is that a serializable object needs to be able to reconstruct itself without any additional information. That means that if you wanted to add encryption to the serialization process, you would need to take additional steps to make sure the key information is stored with the object. This negates the additional security of the encryption—in fact, now the object becomes a dangerous security risk!

That leaves you with two options. First and most obviously, you could perform the encryption manually while serializing the object to disk, by wrapping the stream you are using for serialization. Here's an example:

```
// Wrap a CyptoStream around the FileStream.
FileStream fs = new FileStream("serialized_object.bin",
  FileMode.Create);
CryptoStream cs = new CryptoStream(fs, key.CreateEncryptor(),
  CryptoStreamMode.Write);

// Save the object using the SoapFormatter.
SoapFormatter f = new SoapFormatter();
f.Serialize(cs, objectToWrap);
cs.FlushFinalBlock();
fs.Close();
```

> **There are two serialization formatters provided in the .NET Framework:** `BinaryFormatter` **and** `SoapFormatter`. `BinaryFormatter` **is more compact, and will be used in most cases. However, we use** `SoapFormatter` **in this example so you can easily compare the output. To use the** `SoapFormatter`, **you must add a reference to the** `System.Runtime.Serialization.Formatters.Soap.dll` **assembly, and import the** `System.Runtime.Serialization.Formatters.Soap` **namespace.**

A more interesting option is to create a special encrypted "package" that can wrap any object. This object would encrypt and decrypt its payload as required – provided you supply the right key. Best of all, this package could generically wrap any object, and could be used before automatic serialization takes effect, allowing you to encrypt data before it is saved to disk, or before it is transmitted in a message to a distributed component.

In turns out that creating this generic package object is quite easy. All you need to do is store the wrapped object internally using a `MemoryStream`. The object can be copied into the `MemoryStream` using .NET serialization, and encrypted at the same time.

```
[Serializable]
public class EncryptedPackage
{
    private MemoryStream serializedObject;

    public void Encrypt(object objectToWrap, SymmetricAlgorithm key)
    {
        // Serialize an encrypted copy of objectToWrap in memory.
        // Encryption takes place at the same time.
        serializedObject = new MemoryStream();
        CryptoStream cs = new CryptoStream(serializedObject,
            key.CreateEncryptor(), CryptoStreamMode.Write);
        BinaryFormatter f = new BinaryFormatter();
        f.Serialize(cs, objectToWrap);
        cs.FlushFinalBlock();
    }

    public object Decrypt(SymmetricAlgorithm key)
    {
        // Decrypt the memory stream into another memory stream.
        MemoryStream ms = new MemoryStream();
        CryptoStream cs = new CryptoStream(ms,
            key.CreateDecryptor(), CryptoStreamMode.Write);
```

This operation transfers (and decrypts) 1K at a time; this is not necessary, but it performs well and makes it easy to report on progress, if needed.

```
      byte[] buffer = new byte[1024];
      int bytesRead;
      serializedObject.Position = 0;
      do
      {
        bytesRead = serializedObject.Read(buffer, 0,
          buffer.Length);
        cs.Write(buffer, 0, bytesRead);
      } while (bytesRead > 0);
      cs.FlushFinalBlock();

      // Now deserialize the decrypted memory stream.
      BinaryFormatter f = new BinaryFormatter();
      ms.Position = 0;
      return f.Deserialize(ms);
    }
  }
```

The interesting detail about the EncryptedPackage class is that it too is serializable.
That means you can serialize an encrypted copy of any object you have simply by
wrapping it in EncryptedPackage, and serializing the EncryptedPackage object.
Note that the EncryptedPackage class uses the BinaryFormatter, ensuring that the
internal data is stored in a relatively compact form. That won't stop us from taking this
binary data and serializing it into a SOAP XML document, because the
SoapFormatter is intelligent enough to automatically perform Base64 encoding.

To make EncryptedPackage even easier to use, you can add a constructor that
accepts the object to wrap and automatically calls Encrypt. Note that you also need to
add a default (parameterless) constructor, or .NET won't be able to deserialize
the EncryptedPackage.

```
public EncryptedPackage()
{
  // Default constructor required for deserialization.
}

public EncryptedPackage(object objectToWrap, SymmetricAlgorithm key)
{
  this.Encrypt(objectToWrap, key);
}
```

Now the class is ready to use. To try a simple test, create a simple serializable type like
the Account class shown here:

```
[Serializable]
public class Account
{
  private string name;
  private decimal balance;
```

```
public string Name
{
  get
  { return name; }
  set
  { name = value; }
}

public decimal Balance
{
  get
  { return balance; }
  set
  { balance = value; }
}

public Account()
{
  // Default constructor required for deserialization.
}

public Account(string name, decimal balance)
{
  this.Name = name;
  this.Balance = balance;
}
}
```

The following code shows how you can directly serialize and restore an Account object:

```
Account account = new Account("Test", 1000);

FileStream fs = new FileStream(Application.StartupPath +
  "serialized.bin", FileMode.Create);

SoapFormatter f = new SoapFormatter();
f.Serialize(fs, account);
fs.Close();

// Restore the object.
fs = new FileStream(Application.StartupPath + "\\serialized.bin",
  FileMode.Open);
account = (Account)f.Deserialize(fs);
fs.Close();
MessageBox.Show("Retrieved account: " + account.Name);
```

On disk, the serialized document looks like this (in slightly abbreviated form):

```
<SOAP-ENV:Envelope>
<SOAP-ENV:Body>
  <a1:Account id="ref-1">
  <name id="ref-3">Test</name>
  <balance>1000</balance>
  </a1:Account>
</SOAP-ENV:Body>
</SOAP-ENV:Envelope>
```

As you can see, all the information from the Account class is plainly exposed. However, you can easily modify the code to use the encrypted wrapper:

```
SymmetricAlgorithm crypt = SymmetricAlgorithm.Create();

Account account = new Account("Test", 1000);
EncryptedPackage encryptedAccount = new EncryptedPackage(account,
  crypt);

FileStream fs = new FileStream(Application.StartupPath +
  "serialized.bin", FileMode.Create);

SoapFormatter f = new SoapFormatter();
f.Serialize(fs, encryptedAccount);
fs.Close();
```

The following code can be used to restore the object:

```
fs = new FileStream(Application.StartupPath + "serialized.bin",
  FileMode.Open);
encryptedAccount = (EncryptedPackage)f.Deserialize(fs);
account = (Account)encryptedAccount.Decrypt(crypt);
fs.Close();
MessageBox.Show("Retrieved account: " + account.Name);
```

The new serialized document is effectively indecipherable. It contains the serialized EncryptedPackage object, the MemoryStream object it refers too, and the buffer of memory stored in the MemoryStream. The buffer contains the Account object data in an encrypted Base64-transformed format.

```
<SOAP-ENV:Envelope>
<SOAP-ENV:Body>
  <a1:EncryptedPackage id="ref-1">
    <serializedObject href="#ref-3"/>
  </a1:EncryptedPackage>
  <a2:MemoryStream id="ref-3">
    <_buffer href="#ref-4"/>
```

```
    </a2:MemoryStream>
    <SOAP-ENC:Array id="ref-4" xsi:type="SOAP-ENC:Base64">guDuGbAQ5mC4sA
2j7BXSBYyeJlkwOhGFW3AfmlNYObFpJmmav8hMBMlAcA4VveeGzxn7xxUjJrFQKyZHftFd
nHFx7Ou0aECCavU7LMQ4TGlvWFTgduM9n1hngV3FfxRsgl1toSAgjn7R92qqTyUGO2xQ2g
Q+uz8xQ5KKF+1TE/VyzNB1jGPoPx90u3V/M6+b3FTJxdB2TEMp1PzKdKvxuZpa79nnEbo8
Ma0HlbIRe0AAAAAAAAAAAAAAAAAAAAAAAAAAAAAAAAAAAAAAAAAAAAAAAAAAAAAAAAAAAAA
AAAAAAAAAAAAAAAAAAAAAAAAAAAAAAAAAAAAAAAAAAAAAAA==</SOAP-ENC:Array>
    </SOAP-ENV:Body>
    </SOAP-ENV:Envelope>
```

The nice part about the `EncryptedPackage` wrapper is that you can use it equally well when sending messages in a distributed system, as we'll discuss in the next chapter. You could also use a similar approach to digitally sign objects (perhaps by creating a `SignedPackage` object). Instead of encrypting the memory stream, the class would simply sign it with the provided key. You would then also have the flexibility to combine both objects to perform sign-and-encrypt or encrypt-and-sign operations.

Interestingly, you might want to develop a variant approach that uses encryption with a database. The trick would be to derive strongly typed data classes from `DataRow`, `DataTable`, and `DataSet`. You could add methods (or create a helper class) that would encrypt data before storing it in the `DataRow`. For more information about strongly typed `DataSet` objects, refer to *Professional ADO.NET*.

The Encrypting File System (EFS)

As you've seen, manual application-level encryption requires a significant amount of work to do properly, and can lead to unexpected problems and dependencies. However, what if there was a way to encrypt information automatically without needing to bake the encryption logic alongside the business code in an application? In fact, Windows 2000, Windows XP, and Windows .NET Server operating systems do include support for automatic user-level encryption of data stored on an NTFS partition. This support, known as Encrypting File System (EFS), can play a complementary role to application-level encryption. It allows you to safeguard your system so that an attacker will not easily be able to retrieve sensitive data from a breached computer (or a stolen hard drive).

With current data systems, there is very little data protection by default. User passwords may prevent a malicious user from successfully booting up the operating system on a stolen computer, but other tools exist that can simply scan the hard drive, identify NTFS file structures, and allow information to be retrieved. Other attempts to protect a computer, like BIOS passwords, can be easily circumvented if the user has physical access to the machine (either by shorting the motherboard battery, or simply transplanting the hard drive to a new computer).

The only real way to stop an intruder from accessing data is with encryption. With EFS, data in specified directories is encrypted on disk. Each file is encrypted with a unique symmetric key (using the DES algorithm), which is generated randomly, and, in turn, encoded using the current user's public key. Thus, the only way to retrieve the symmetric key needed to decrypt a file is to have access to a user's private key. Users who have access to this key can access the file, while others will be denied.

The EFS is notable in the fact that it is transparent to implement and secure (it always generates strong keys, and never stores them in paged memory that could be swapped to disk and discovered). In fact, EFS is based on the same CryptoAPI library that underlies most of the types in the `System.Security.Cryptography` namespace. In a network environment with a Windows 2000 or Windows .NET Server domain controller, you can also configure a recovery policy that will allow a domain administrator to recover the randomly generated symmetric key used to encrypt an individual file (although never the user's private asymmetric key). For more information, refer to http://www.microsoft.com/windows2000/techinfo/howitworks/security/encrypt.asp.

With EFS, data in specified directories is encrypted on disk. Each file is encrypted with a unique symmetric key (using the DES algorithm), which is generated randomly, and, in turn, encoded using the current user's public key. Thus, the only way to retrieve the symmetric key needed to decrypt a file is to have access to a user's private key. Users who have access to this key can access the file, while others will be denied. In a network environment, the root key will be signed by some Certificate Authority on the network, and so won't be recoverable directly from the hard drive.

Using EFS is quite easy. You can choose a folder for automatic encryption using Windows Explorer. Simply right-click on a folder and select Properties, and then click the Advanced button. In the Advanced Attributes window, choose Encrypt contents to secure data, and click OK.

Any existing files in the directory will be automatically encrypted. If there are subdirectories, you will be prompted as to whether you want to encrypt them as well.

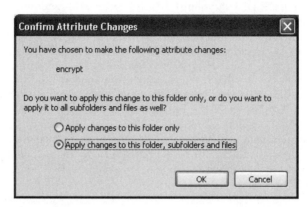

All encrypted folders and files are displayed in Windows Explorer using special green lettering. EFS encryption adheres to the following rules:

❑ New files moved into an encrypted directory will be automatically encrypted.

❑ Files moved from an encrypted directory will remain encrypted.

❑ Files moved from an encrypted directory to a location that does not support encryption (like a non-NTFS partition or removable media) will generate a warning informing you that encryption will be lost. If you choose to click Ignore you can bypass the warning and create an unencrypted copy of the file.

You can choose to encrypt individual files, but it is not recommended. The key problem is that an application might copy data into an unencrypted file (like a temporary file in the same directory), because it will not be aware that the original file is encrypted. If you choose to encrypt a single file, you will receive a warning message first.

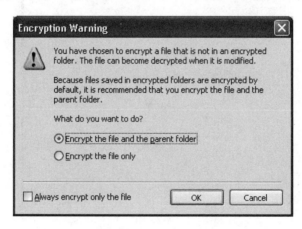

Finally, it is possible to access the EFS cryptographic services from the command line using a tool called `cipher.exe`, which is found in the system directory (for example C:\Windows\System32). Using `cipher.exe`, you could encrypt a directory with this command line:

```
> cipher /e MyDirectory
```

and decrypt it with this command:

```
> cipher /d MyDirectory
```

This makes encryption possible as part of an application install script. For the full list of supported cipher parameters, enter the following command:

```
> cipher /?
```

Remember, EFS is a complementary technology to application-level encryption, not a replacement. One limitation in EFS is that fact that you can't enforce it from inside your code, or even verify that it is properly in effect before writing sensitive data. Depending on the application and the type of environment it is deployed in, this level of protection may be inadequate. Similarly, if data leaves the computer or is sent in a message to another component, it won't be encrypted, and it may be subject to other types of attacks (such as eavesdropping).

Using Triple DES

By default, EFS uses DESX encryption, which although more secure than plain DES isn't considered very secure by modern standards. The good news is that on Windows XP (Professional), .NET Server and Windows 2000 using the high encryption pack, you can enable the much more secure Triple DES if you feel extra security is required. This can be enabled using a group policy – this also enables triple DES for IP security. You can edit group policies for a machine using the Group Policy Object Editor MMC snap-in.

❑ Select the Computer Configuration | Windows Settings | Security Settings | Local Policies | Security Options pane in the MMC window.

❑ Double-click System cryptography: Use FIPS compliant algorithms for encryption, hashing and signing

❑ Select Enabled, and then click OK.

Storing Data in Databases

Many organizations make the mistake of assuming their server environment is an impenetrable fortress. Although an attacker who gains access to the server will be difficult to stop, you can dramatically reduce the damage caused by a brief break-in by locking down resources like database information. (and following some of the best practices discussed in Chapter 8). This way, a user can't easily walk off with a list of credit card numbers or passwords that can be used for future attacks.

Storing encrypted data in a database is easy. You simply need to create a binary field. However, storing encrypted in a database does force you to sacrifice some flexibility: For example:

❑ You can't easily manipulate the fields in stored procedures or SELECT statements. Typically, this isn't required.

❑ You lose any information about what the unencrypted data type should be. For example, it may not be clear whether the decrypted binary data should be converted to a decimal or integer. Similarly, it won't be obvious what encoding you use with strings. You can mitigate some of these problems with careful documentation, and you can encapsulate all the details in a dedicated database component, but it will still complicate life.

You'll also sacrifice niceties like fixed-length strings. The size of the binary field in the database must be dictated by the key size used for encryption. If you use RSA asymmetric encryption, blocks of data will be 1024 bits (or 128 bytes) long by default. With asymmetric encryption with Rijndael, the default block size is 256 bits (or 32 bytes). The following screenshot defines a binary field for storing passwords that is large enough to hold a single block of Rijndael-encrypted data.

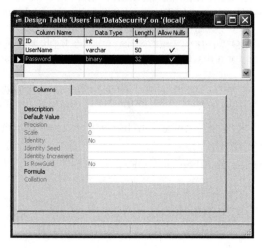

Consult the tables in Chapter 1 for more information about the algorithm block size.

Storing Encrypted Data

The easiest way to deal with binary data in the database is by using stored procedure calls or parameterized commands. Both of these options use parameters instead of dynamically inserted SQL clauses, which will prevent most SQL injection attacks. Using parameters makes life easier because the provider handles the necessary escaping. This means that you won't have to waste time crafting a subroutine that allows you to convert a byte array into a string representation.

We'll create a simple test application (Database Storage) to demonstrate this principal. The application can generate a password-based key using the Generate Key button, save encrypted data to the database via the Save button, and verify a username-password combination against the database with the Verify button.

Remember, in order for this approach to work, you must use the same key when creating the password record as you do when validating it. You'll need to find an extremely secure location to store this key information – ideally in a separate ROM hardware device like a smart card. (In the best-case scenario, you'll have a dedicated CSP or .NET class that extends the cryptography system and wraps the key information, so that your code will be able to encrypt and decrypt data without accessing the information directly). For some more information about storing and managing keys, refer to Chapter 6.

> **Under no circumstances should you use the undocumented SQL Server encryption functions, (like `pwdencrypt`). These are intended for internal use only, are subject to change, and may suffer from vulnerabilities that are not known.**

For test purposes we'll generate a password-derived key using the same technique we described in Chapter 1. Clearly this isn't the most secure approach in the world but it works well enough for demonstration purposes.

```
private void cmdGenerateKey_Click(object sender,
                                  System.EventArgs e)
{
   // Here we have hard-coded the salt value and password value
   ulong hexSalt = ulong.Parse(txtSalt.Text);
   byte[] saltValue = BitConverter.GetBytes(hexSalt);
   crypt = Rijndael.Create();
   // Generate Password-Based Key
   RNGCryptoServiceProvider rng = new RNGCryptoServiceProvider();
   PasswordDeriveBytes pdb = new
      PasswordDeriveBytes(txtKeyGenPassword.Text, saltValue);
   byte[] key = pdb.GetBytes(32);
   crypt.Key = key;
   crypt.IV = new byte[16];
   //
   // TODO: Add any constructor code after InitializeComponent call
   //
   MessageBox.Show("Key Generated");
}
```

As an example, consider the following code behind the Save button, which uses a parameterized command with the SQL Server provider to insert a new user. Before the password information is added, it is encrypted with the Rijndael algorithm.

```
private void cmdSave_Click(object sender, System.EventArgs e)
{

   if (crypt == null)
   {
      MessageBox.Show("Generate Key First!");
   }
   else
   {

      // Create a cryptographic stream for encryption.
      MemoryStream ms = new MemoryStream();
      CryptoStream cs = new CryptoStream(ms,
         crypt.CreateEncryptor(), CryptoStreamMode.Write);

      // Write the password text to an encrypted memory stream.
      System.Text.UTF8Encoding enc = new System.Text.UTF8Encoding();
      byte[] password = enc.GetBytes(txtPassword.Text);
      cs.Write(password, 0, password.Length);
      cs.FlushFinalBlock();
```

```
    // Now move the information out of the stream
    // and into an array of bytes.
    password = new Byte[ms.Length];
    ms.Position = 0;
    ms.Read(password, 0, (int)ms.Length);

    // Define the database you want to connect to
    string connectionString = "Data Source=localhost;" +
      "Initial Catalog=DataSecurity;Integrated Security=SSPI";

    // Create a parameterized command with placeholders
    string SQL = "INSERT Users (UserName, Password) " +
      "VALUES (@UserName, @Password)";

    SqlConnection con = new SqlConnection(connectionString);
    SqlCommand cmd = new SqlCommand(SQL, con);

    // Add a @UserName parameter of "TestUser"
    SqlParameter param;
    param = cmd.Parameters.Add("@UserName", SqlDbType.VarChar,
                              50);
    param.Value = txtUserName.Text;

    // Add the encrypted data to a @Password parameter
    param = cmd.Parameters.Add("@Password", SqlDbType.Binary, 32);
    param.Value = password;

    try
    {
      // Insert the record
      con.Open();
      int rows = cmd.ExecuteNonQuery();
      MessageBox.Show(rows.ToString() + " row inserted.");
    }
    catch (Exception err)
    {
      MessageBox.Show(err.ToString());
    }
    finally
    {
      con.Close();
    }
  }
}
```

> **If you are using the OLE DB provider, you can't use named placeholders (like @UserName) in a parameterized command. Instead, you must use a simple question mark (?) placeholder. In this case, make sure that you add the parameters to the Command.Parameters collection in the same order that they are listed in the command text.**

This example works directly with a string that is converted to a byte array, but you could also combine this code with some of the earlier examples to write a serialized and encrypted object or XML document to a database field. The following graphic shows what the data looks like in the database (as shown in Query Analyzer).

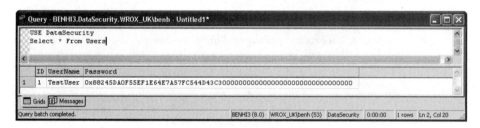

The code uses another parameterized command to select a record with the matching user name and password. Before attempting to match the password, however, the user-supplied value must be converted to a byte array, and encrypted using the same key and algorithm.

```csharp
private void cmdVerify_Click(object sender, System.EventArgs e)
{
    if (crypt == null)
    {
        MessageBox.Show("Generate Key First!");
    }
    else
    {
        // Create a cryptographic stream for encryption.
        MemoryStream ms = new MemoryStream();

        CryptoStream cs = new CryptoStream(ms,
            crypt.CreateEncryptor(), CryptoStreamMode.Write);

        // Write the password text to an encrypted memory stream.
        System.Text.UTF8Encoding enc = new System.Text.UTF8Encoding();
        byte[] password = enc.GetBytes(txtPassword.Text);
        cs.Write(password, 0, password.Length);
        cs.FlushFinalBlock();
```

```csharp
      // Now move the information out of the stream,
      // and into an array of bytes.
      password = new Byte[ms.Length];
      ms.Position = 0;
      ms.Read(password, 0, (int)ms.Length);

      // Define the database you want to connect to.
      string connectionString = "Data Source=localhost;" +
        "Initial Catalog=DataSecurity;Integrated Security=SSPI";

      // Create a parameterized SELECT command with placeholders.
      string SQL = "SELECT * FROM Users " +
        "WHERE UserName=@UserName and Password=@Password";
      SqlConnection con = new SqlConnection(connectionString);
      SqlCommand cmd = new SqlCommand(SQL, con);

      // Add parameters
      SqlParameter param;
      param = cmd.Parameters.Add("@UserName", SqlDbType.VarChar,
                                 50);
      param.Value = txtUserName.Text;
      param = cmd.Parameters.Add("@Password", SqlDbType.Binary, 32);
      param.Value = password;

      try
      {
        con.Open();
        SqlDataReader r = cmd.ExecuteReader();
        if (r.Read())
        {
          // A row was returned
          MessageBox.Show("Authentication succeeded.");
        }
        else
        {
          // A row was not returned.
          // You may want to log this error to a security log
          MessageBox.Show("Authentication failed.");
        }
        r.Close();
      }
      catch (Exception err)
      {
        MessageBox.Show(err.ToString());
      }
      finally
      {
        con.Close();
      }
    }
}
```

One nice fact about using encrypted data with a database is that all text comparisons become case sensitive. By default, string comparison in SQL in not case-sensitive, so "OpenSesame" and "OPENsesame" would be deemed the same. If you want case to be ignored, simply convert all your passwords into a canonical form (for example, all lowercase) before storing them in the database, and do the same with any user-supplied values. The key weakness of password encryption is that the encrypted value is likely to be very short, which makes it easier to crack by brute force. One solution would be to use a class like `PasswordDeriveBytes` as an intermediary to generate binary information from a password, and encrypt that data instead.

Authenticating with Password Hashes

If you store an encrypted version of the password in the database, the password will always exist, and you will be able to retrieve and decrypt it if needed. However, if you simply need to validate users, but you don't need to decipher an existing password, you can use a one-way hashing function instead, and store the password hash in the database. There are several advantages to this approach:

❑   You won't require a secret value to generate the hash.

❑   There is no way to determine the password without a computationally expensive brute force attack, because there is no secret key that could be discovered.

❑   The code is slightly simpler, because you can call `ComputeHash()` instead of using streams.

You also won't lessen your security, as finding another value that can generate an identical hash is theoretically as difficult as decrypting a password. The following code snippet demonstrates the minor changes you'd need to store a hash code in the database. Remember, you should set the size of the field to match the size of the hash to avoid wasted space. The bit size of the hash is available as the `HashAlgorithm.HashSize` property (divide in by 8 for a number in bytes).

```
// Generate the hash.
System.Text.UTF8Encoding enc = new System.Text.UTF8Encoding();
byte[] password = enc.GetBytes("OpenSesame");
password = HashAlgorithm.Create().ComputeHash(password);
```

Authenticating with Salted Password Hashes

An even more secure approach is to use a salted hash. This is the approach taken by many operating systems (including Unix) when storing passwords, and it has the advantage of making dictionary attacks more difficult. The basic principle is that the hash value is generated using a random series of bytes (the "salt"). In a table of passwords, each password would have a different salt value. This means that if the an attacker retrieved an entire list of passwords and wanted to find a matching value using brute force, the attacker would need to attack each hash separately. This would greatly increase the amount of time required to crack all the passwords.

One approach to hashing and salting is shown below. Essentially, it works as follows. When a password hash is created, these steps are taken:

1. The password is converted to a byte array.

2. The password is hashed normally.

3. The random salt is added to the password, and it is hashed again.

4. The random salt is appended to the hash data. The result can then be stored in the database.

Figure 1

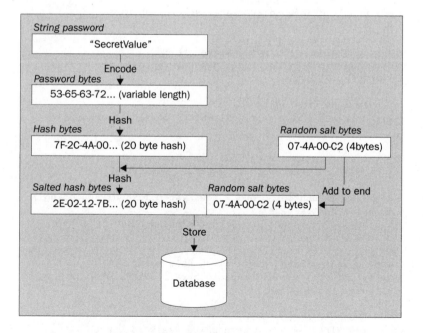

You can create a utility class to encapsulate these steps:

```
using System;
using System.Security.Cryptography;

public sealed class HashHelper
{
  private const int saltLength = 4;

  // (Code omitted.)
}
```

This class provides a `CreateDBPassword()` method that creates a salted password by taking the password, converting it to a hash (using the `CreatePasswordHash()` method), and then hashing with a random salt value (using the `CreateSaltedPassword()` method). You will use this method only once, when first creating the user record to store in the database. (If you use this method multiple times with the same password, you will receive a different hash each time, because a different random salt value would be chosen).

```
// Creates a salted password to save in the database.
public byte [] CreateDBPassword(string password)
{
  // Create the unsalted password hash.
  byte[] unsaltedPassword = CreatePasswordHash(password);

  // Generate a random salt value.
  byte[] saltValue = new byte[saltLength];
  RNGCryptoServiceProvider rng = new RNGCryptoServiceProvider();
  rng.GetBytes(saltValue);

  // Create a salted hash.
  return CreateSaltedPassword(saltValue, unsaltedPassword);
}

// Creates a basic (unsalted) password hash.
public byte[] CreatePasswordHash(string password)
{
  System.Text.UTF8Encoding enc = new System.Text.UTF8Encoding();
  SHA1 sha1 = SHA1.Create();
  return sha1.ComputeHash(enc.GetBytes(password));
}

// Create a salted hash with a given salt value.
private byte[] CreateSaltedPassword(byte[] saltValue,
    byte[] unsaltedPassword)
{
  // Add the salt to the hash.
  byte[] rawSalted  = new byte[unsaltedPassword.Length +
    saltValue.Length];
```

```
    unsaltedPassword.CopyTo(rawSalted, 0);
    saltValue.CopyTo(rawSalted, unsaltedPassword.Length);

    // Create the salted hash.
    SHA1 sha1 = SHA1.Create();
    byte[] saltedPassword = sha1.ComputeHash(rawSalted);

    // Add the salt value to the salted hash.
    byte[] dbPassword  = new byte[saltedPassword.Length +
      saltValue.Length];
    saltedPassword.CopyTo(dbPassword, 0);
    saltValue.CopyTo(dbPassword, saltedPassword.Length);

    return dbPassword;
}
```

A client who wants to become authenticated with a password would call just the
CreateSaltedPassword() method to generate a password hash. This password hash
could then be sent over the network (although it should still be encrypted to
prevent eavesdropping).

The server can then retrieve the salted hash from the database, and call the
HashHelper.CompareHash() method with both the salted hash and the user-
supplied the hash. This method works like this:

1. It extracts the original salt value from the end of the salted hash.

2. It takes the user-supplied hash, and uses it (with the salt value), to calculate
    the salted hash.

3. It then compares both versions of the salted hash, byte-by-byte.

```
// Compare the hashed password against the stored password
public bool ComparePasswords(byte[] storedPassword,
  byte[] unsaltedPassword)
{
  if (storedPassword == null || unsaltedPassword == null ||
    unsaltedPassword.Length != storedPassword.Length - saltLength)
    return false;

  // Retrieve the salt value.
  byte[] saltValue = new byte[saltLength];
  int saltOffset = storedPassword.Length - saltLength;
  for (int i = 0; i < saltLength; i++)
  saltValue[i] = storedPassword[saltOffset + i];

  // Convert the hashed password to a salted password.
  byte[] saltedPassword = CreateSaltedPassword(saltValue,
    unsaltedPassword);
```

```
      // Compare the two salted hashes (they should be the same).
      return CompareByteArray(storedPassword, saltedPassword);
  }

  // Compare the contents of two byte arrays.
  private bool CompareByteArray(byte[] array1, byte[] array2)
  {
    if (array1.Length != array2.Length)
      return false;

    for (int i = 0; i < array1.Length; i++)
    {
      if (array1[i] != array2[i])
        return false;
    }
    return true;
  }
```

> **To see this approach in action in a distributed application,
> refer to Chapter 8, which uses it in a full end-to-end example.**

Creating Tamper-Proof Files

In Chapter 3, we looked at how to create hashes, keyed hashes, and digital signatures to verify that the content of data does not change. Hashes are often used in a distributed communication scenario, but they are equally useful when storing persisted data.

The important detail to remember is that a simple hash code alone is not enough to verify data, because a malicious user could generate new data and a new matching hash code. Instead, you must use some form of encryption (for example, with a keyed hash or digital signature), or you must store hashes in a secure location. One option is to store a list of hash codes in a database. Before using the data in a file, you could quickly compute its hash code and compare it to the last recorded value.

Hashing doesn't necessarily need to be restricted to data files. You can also use hashing to protect executable files. By default, .NET uses asymmetric encryption to allow publishers to sign their assemblies, and allows you to set security policies based on allowed publishers. The signature, if present, is verified before the assembly is executed. However, this digital signature system does not provide any way to protect against key theft. Malicious users that acquire your key can publish hostile code that looks like your own. You can avoid some of these problems by applying an Authenticode Publisher signature after the strong name signature. However, in a mission-critical environment a publisher-based model of trust may not be sufficient. For example, it can't defend against a bug-ridden update to an existing application by the same publisher.

One solution is to authorize code not based on who signed it, but what it contains – in other words, to take a digital fingerprint of the code assembly using a hashing algorithm. Windows 2000 introduced this feature with Windows File Protection (WFP). WFP uses a hashing mechanism that compares hash codes to the allowed values in a digitally signed catalog file. It protects operating system files, and third-party code that has been certified by Microsoft as Windows Compatible. Using this hashing approach makes it extremely difficult to alter these protected files. You can't simply "fake" the correct file header or version information; instead, you must replace the digitally signed catalog of hashes with a catalog containing the hashes of the malicious operating system file replacements. For more information about WFP and how it is implemented, refer to http://www.microsoft.com/hwdev/driver/digitsign.asp and the MSDN knowledge base.

Is it possible to use a similar approach to lock down a production server environment? It depends on the type of application you are creating and the amount of additional work you are willing to undertake. In the next two sections we'll consider two approaches.

Using Hashes with Code-Access Security

.NET provides a rich code-access security system that allows you to grant permissions based on a variety of factors (collectively known as *evidence*). By default, all local code (code that executes from the local hard drive) is given full permission. However, it is possible to tighten security, and only grant permissions based on the hash code of the assembly.

Of course, this isn't a book about code-access security (for that topic you are well advised to read Eric Lippert's excellent *Visual Basic .NET Code Security Handbook*). However, we will present a quick example that shows how you would use the caspool.exe command-line utility to configure .NET security to use hash codes.

First of all, to determine your security level you can use the following command:

```
> caspol -lg
```

A typical summary is as follows:

```
Security is ON
Execution checking is ON
Policy change prompt is ON

Level = Machine

Code Groups:

1.  All code: Nothing
    1.1.  Zone - MyComputer: FullTrust
        1.1.1.  StrongName - Microsoft : FullTrust
```

```
      1.1.2.  StrongName - ECMA : FullTrust
   1.2.  Zone - Intranet: LocalIntranet
      1.2.1.  All code: Same site Web.
      1.2.2.  All code: Same directory FileIO - 'Read, PathDiscovery'.
   1.3.  Zone - Internet: Internet
      1.3.1.  All code: Same site Web.
   1.4.  Zone - Untrusted: Nothing
   1.5.  Zone - Trusted: Internet
      1.5.1.  All code: Same site Web.
```

The most important part of this default policy is the code group tree at the end. .NET tries to match code to one of these code groups to grant permission. By default, zone 1.1 is used for all code on the local hard drive, which grants the FullTrust permission set.

To authorize assemblies based on hash codes, you would probably first begin by removing this FullTrust permission set from zone 1.1 (although this is necessarily true – for example, you might use hash codes to authenticate code downloaded from the Internet or intranet, in which case you would add it as a subgroup to 1.3 or 1.2). In this case, local code is given the LocalIntranet permission set, which is greatly restricted (it includes execution but restricts almost everything else, including file or system access).

```
> caspol -cg 1.1 LocalIntranet
```

Next, you explitly add groups that include assemblies based on their hash code. Here's how you might grant full permission to ensure than an assembly MyLibrary.dll:

```
> caspol -ag 1.1 -hash MD5 -file MyLibrary.dll FullTrust
```

Now if you list the policy again you will see a new policy tree:

```
 1.  All code: Nothing
    1.1.  Zone - MyComputer: LocalIntranet
       1.1.1.  StrongName - Microsoft: FullTrust
       1.1.2.  StrongName - ECMA : FullTrust
       1.1.3.  Hash -
System.Security.Cryptography.MD5CryptoServiceProvider, =
D41D8CD98F00B204E9800998ECF8427E: FullTrust
    1.2.  Zone - Intranet: LocalIntranet
       1.2.1.  All code: Same site Web.
       1.2.2.  All code: Same directory FileIO - 'Read, PathDiscovery'.
    1.3.  Zone - Internet: Internet
       1.3.1.  All code: Same site Web.
    1.4.  Zone - Untrusted: Nothing
    1.5.  Zone - Trusted: Internet
       1.5.1.  All code: Same site Web
```

Now all code running on the computer will be granted the LocalIntranet permission set, unless it is from Microsoft, from ECMA, or has the same MD5 hash as `MyLibrary.dll`. Note that you can add and configure code groups using the .NET Framework security tools. However, using `caspool.exe` is an easy way to see the entire code group tree at-a-glance.

This approach is quite powerful, and allows a good deal of flexibility when assigning permissions to assemblies based on a range of criteria. Of course, it requires some time-consuming policy tweaking and testing.

Checking Hashes Programmatically

Another approach first presented by Jason Coombs (*MSDN Magazine*, September 2002, *Cryptographic Hash Algorithms Let You Detect Malicious Code in ASP.NET*), is to secure web services and web applications using a custom HTTP module. This module would react to the `AuthorizeRequest` event, and would automatically verify the hash codes of any files that are required to serve the current request before allowing it to continue. The prototype code is shown below. In this case, the assumption is made that you are using an ordinary hash code; although you could substitute a keyed hash or digital signature if you are afraid the list of hashes could be easily tampered with.

```
using System;
using System.IO;
using System.Web;
using System.Security.Cryptography;

public class HashVerificationModule : System.Web.IHttpModule
{
    public void Init(HttpApplication context)
    {
        context.AuthorizeRequest += new
        EventHandler(this.HashAuthorization);
    }

    public void Dispose() {}

    public void HashAuthorization(object sender,EventArgs e)
    {
        HttpApplication app = (HttpApplication)sender;

        FileStream f = File.Open(app.Request.PhysicalPath,
          FileMode.Open,FileAccess.Read, FileShare.ReadWrite);
        HashAlgorithm hash = HashAlgorithm.Create();
        byte[] hashValue = hash.ComputeHash(f);
        f.Close();

        // Compare the computed hash code with a value stored
        // in a database, and throw an error if it does not agree.
    }
}
```

You can register this module for automatic request processing by adding a new <add> element to the <httpModules> section of the machine.config configuration file. First, you will need to assign the assembly a strong name and add it to the GAC. Then, in the add element, specify the full strong name information as shown here:

```
<httpModules>
  <add name="HashVerification"
  type="HashVerification.HashVerificationModule, HashVerification,
  Version=1.0.3300.0, Culture=neutral,
  PublicKeyToken=b77a5c561934e089" allowLocation="false""/>
</httpModules>
```

You would also create a carefully restricted utility application that can update the database with the new hash information.

Unfortunately, this system has two significant limitations:

❑ Currently, the only file that is validated is the request target, which is the .aspx file. Code-behind assembly files and any components the page may use are not validated. Thus, the system is only effective (as written) if you are using inline coding with no components, which is a decidedly poor design.

❑ The IHttpModule scans the precompiled pages, not the machine code ASP.NET generates automatically. If an attacker could find a way to replace these files without altering the .aspx pages, the validation would succeed, but the invalid code would be executed.

These drawbacks compromise the security of code, but you may be able to provide similar security with hashing using a slightly different approach. For example, you could create a component that periodically scans through a catalog of application files on the server and validates them. Or, you might extend the IHttpModule to read a catalog of dependency information from a database. Finally, you might use global.asax event to scan and validate application binaries in the bin directory when an ASP.NET application or session begins. This code could be implemented asynchronously; ensuring that the user would not need to wait and the performance overhead would be as small as possible.

Summary

This chapter looked at a wide range of issues that you face when planning how to store data in a secure manner. These include application issues like securely persisting objects, and using selective encryption. We also considered the best ways to work with encrypted data in a database, and how you might use hash codes with .NET to protect code assemblies as well as data, and thereby prevent unrecognized or altered code from executing. Of course, you should always remember to plan in layers. For maximum success, the techniques in this chapter should be combined with other measures, like the best practices in Chapter 8, to ensure that no exploitable gap is left in your code.

In the next chapter, we'll expand our perspective, and look at the role cryptography can play in a large distributed system based on remoting or web services.

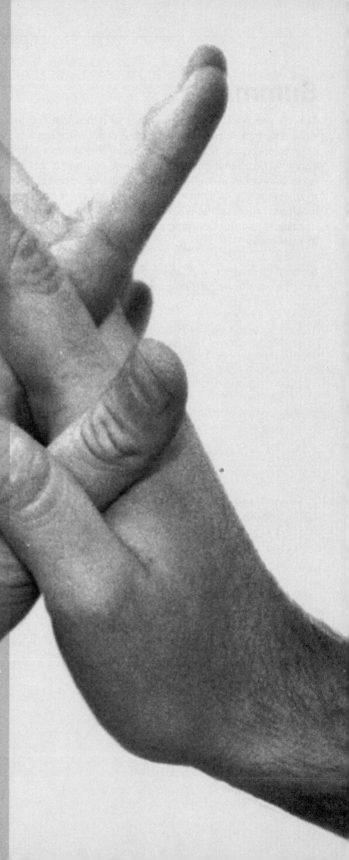

C#

Data Security

Handbook

5

Securing Data Over the Wire

In this chapter, we focus on how to use encryption and authentication to secure communication between components in a distributed system. These steps ensure that intercepted messages can't be read or altered, whether communication is over a local area network or that network of networks, the Internet. They also work equally well for any message format and transport protocol, which means you can use these techniques with raw sockets, .NET web services, or remoting.

From the application programmer's point of view, there are two approaches when using encryption to protect data:

❑   Use a form of automatic (or transparent) encryption that is built into your transport format. For example, you might use SSL or IPSec. In this case, the entire message is automatically encrypted, and you have little control over the process. However, you also have the benefit of a tested, industrial-strength encryption process.

❑   Use .NET's cryptographic classes to selectively encrypt portions of the data before it is sent in a message. Here you have to code carefully to ensure you don't introduce security vulnerabilities, but you have unlimited flexibility.

The first approach is often easier to implement, and it has the advantage that you don't need to insert encryption code alongside your application logic. However, it is also subject to availability: depending on the application, automatic encryption services may not be available to you. Also, you lose the flexibility of encoding just some portions of a message exchange. We'll consider automatic encryption in this chapter with SSL.

The second approach leverages what you've already learned about the .NET Framework and its support for encryption. It allows you to optimize your encryption logic by reducing the amount of information that needs to be encrypted. However, in order to implement this logic properly, you'll usually need to modify the interface of the system. For example, data that was passed as strings must now be sent as byte arrays. These steps run the risk of tightly coupling your application to a specific encryption strategy. In this chapter, we'll consider how to use selective encryption in a distributed application, and some of the strategies you might use to minimize the tight coupling problem.

Of course, the question remains – which approach is better? The answer depends on your environment, the value of your data, the types of attackers, and the probabilities of various threats. SSL is ideal in mission-critical applications because it encrypts everything, thereby preventing attackers from being able to detect any patterns of usage that might allow them to exploit your system. If you use selective encryption, you might inadvertently leave certain data unencrypted which, while not valuable on its own, could be used to determine application weaknesses. However, automatic encryption also needs an environment that supports it (like IIS), and it typically requires more CPU processing. This can slow down a server that needs to handle hundreds of SSL requests at a time, although hardware SSL accelerators are available (and often used for web servers).

When considering transport-layer security, it's important to understand the possible attacks you will face. These are described in much more detail in Chapter 7, but here is a brief overview of some of the most common:

❑ **Eavesdropping** allows an attacker to retrieve sensitive information as it travels between the client and the server. You typically protect against eavesdropping by encrypting the message.

❑ **Tampering** is when an attacker tries to alter a message, potentially causing an error in your application. To prevent tampering, you can use some sort of signature or keyed hash code to verify that data hasn't been modified.

❑ **Man-in-the-middle** is when an attacker impersonates either the client or server, possibly with the goal of gaining privileged data or just causing an application error. To defend against man-in-the-middle attacks you need all of the above techniques, along with some form of identity validation, like digital certificates.

❑ **Replay attacks** occur when an attacker intercepts a message and tries to reuse it later. For example, even if an attacker can't understand or tamper with a login message, the attacker might attempt to use it to gain access later. Replay attacks are generally protected against using some sort of sequence number or date stamping system to detect old or out-of-sequence messages.

> Many of the following examples assume that you already
> know how to create web services and expose components
> through remoting with a component host. If you are new to
> web services or remoting, it's recommended that you first
> read a dedicated book on the subject, and then read this
> chapter to learn how to combine remote components
> with .NET encryption. You might look at Wrox's *C# Web
> Services: Building Web Services with .NET Remoting and
> ASP.NET* (1-86100-439-7).

SSL

Secure Sockets Layer (SSL) technology is used to encrypt communication over the
HTTP protocol. It's commonly used to encrypt data exchanged between a client and a
web site. In order for a server to support SSL connections, it must have an installed
X.509 certificate. A *certificate* is a digital document used to establish identity.
Certificates can be purchased from a trusted third-party like VeriSign, and are discussed
in much more detail in Chapter 6.

SSL can be used in a distributed system in two cases:

❑　You are using web services. Because web services are hosted by IIS
　　(Internet Information Server), they support SSL encryption.

❑　You are using remoting, and your remote components are hosted in IIS.

Both of these cases leverage the ability of IIS to use SSL. In addition, there are other
lower-level options. For example, you could interface directly with Microsoft's
unmanaged Security Support Provider Interface (SSPI) API to use SSL outside of IIS.
This task is beyond the scope of this book, and generally discouraged because it
requires a high level of technical expertise to implement correctly (with no unnoticed
security flaws). You can find more information about SSPI on MSDN at
http://www.microsoft.com/technet/prodtechnol/windows2000serv/maintain/security/sspi2k.asp.

To use IIS with SSL, you need to first purchase or generate a certificate and install it. You
can then configure one or more virtual directories in IIS to require secure communication.
Clients that connect to web pages, web services, or remoted objects exposed through
these virtual directories will need to use URLs that begin with https:// instead of http://.
We'll cover these steps in the following sections with a sample web service.

It is fairly easy to configure a remoting component to be hosted in IIS, but we won't cover the specific steps here. For more information about remoting, refer to *C# Web Services: Building Web Services with .NET Remoting and ASP.NET* (Wrox Press, 1-86100-439-7). IIS supports SSL 3.0.

Understanding Certificates

In many distributed application scenarios, a client must decide whether to trust a web site before sending sensitive data. Certificates were designed to serve this purpose, by establishing a trust relationship with the help of a third party. Conceptually, a certificate is analogous to a driver's license. A driver's license establishes that the department of motor vehicles vouches for your identity (and your ability to drive). Similarly, a certificate establishes that a Certificate Authority (CA) vouches for your identity. Just as a credit card company may decide to accept an application based on a valid driver's license, a client may choose to submit sensitive data to a web sever, based on whether it has a certificate signed by a trusted third-party.

To use SSL, an organization must purchase a certificate from a known Certificate Authority, and install it on their web server. The client trusts the certificate authority, and is therefore willing to implicitly trust certificate information validated by the CA. This model works well because it is unlikely that a malicious user will go to the expense of purchasing and installing a certificate with a falsified identity. Even if it did, the CA also retains information about each registered user, and can revoke certificates. However, a certificate does not in any way ensure the trustworthiness of the server, the safety of the application, or the legitimacy of the business. Certificates are fundamentally limited in scope – not only could a malicious application be legitimately registered, but a chain of trust can, in some situations, allow a client to trust a server it otherwise would not (and should not).

The certificate itself contains certain identifying information. It is signed with the certificate authority's private key to guarantee that it is authentic and has not been modified. The industry-standard certificate type, known as x.509v3, contains the following basic information:

❑ The holder's name, organization, and address

❑ The holder's public key

❑ The certificate's validation dates

❑ The certificate's serial number

In addition, a certificate might also include business-specific information, like the certificate holder's industry, the length of time they have been in business, and so on. Chapter 6 has much more information about certificates, and how they establish chains of trust. It also explains how certificates are revoked, and how a computer makes trust decisions based on the installed root certificates.

Understanding SSL

As you can see, every certificate includes a public key. This allows asymmetric encryption to take place. Any information the client encodes with the public key will only be decipherable by the server. This is the basis for establishing a session with SSL. The client establishes a trust relationship with the server and securely exchanges a symmetric encryption key to be used to encrypt the rest of the traffic. In detail, the process works like this:

1. The client sends a request to connect to the server.

2. The server signs its certificate and sends it to the client. This signing (performed with the server's private key) ensures that the message can't be tampered with. This concludes the handshake portion of the exchange.

3. The client checks whether the certificate was issued by a CA it trusts. If so, it proceeds to the next step. In a web-browser scenario, the client may warn the user with an ominous sounding message if it does recognize the CA, and allow them to decide whether to proceed. Note that the client uses the CA's public key to verify the certificate signature.

4. The client compares the information in the certificate with the information received from the site (including its domain name and its public key). The client also verifies that the server-side certificate is valid, has not been revoked, and is issued by a trusted CA. Then the client accepts or rejects the connection.

5. The client tells the server what types of encryption key it supports for communication.

6. The server chooses the strongest key length that can be used by both the client and server, and informs the client.

7. The client randomly generates a symmetric encryption key of the indicated length. This key is called the session key. This will be used for the duration of the transaction between the server and the client. It ensures better performance, because symmetric encryption is much faster than asymmetric encryption.

8. The client encrypts the session key using the server's public key (from the certificate), and then it sends the encrypted session key to the server.

9. The server receives the encrypted session key and decrypts it using its private key. Both the client and server now have the shared secret they can use to encrypt all communication for the duration of the session.

It's important to understand these steps if you are planning to implement selective encryption, because you will probably follow the same pattern. The only difference is that the encryption and authentication logic will take place inside your application code. There are a few important points that you should note:

❑ Asymmetric encryption is only used for exchange of a symmetric key. This ensures better performance.

❑ The symmetric key is generated randomly, and only used for the duration of a session. This limits the security risk. First of all, it's harder to break encrypted messages using cryptanalysis, because messages from other sessions can't be used. Secondly, even if the key is determined by a malicious user, it will only remain valid for the course of the session.

❑ The client must generate the symmetric key. This is because the client has the server's public key, which can be used to encrypt a message that only the server can read. The server does not have corresponding information about the client, and thus cannot yet encrypt a message.

The last point is particularly interesting. If the client supplies a weak key, the entire interaction could be compromised. For example, older versions of the Netscape browser used a weak random number generator to create the symmetric key. This would make it much easier for a malicious user to guess the key using a brute force attack.

Two-Way Certificate Authentication

In any SSL scenario, encryption always works in both directions, and is used for messages sent to the server and sent to the client. However, the authentication we described above is one-way: the server provides a certificate that substantiates its identity, and the client agrees to start the session.

This doesn't address the question of how the client is authenticated. There are several possibilities:

❑ Use some sort of application-specific custom authentication that compares client-submitted information against a database. Chapter 8 demonstrates a basic example of this technique.

❑ Use one of the authentication schemes provided by IIS, such as Integrated Windows authentication (which is by far the most secure). If you enable IIS authentication, IIS will attempt to authenticate the client automatically against a Windows domain server when the client requests a resource in a specific virtual directory. The request will be refused if the client cannot be authenticated.

❑ Use client-side certificates. In this case, the connection will be refused if the client cannot produce a certificate validated by a trusted CA.

The last option is particularly interesting because it is a part of the SSL standard. However, it's rarely used in web service scenarios because the overhead involved with distributing certificates to all possible clients is enormous. That said, two-way authentication *is* useful in some B2B (business-to-business) scenarios.

With two-way authentication, the server provides the client with a list of Certificate Authorities that it trusts. If the client possesses a certificate issued by one of these Certificate Authorities, it sends a copy of that certificate to the server for verification. If the certificate is valid, IIS then authenticates the user that maps to the provided certificate.

All IIS authentication is enabled on a virtual directory basis. To enable two-way certificate authentication, find the corresponding virtual directory in IIS, right-click it, and select properties. On the Directory Security tab, under Secure Communications, click Edit. You can then specify the certificate to account mappings. For more information about mapping rules, see the IIS documentation at http://www.microsoft.com/windows2000/en/server/iis/htm/core/iimapsc.htm.

Using Certificates

General information on how to obtain (or generate) a certificate to use with the applications described in this chapter can be found in Chapter 6, *Key and Certificate Management.*

.NET includes a `System.Security.Cryptography.X509Certificates` namespace with classes that allow you to read certificate information. The `X509Certificate` class provides two static members: `CreateFromFile()` and `CreateFromSignedFile()`, both of which allow you to instantiate an `X509Certificate` object and fill it with the information from the certificate file. The `X509Certificate` class does not provide any properties, but it does provide a number of instance methods that allow you to retrieve information about the certificate, like `GetIssuerName()` and `GetKeyAlgorithm()`.

The `X509Certificate` class is fairly limited, and only designed for informational purposes. The public key data is exported as a byte array (or Base64-encoded string), which cannot be used to directly construct an `AsymmetricAlgorithm` object. A much more powerful version of the same class is provided with Microsoft's WSE (Web Services Enhancements for Microsoft .NET), and can be downloaded from http://msdn.microsoft.com/webservices/building/wse. Using the WSE, you can retrieve a key from a certificate and use it to perform programmatic encryption in .NET. You can also retrieve a certificate from the computer's key store (not just the file). This technique was demonstrated at the end of Chapter 2, with the `X509CertificateStore` and `X509Certificate` classes from the `Microsoft.Web.Services.Security.X509` namespace. This may be incorporated into the core .NET Framework in a future release.

> If you are programming a web application with ASP.NET, or a web service or remoting component hosted in IIS, you can also retrieve certificates sent to authenticate the client using the `HttpRequest.ClientCertificate` property. However, these certificates use the `System.Web.HttpClientCertificate` class, not the `X509Certificate` class.

Installing Certificates in IIS

When deploying an application, you will probably want to purchase certificates from a genuine certificate authority like VeriSign (see, for example, http://www.verisign.com). IIS Manager allows you to create a certificate request automatically. First, start Internet Services Manager (also known as IIS Manager). Expand the Web Sites group and right-click on your web site item (often titled Default Web Site) and choose Properties. Under the Directory Security tab, you'll find a Server Certificate button. Click this button to start IIS Certificate Wizard, which requests some basic organization information, and generates a request file. You'll also need to supply a bit length for the key – the higher the bit length, the stronger the key. This is the bit length of the asymmetric key that will be assigned to the certificate (not the session keys that will generated dynamically).

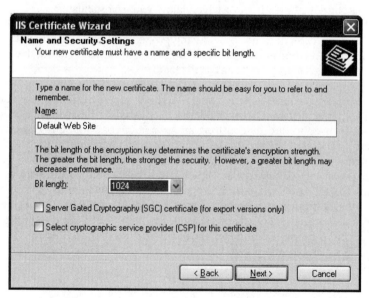

The generated file can be saved as a text file, but it must ultimately be e-mailed to a certificate authority. The certificate request data is automatically encrypted. A sample (slightly abbreviated) request file is shown here:

166

```
-----BEGIN NEW CERTIFICATE REQUEST-----
MIIB1DCCAT0CAQAwgZMxCzAJBgNVBAYTAlVTMREwDwYDVQQIEwhOZXcgWW9yazEQ
MA4GA1UEBxMHQnVmZmFsbzEeMBwGA1UEChMVVW5pdmVyc2l0eSBhdCBCdWZmYWxx
MRwwGgYDVQQLExNSZXNlYXJjaCBGb3VuZGF0aW9uMSEwHwYDVQQDExh3d3cucmVz
ZWFyY2guYnVmZmFsby5lZHUwgZ8wDQYJKoZIhvcNAQEBBQADgY0AMIGJAoGBALJO
hbsCagHN4KMbl7uz0GwvcjJeWH8JqIUFVFi352tnoA15PZfCxW18KNtFeBtrb0pf
-----END NEW CERTIFICATE REQUEST-----
```

The certificate authority will return a certificate that you can install according to their instructions. By convention, you should run all SSL communication over port 443, and serve normal web traffic over port 80.

By default, you won't be able to use certificates you generate with makecert with IIS. Instead, it's recommended that you purchase a certificate from a known certificate authority, or use Certificate Server from Windows 2000 Server or Windows .NET Server. Microsoft provides full step-by-step instructions to setting up these certificates in its knowledge base (http://support.microsoft.com/default.aspx?scid=kb;EN-US;q299525).

Encoding Information with SSL

Once you've installed the certificate, it's fairly easy to use SSL communication. For example, consider the very basic web service shown below. It provides a single method called TestSSL(), which verifies that SSL is being used for the current connection by checking the HttpRequest.IsSecureConnection property.

```
public class SecureService : WebService
{
    [WebMethod()]
    public bool TestSSL()
    {
        if (!Context.Request.IsSecureConnection)
        {
            // In this case, we throw a security error (because this is a
            // web service). In the case of a web page, you might just want
            // to redirect the user to a non-secure page.
            throw new SecurityException(
                "This method requires SSL.");
        }

        // (In a real web service, you would place your application
        // code here.)
        return true;
    }
}
```

The only other step is to modify client requests to use a URL that starts with `https://` instead of the `http://` prefix. In a remoting scenario, you will probably modify the URL in the client's configuration file. In a web service, you can modify the base `Url` property of the generated proxy class, which is inherited from `WebClientProtocol` class in the `System.Web.Services.Protocols` namespace.

```
SecureTest.SecureService proxy;
proxy = new SecureTest.SecureService();
proxy.Url = "https://WebServer/SecureTest/SecureService.asmx";

// You can now send an SSL-encrypted message.
// This method will return true.
Console.WriteLine(proxy.TestSSL());

proxy.Url = "http://WebServer/SecureTest/SecureService.asmx";

// You can now send normal unencrypted requests.
// This method will generate an error.
Console.WriteLine(proxy.TestSSL());
```

This technique is particularly useful when working with a service that uses authentication for some, but not all methods. In this case, you might want to use SSL only when calling the `Login()` method. To perform the required URL manipulations without hard-coding the URL, you can use the `System.Uri` class:

```
SSLTest.SSLService proxy = new SSLTest.SSLService();
Uri uri = new Uri(proxy.Url);

// Use SSL.
Proxy.Url = "https://" + uri.Host + uri.AbsolutePath;

// Use ordinary HTTP.
proxy.Url = "http://" + uri.Host + uri.AbsoultePath;
```

> **A common mistake is to use localhost or any other aliases for the server host name in an SSL connection. This will not work, because the client attempts to verify that the Common Name (CN) part of the Subject name of the server certificate matches the host name found in the HTTP request during the handshake portion of the SSL exchange. Thus, you should use the server name, even when testing.**

Because all the encryption and decryption occurs just before the message is sent (or immediately after it is retrieved), your application does not need to worry about deciphering the data manually, manipulating byte arrays, using the proper character encoding, and so on.

At the server side, you can also enforce SSL connections, so that it is impossible to interact with a web service without encrypting communication. Simply right-click the web site in IIS Manager, and select the Directory Security tab. In the Secure Communications section, click the Edit button (which is only available after a certificate is installed). Then, choose Require Secure Channel (SSL).

Keep in mind that there are good reasons *not* to enforce an SSL connection. For example, you might want to secure some method calls in a web service, but not secure others that don't return sensitive information. This allows you to increase performance and reduce the work performed by the server.

Remember, with SSL, all traffic will be encrypted, not just the sensitive data. For this reason, many web servers use a hardware accelerator to improve the performance of encryption with SSL.

> **For information about other forms of transport-level security, refer to Appendix A, which discusses IPSec.**

Application-Level Encryption

With SSL the code requires only minor optional modifications, which allow you to check if communication is currently being encrypted. If you want to perform your own selective encryption, a significant amount of extra code is required. However, you can simplify coding and maintenance by following the design patterns outlined here, and moving your encryption logic into a dedicated, reusable assembly.

Before you implement application-level encryption, it's important to verify that you are doing it for the right reasons. Here are two reasons that you should *not* use application-level encryption:

❏   To replace an industrial-strength authentication or encryption protocol like Kerberos or SSL

❏   As the best way to protect mission-critical data

On the other hand, you may want to use application encryption to prevent individual pieces of information in a sea of unprotected data, or when you need a highly flexible solution, and the threat of attack (and consequences of a successful attack) are more modest. This is particularly the case with man-in-the-middle attacks where an attacker uses privileged access to your network, which are notoriously difficult to protect against properly.

> **We're not suggesting here that application-based cryptographic code is useless – far from it – but for the task of encrypting client-server communications, you should use SSL whenever it is appropriate. For encrypting information on the client that is not intended for the server program, or other application-level cryptographic tasks, you will need to use the .NET cryptography facilities.**

Application-level encoding requires nothing more than the .NET Framework, and can therefore work with almost any type of distributed application. Application-level encoding is ideally suited to ASP.NET web services, because they include other services, like caching and session state, that make it easier to implement.

We'll begin by considering how you can use asymmetric encryption to protect information sent to the server, and then explore how you can use sessions with symmetric encryption to increase performance. At the end of this section, we'll analyze the risks presented by the custom approach, and some attack types that might be used. We'll then look at how these security holes can be patched with further enhancements, and look forward to the end-to-end solution shown in Chapter 8.

Simple Asymmetric Encryption

The following example shows a simple web service that allows clients to encrypt data in a way that only it can decipher.

```
public class SecuredService : WebService
{ ... }
```

The web service uses a private method to create a new public-private key pair by instantiating the RSACryptoServiceProvider object. This object is stored in ASP.NET application state, which ensures that it will remain in memory even when the web service is not running, and only be removed when the web server is rebooted or the application domain is recycled (possibly in response to newly compiled web service assemblies). Optionally, you could construct the RSACryptoServiceProvider object using information read from a secured location, like the local certificate store or a smart card, as discussed in Chapter 6.

```
private RSACryptoServiceProvider GetKeyFromState()
{
  RSACryptoServiceProvider crypt = null;

  // Check if the key has been created yet.
  // This ensures that the key is only created once.
  if (Application["Key"] == null)
  {
    // Create a key for RSA encryption.
    CspParameters param = new CspParameters();
    param.Flags = CspProviderFlags.UseMachineKeyStore;
    crypt = new RSACryptoServiceProvider(param);

    // Store the key in the server memory.
    Application["Key"] = crypt;
  }
  else
  {
    crypt = (RSACryptoServiceProvider)Application["Key"];
  }
  return crypt;
}
```

Note that some additional steps are required to access a key container, because the ASP.NET process is designated as a non-interactive user. For more information, refer to Chapter 2.

Next, a method is added that allows the client to retrieve just the public portion of the key.

```
[WebMethod()]
public string GetPublicKey()
{
  // Retrieve the key object.
  RSACryptoServiceProvider crypt = GetKeyFromState();

  // Return the private portion of the key only.
  return crypt.ToXmlString(false);
}
```

Finally, you can create a web method that requires encrypted information. The easiest way to do so is to accept raw binary data for all encrypted parameters. This way, the client won't be able to mistakenly submit the original unencrypted values. It's also a good idea to add a description through the WebMethod attribute that indicates that the method includes encrypted parameters, and indicates the appropriate underlying data type. There is currently no standard way to flag these parameters.

```
[WebMethod(Description = "Parameters to this method " +
  "must be encrypted with the web service public key. " +
  "encryptedAccountNumber is an encrypted String; " +
  "encryptedAmount is an encrypted String (containing a decimal).")]
  public bool DepositFunds(byte[] encryptedAccountNumber,
                           byte[] encryptedAmount)
  { ... }
```

The web service itself might also include the following documentation:

```
[WebService(Description = "All encrypted strings use " +
  "UTF-8 Unicode encoding")]
public class SecureService : WebService
  { ... }
```

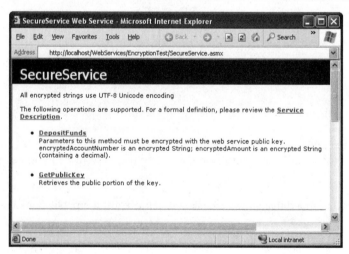

Note that the string data type is used for encryptedAmount, even though it is really a decimal value. The reason is that decimals are difficult to encode into bytes in a standardized fashion. The quickest approach is to simply convert them into a string, and then covert the string into bytes. Another, more involved approach would be to use the Decimal.GetBits() method, which returns an array of four integers representing different information about the decimal value. Then, you could convert these integers into bytes using the overloaded GetBytes() method of the System.BitConverter class on each one. Or, you could use the BinaryWriter and BinaryReader classes, which support decimal types.

The client can now retrieve the key, and use it to encrypt the method parameters before calling the DepositFunds() web method.

```
EncryptionTest.SecureService proxy =
  new EncryptionTest.SecureService();

// Instantiate a cryptographic object using the web service key.
RSACryptoServiceProvider crypt = new RSACryptoServiceProvider();
crypt.FromXmlString(proxy.GetPublicKey());

// Create some sample parameters for DepositFunds().
string accountNumber = "000-M334";
string amount = "1000.42";

// Encrypt the parameters.
byte[] encryptedAccountNumber, encryptedAmount;
System.Text.UTF8Encoding enc = new System.Text.UTF8Encoding();
encryptedAccountNumber = crypt.Encrypt(enc.GetBytes(accountNumber),
    false);
encryptedAmount = crypt.Encrypt(enc.GetBytes(amount), false);

// Call the method with the encrypted parameters.
proxy.DepositFunds(encryptedAccountNumber, encryptedAmount);
```

Because the information is sent as a byte array, .NET will automatically convert it to the required Base64 encoding for insertion in a SOAP message. However, if you manually converted this information into a string (without Base64 encoding), and sent that string, the Base64 encoding would not be performed, and the SOAP message would likely include special characters that are not XML-legal. Thus, in the rare case that you need to send encrypted data as a string, it's recommended that you use the Convert.ToBase64String() method instead of the BitConverter.ToString() method when converting the byte array.

Finally, the server uses its private key to decode the parameters.

```
// Retrieve the key object.
RSACryptoServiceProvider crypt = GetKeyFromState();

// Decrypt the parameters.
string decryptedAccountNumber;
decimal decryptedAmount;
System.Text.UTF8Encoding enc = new System.Text.UTF8Encoding();
decryptedAccountNumber = enc.GetString(
   crypt.Decrypt(encryptedAccountNumber, false));
decryptedAmount = Decimal.Parse(enc.GetString(
   crypt.Decrypt(encryptedAmount, false)));

// (Use decryptedAccountNumber and decryptedAmount.)
```

So far, we've considered web services, but this technique can be easily applied to a component exposed over .NET remoting. The only difference is that you will need to use a singleton or client-activated remote object. This way, the object will continue to exist under a fixed lifetime policy after the client accesses it. This ensures that the public key associated with the component will not change. Another approach would be to simply read the public key information from a secure location at the start of every method call (perhaps a hardware device). This would replace the code currently used to access application state, which is only available through ASP.NET.

It may occur to you at this point that you could extend this approach to support bi-directional encryption. The client would simply need to submit its public key when calling a method. That public key could then be used to encrypt any return value.

```
public bool DepositFunds(byte[] encryptedAccountNumber,
   byte[] encryptedAmount, string clientKeyXml)
```

However, asymmetric encryption is inherently slow – hundreds of times slower than symmetric encryption. A better way to extend this model is to use sessions and dynamically generated symmetric keys, much as the SSL protocol does. We'll consider this approach in the next section.

Using Sessions

SSL introduced the idea of a *session* that begins when a client accesses a page over SSL. During the course of a session, all communication is governed by the same randomly generated symmetric key. With selective encryption, you will want to follow the same design. This reduces overhead, because it ensures that you will only need to use asymmetric encryption once, when first negotiating the shared key. After this point, all interactions will use symmetric encryption.

In order for this design to work, the server must store some basic information in memory: a list of current client sessions, and the symmetric keys they are using. In an ASP.NET web service, you can store this information in session state or the cache. The ASP.NET process retains the information on your behalf, allowing your web service class to execute in a stateless fashion. In a remoting component, you may need to take extra steps to retain session information, such as storing this information in a back-end database, or using a client-initiated object so that each remote object will only serve one client. Neither of these options is perfect; database storage will impose additional overhead to every method call, and a client-initiated object is not suitable for all situations, and not as robust as a stateless implementation.

> **Session-based encryption is a perfect example of how you should implement security in layers. Because the symmetric key is only used for a short period of time, it will no longer be valid by the time a malicious user can crack it using a brute force approach. Similarly, if a malicious user attempts to capture and resend the same messages later (a "replay" attack), the attack will fail, because the key will have changed.**

In a session-based system, you will usually dedicate a special method that the client will call to initiate a session. Often, this will be a Login() method that validates client-supplied credentials like a user name and password. This method will also return a *ticket*, which is used to uniquely identify the session. Usually, this ticket will be a GUID created by the web service using the Guid.NewGuid() method. For the remainder of the session, the client will resubmit this ticket with every method call. The web service will look up the corresponding symmetric key information, and use it to decrypt any submitted parameters. Thus, the ticket serves as a way to authenticate the client for a session, and a way to track the key information on the server.

The method that the server-side component uses to store the ticket and key information is entirely up to you. However, there are three approaches that are commonly used:

❑ ASP.NET's application state. This is the most convenient method. However, you will need to take additional steps to ensure that the information is removed properly when the session is over. If not, a significant amount of server memory could be wasted.

❑ ASP.NET's built-in session state facility. In this case, the information is uniquely identified with a specific user by an automatically generated cookie. However, if the web service client is configured to not accept the cookie and resubmit it on subsequent requests, the information will be lost. With session state, session will timeout depending on web.config settings, which usually set the session limit to twenty minutes of disuse.

❏ A database, which can optionally be combined with caching. This provides long-term storage (and storage of large amounts of information if needed). Usually, you will insert the key into ASP.NET's data cache as well. When looking up the key, you can use the cache first, and query the database only if the required information is not found. You should never use the cache without storing information in another more permanent store (like a database), because information could be removed arbitrarily if server memory becomes scarce, even if only seconds have elapsed.

In this chapter, we'll use the first approach, although you can easily modify the code to use either of the others. The third approach is useful in cases where you want to allow sessions that last long periods of time (for example, several days) and are still highly scalable. Keep in mind that in this case, you must note a creation date or an expiration date in the database, and decide programmatically when the session should be expired.

Using Sessions with a Web Service

Below is a sample Login() method that pulls these concepts together. It accepts a symmetric key that has been encrypted using the public web service key. The key is decrypted, and stored in application state, indexed using the randomly generated GUID value.

```
[WebMethod(Description = "The encryptedClientKey should be a " +
    "secret value for Rijndael encryption. It should be encrypted " +
    "using the web service public key.")]
public string Login(byte[] encryptedClientKey)
{
    // Retrieve the server key.
    RSACryptoServiceProvider serverKey = GetKeyFromState();
    SymmetricAlgorithm clientKey = Rijndael.Create();
    clientKey.Key = serverKey.Decrypt(encryptedClientKey, false);

    // The initialization vector is not used.
    clientKey.IV = new byte[clientKey.IV.Length];

    // Create a new ticket.
    string ticket = Guid.NewGuid().ToString();

    // Store this key in application state.
    Application[ticket] = clientKey;

    return ticket;
}
```

For simplicity's sake, this Login() method does not require any additional user information, and does not perform user authentication before creating the session. This is keeping with our focus on data security, not user authentication services. However, in a real-world scenario, you would probably perform both these tasks at once, and your login method might take the following form:

```
[WebMethod(Description = "The encryptedClientKey should be a " +
   "secret value for Rijndael encryption. It should be encrypted " +
   "using the web service public key.")]
public string Login(byte[] encryptedUserName,
   byte[] encryptedPassword,  byte[] encryptedClientKey)
{
   // (Decrypt the user name and password.)

   // Verify that the user name and password are in the database
   // using a private member function.
   if (ValidateUser(decryptedUserName, decryptedPassword))
   {
     // (Create and store the ticket here.)
   }
   else
   {
      throw new SecurityException("Unrecognized user. " +
       "Cannot start session.");
      return null;
   }
}
```

In addition, you might want to store a custom object in application state that aggregated multiple pieces of information about the client (for example, the symmetric session key and the user name).

The application state information is never released unless the application is restarted. Thus, you should add a corresponding Logout() method that the client can call when the session is complete in order to remove the server-side information.

```
[WebMethod()]
public void Logout(string ticket)
{
   Application[ticket] = null;
}
```

Of course, this Logout() method won't be invoked if a network problem occurs that prevents the client from calling the web service and terminating the session, or if the client simply neglects its responsibilities. This is one of the problems with using application state to store this type of information. Depending on how heavily trafficked your web service is, you can solve this problem by setting machine.config options that periodically recycle the application domain, or switch to another approach that stores key information in the cache and a back-end database, not application state.

Next, every other method in the web service should be modified to accept the ticket parameter. Note that the ticket parameter is never encrypted.

```
public bool DepositFunds(byte[] encryptedAccountNumber,
   byte[] encryptedAmount, string ticket)
{
    // Validate ticket.
    SymmetricAlgorithm clientKey = (clientKey)Application[ticket];

    if (clientKey == null)
    {
        throw new SecurityException("Invalid ticket.");
    }

    // (Application specific logic goes here.)
}
```

> **You can simplify this design with a SOAP header, or, in the case of remoting, a call context setting. In this case, the ticket is submitted automatically with every method call, and you don't need to add it as a separate method parameter. For more information about these conveniences, consult a dedicated book about web services or remoting.**

Here's how the client might interact with the server:

```
EncryptionTest.SecureService proxy =
   new EncryptionTest.SecureService();

// Instantiate a cryptographic object using the web service key.
RSACryptoServiceProvider crypt = new RSACryptoServiceProvider();
crypt.FromXmlString(proxy.GetPublicKey());

// Create a random symmetric key.
SymmetricAlgorithm clientKey = Rijndael.Create();

// The initialization vector is not used.
clientKey.IV = new byte[clientKey.IV.Length];

// Start a new session by sending an encrypted copy of the random
// symmetric key to the server.
string ticket = proxy.Login(crypt.Encrypt(clientKey.Key, false));

// Create some sample parameters for DepositFunds().
string accountNumber = "000-M334";
string amount = "1000.42";
```

```
// Encrypt the parameters with the symmetric key.
byte[] encryptedAccountNumber, encryptedAmount
encryptedAccountNumber = this.EncryptString(accountNumber, clientKey);
encryptedAmount = this.EncryptString(amount, clientKey);

// Call the method with the encrypted parameters.
proxy.DepositFunds(encryptedAccountNumber, encryptedAmount, ticket);
```

Remember, with symmetric encryption you must write to a CryptoStream. With web services or remoting, you cannot access the request and response streams directly. Instead, you must encrypt the data using an in-memory stream before you attempt to send it. To simplify this code, we've created and used a helper function called EncryptString(), which is shown below.

```
private static byte[] EncryptString(string text,
  SymmetricAlgorithm crypt)
{
  UTF8Encoding enc = new UTF8Encoding();

  // Create a memory stream.
  MemoryStream ms = new MemoryStream();

  // Encrypt information into the memory stream.
  CryptoStream cs = new CryptoStream(ms,
    crypt.CreateEncryptor(), CryptoStreamMode.Write);
  StreamWriter w = new StreamWriter(cs);
  w.WriteLine(text);
  cs.FlushFinalBlock();

  byte[] encryptedBytes = new byte[ms.Length];
  ms.Position = 0;
  ms.Read(encryptedBytes, 0, ms.Length);
  ms.Close();

  // Return the final byte array of encrypted data.
  return encryptedBytes;
}
```

The server can perform the same steps in DepositFunds() to decrypt the parameters, this time with the help of a DecryptString() method:

```
// Retrieve the key object.
SymmetricAlgorithm clientKey =
  (SymmetricAlgorithm)Application[ticket];

// Decrypt the parameters.
string decryptedAccountNumber;
decimal decryptedAmount;
```

```
decryptedAccountNumber = DecryptString(encryptedAccountNumber,
clientKey);
decryptedAmount = DecryptString(encryptedAmount, key);

// (Use decryptedAccountNumber and decryptedAmount.)
```

The DecryptString() method is shown here:

```
private static string DecryptString(byte[] encryptedText,
 SymmetricAlgorithm crypt)
{
  System.Text.UTF8Encoding enc = new System.Text.UTF8Encoding();

  // Create a memory stream.
  MemoryStream ms = new MemoryStream();
  CryptoStream cs = new CryptoStream(ms, crypt.CreateDecryptor(),
                                     CryptoStreamMode.Write);

  // Place the array of bytes into a memory stream.
  cs.Write(encryptedText, 0, encryptedText.Length);
  cs.FlushFinalBlock();

  // Decrypt and display the data.
  StreamReader r = new StreamReader(ms);
  ms.Position = 0;
  return r.ReadToEnd();
}
```

The effect is the same as the asymmetric example presented earlier, but the code will execute much faster, and the burden on the server will be lessened. We'll return to this approach to construct a more full-featured example in Chapter 8. However, first we need to explore some of the security risks it presents.

Security Risks in the Custom Approach

The custom cryptography solution shown so far may behave somewhat like SSL, but it's important to remember that it isn't SSL. In particular, our implementation suffers from a few serious security flaws. Some of these are fairly easy to resolve, while others are extremely complex (and are better accomplished through SSL). In the following sections, we'll analyze these issues more closely, and in Chapter 8 we'll resolve many of them with a significant amount of additional code. You may also find it interesting to compare our basic approach to authentication with a more robust industry standard, like Kerberos. Surf to http://web.mit.edu/kerberos/www/dialogue.html to read a description of Kerberos and the security problems it solves that's written in a very unique dialogue format.

Passwords and Hashes

Currently, the user's entire password is encrypted and sent over the wire. The password is stored in clear text in the database, which makes it easy to enter and update, but also renders it an easy target for any attacker that gains access to the server. A better approach is to store a salted hash of the password in the database. This technique was first presented in Chapter 4, and is incorporated into the custom web service approach in the end-to-end example you'll see in Chapter 8.

Guessable GUID Tickets

Currently, GUIDs are used as tickets. The problem with this approach is that the algorithm for creating a GUID is not known to be cryptographically secure. In other words, the Guid class might allow you to generate GUIDs that are statistically unique, but it can't guarantee that an attacker won't be able to predict the GUID that will be generated at a specific point in time based on some knowledge of the GUID-generating algorithm. This topic is explored in more detail in Appendix B.

To remedy this problem, you can replace the GUID with any string of random bytes, which you can derive (in a cryptographically random fashion) from the RNGCryptoServiceProvider class. It's a good idea to use 16-bytes (the same number as a GUID) to prevent collisions. You can return the random bytes to the client as a Base64 string (using the Convert.ToBase64() method) or a hexadecimal string (using the BitConverter.ToString() method).

```
// Create a new ticket.
byte[] ticketBytes = new byte[16];
RNGCryptoServiceProvider rng = new RNGCryptoServiceProvider();
rng.GetBytes(ticketBytes);
string ticket = BitConverter.ToString(ticketBytes);
```

Alternatively, you can still use a GUID, but create it based on the random data. This is the technique used in Chapter 8.

```
// Create a new ticket.
byte[] ticketBytes = new byte[16];
RNGCryptoServiceProvider rng = new RNGCryptoServiceProvider();
rng.GetBytes(ticketBytes);
Guid ticketGuid = new Guid(ticketBytes);
string ticket = ticketGuid.ToString();
```

Message Authentication

Encryption makes it difficult for attackers to decipher messages, but it won't stop them from corrupting them. Currently, the web service lacks any way to stop this type of message tampering (except through the runtime errors that will appear when the tampered data cannot be successfully decrypted and converted to the expected data types). A more robust approach is to use a message authentication code to sign the encrypted data. In this case, you would either need to combine all the data in one encrypted package, or sign each encrypted piece of data separately.

A good choice for a message authentication hash code is the HMAC keyed hash algorithm. You could use this in conjunction with the session key. This approach was demonstrated in detail in Chapter 3, and we'll demonstrate it with a complete web service example in Chapter 8.

Replay Attacks

One specialized type of attack is possible with the custom web service if a malicious user is able to intercept the login message and save it to disk. The attacker could then reuse this message (without being able to decrypt it) to log into the service at a later point in time. One way to avoid this risk is to encrypt some data about the date and time a package was created along with the package itself. The server can then validate that this is the expected data. This approach is explained in more detail in Chapter 7, and demonstrated in the complete Chapter 8 example.

Identity and the Man in the Middle

One of the most difficult problems in the web service example is the question of authentication and identity. For example, consider what might happen if an attacker were able to rewire the network and launch a man-in-the-middle attack by pretending to be the server. When the client called methods like `GetPublicKey()`, it would have no way of knowing that it's not communicating with the real server. The data would still be encrypted, but using the attackers public key!

As discussed at the beginning of this chapter, the only way to solve these identity problems is to rely on a third party, like a Certificate Authority. Unfortunately, even if the web service did transmit signed certificate data to the client when the session is first created, the client would have no easy way to validate this information, because .NET does not expose an API for validating certificate data. This lack of real identity validation is one of the key problems with the custom cryptography approach, and one of the key differences between it and the SSL protocol. Of course, you may decide in your risk assessment that such an attack is relatively unlikely – in practice, it is much less common that eavesdropping, impersonation, bug exploits, or denial-of-service attacks.

One solution to this problem would be for the client to perform its own key verification without the help of a certificate authority. For example, every client could store a list of trusted server keys. If it received a key that was not on this list, it could decide not to start the session. The server could also take the same approach to authenticating clients. This would also provide a nice solution for message integrity authentication, because each message could be digitally signed using the appropriate asymmetric key.

> **Remember, the goal of custom encryption is not to reinvent the wheel. Your custom encryption code can be more flexible and customizable for specific applications, but it will not duplicate SSL.**

Objects and Serialization

Currently, this web service only supports primitive data types that can be converted directly into bytes. A better and more extensible approach is to use object serialization and encrypt the resulting binary data, as demonstrated in Chapter 4. We'll use this approach to encrypt entire objects in Chapter 8. Custom objects will also allow your code to store more client authentication information.

Using Sessions with Remoting

As explained earlier, remoting does not include any built-in facility for storing shared memory. That means that you can't use the approach discussed in the previous section with a stateless (SingleCall) component over remoting. However, you can easily use it with a client-activated object. In this scenario, the Login() method would store the symmetric key in a class member variable. A collection is not necessary, because only one user can interact with any given instance of a client-activated object. However, you will need to take special care in configuring the appropriate lifetime lease. Once the server-side object is destroyed, the client will need to recreate it, and start a new session by calling Login().

If needed, you could also use a session-based approach with a singleton object. In this case, every client uses the same instance, and you would need to store client information in a hashtable collection, which would be included as a member variable of the remote object. However, this approach is the most complicated. You will need to add locking code to ensure that multiple users cannot access the collection at the same time on different threads.

When using remoting, you don't need to rely on byte arrays to transmit encoded data. Instead, you can use a custom object that stores the data, and has the functionality required to encrypt or decrypt it. The previous chapter presented one example that you could use to transmit secure information: the `EncryptedPackage` object. By centralizing the decryption logic in one class, you remove the possibility for encoding errors and other annoyances. The only way that a problem can occur is if the client and server are using incompatible versions of the same object and have disabled strict version checking. However, this approach won't work in the web service scenario, because web services only support a limited set of common data types. You can create a custom type to use in a web service, but the client will only receive a structure with the public data members. All methods, constructors, and property procedure code will be ignored.

The Key Exchange Classes

One of the most common sources of error when using cryptography with distributed communication is performing the key exchange incorrectly. If you do not properly generate a random value, or if you fail to encode the secret value information correctly, your entire session could be compromised. To make life easier, the .NET Framework includes special key exchange classes that are designed to ensure a secure key exchange.

With an RSA public key, you have two choices for exchanging keys, both of which derive from `AsymmetricKeyExchangeFormatter`:

❑ `RSAOAEPKeyExchangeFormatter` creates encrypted key exchange data using Optimal Asymmetric Encryption Padding (OAEP). `RSAOAEPKeyExchangeDeformatter` decrypts this key exchange data.

❑ `RSAPKCS1KeyExchangeFormatter` creates encrypted key exchange data using PKCS#1 padding. `RSAPKCS1KeyExchangeDeformatter` decrypts this key exchange data.

These key exchange formatters provide a `CreateKeyExchange()` method that randomly generates a session key, and then encrypts it using asymmetric encryption. The only required piece of information is the public key that should be used to encrypt the random symmetric key. You specify the key by calling `SetKey()` before you generate the key exchange data.

Below is the revised client code, which submits a session key using the `Login()` method. Now, the key data is not created and encrypted manually, but exported directly from the `RSAPKCS1KeyExchangeFormatter`.

```
EncryptionTest.SecureService proxy =
  new EncryptionTest.SecureService();
```

```
// Instantiate a cryptographic object using the web service key.
RSACryptoServiceProvider crypt = new RSACryptoServiceProvider();
crypt.FromXmlString(proxy.GetPublicKey());

// Instantiate the key exchange formatter.
RSAPKCS1KeyExchangeFormatter exchange =
  new RSAPKCS1KeyExchangeFormatter();

// Specify the public key to use for encryption.
exchange.SetKey(crypt);

// Create a random symmetric key.
SymmetricAlgorithm clientKey = Rijndael.Create());

// Create the key exchange data.
byte[] exchangeData = exchange.CreateKeyExchange(clientKey.Key);

// Start a new session by sending the key exchange data.
proxy.Login(exchangeData);
```

On the server side, the Login() method must now use the corresponding deformatter to retrieve the secret value from the key exchange data:

```
[WebMethod()]
public string Login(byte[] encryptedClientKey)
{
  // Instantiate the key exchange deformatter.
  RSAPKCS1KeyExchangeDeformatter exchange =
    new RSAPKCS1KeyExchangeDeformatter();

  // Specify the server key.
  exchange.SetKey(GetKeyFromState());

  // Decrypt the symmetric key.
  SymmetricAlgorithm clientKey =
    (SymmetricAlgorithm)(new RijndaelManaged());
  clientKey.Key = exchange.DecryptKeyExchange(encryptedClientKey);

  // Create a new ticket.
  string ticket = Guid.NewGuid().ToString();

  // Store this key in application state.
  Application[ticket] = clientKey;

  // Return the ticket.
  return ticket;
}
```

Note that this approach still suffers from the security weaknesses identified earlier.

Advanced Choices

This chapter has considered two basic levels of encryption support. At the transport level you can use SSL, which encrypts and decrypts data outside your application, isolating you from the cryptography details.

Figure 1

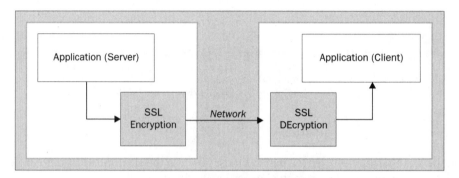

The other approach considered in this chapter was application-level encryption, where all the work is performed under the supervision of your code.

Figure 2

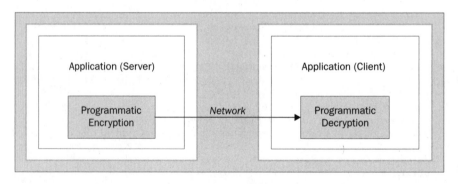

There are also additional options that fall somewhere in between these two levels. These are generic .NET code modules that perform the encryption work manually, but work for the most part without any interaction from the application. Two commonly cited examples are:

❑ A custom SOAP extension, which automatically encrypts SOAP messages just before they are sent and decrypts them just after they are received. This approach will become less common now that WSE has been released.

❑ A custom remoting channel sink that encrypts messages before they are sent and decrypts them just after they are received. This technique is developed in detail in the book *C# Web Services: Building Web Services with .NET Remoting and ASP.NET*, ISBN 1-86100-439-7.

Both of these examples are technology-specific, and must run at both the client and the server end. They have important specialized uses (for example, adding transparent encryption to remoting without using IIS, or automating custom algorithms like combined encryption, compression, and validation). These approaches also require significantly more work, and tightly couple your solution to a specific technology. Usually, they need to encrypt the entire message, which means they may perform slower than selective encryption. The greatest danger, however, is that you may implement these pieces of infrastructure insecurely. Remember, most attacks don't use brute force or a weakness in a specific encryption algorithm, but depend on procedural problems (for example, a list of unencrypted passwords in an unsecured database), or weaknesses in the software that implement the encryption. If you design a custom SOAP encryption method or remoting encryption channel, you may accidentally leave a secret key value exposed in memory, or allow an unhandled error to expose sensitive unencrypted information.

For these reasons, I heartily recommend that you don't try to develop these pieces of infrastructure on your own, but leave it to the experts at companies such as Microsoft. Security is complicated, and it's all too easy to leave a gaping hole when you develop a piece of the infrastructure on your own, especially when programming under time constraints and with limited resources.

WSE and the Future of SOAP Security

The SOAP standard, which is used to send request and response messages to a .NET web service, is evolving rapidly. Many proposed extensions haven't been incorporated into the .NET Framework yet, including WS-Security. As these standards become more concrete, Microsoft is working to provide an object model that allows developers to use them easily and securely. One such tool is the Web Services Enhancements to Microsoft .NET (WSE), which is available for download at http://msdn.microsoft.com/webservices/building/wse. WSE does give insight into the future of secure web service programming with .NET and may be incorporated into the core framework in the future.

Currently, the WSE is structured as a set of extensions that apply transformations to SOAP request and response messages. They work through a custom HttpModule that the WSE installs. In the area of security, these extensions include several interesting features:

❑ Support for automatic encryption. You set the encryption parameters through WS-Security headers, and the SOAP message body is encrypted automatically.

❑ Similar support for automatic digital signatures. Once again, you create and add token objects to the current message, and the signing takes place automatically.

❑ Support for hashed secret values (like passwords), which can be combined with a timestamp to prevent a malicious user from intercepting and reusing them.

❑ Enhanced support for digital certificates and certificate stores. As you learned earlier, the .NET framework provides classes for manipulating reading certificates from a file and retrieving their properties, but no way to retrieve them from a certificate store on the current computer.

The most significant challenges faced are in application interoperability, especially with non-.NET clients. Currently, if you were to base a system on the WSE, both your server and client would need to follow exactly the same protocol to successfully work with encryption or validation. Currently there is no way to automatically determine what steps need to be performed by reading the SOAP message metadata.

Summary

This chapter has delved deeply into the techniques you need to apply to properly secure communication in a distributed environment. You've seen how to protect sensitive data sent over the wire with SSL or the .NET cryptography classes. For the most part, we've focused on remoting and web services, but the same techniques apply over any protocol.

One important fact to realize about secure distributed programming is that you need to plan for it starting with the initial stage of a project. Introducing encryption can change the interface of your server-side components, it can require a different deployment strategy, and in some cases it may need the development of a special piece of infrastructure like a custom encryption channel. These details can (and must) be controlled using shared components and careful organization, or they will muddle the business-specific parts of your application. In the future, as web services evolve and Microsoft builds new features into the .NET Framework, these security tasks may become more transparent, and are likely to require less and less custom code. Today, however, they still require a good deal of developer investment and effort.

Chapter 6 continues with a deeper look into certificates and trust chains, and Chapter 8 picks up with an end-to-end web service example that shows how to manage some of the complexity of encryption in your custom code. We'll also explore how to defend further against the attacks we discussed in Chapter 7.

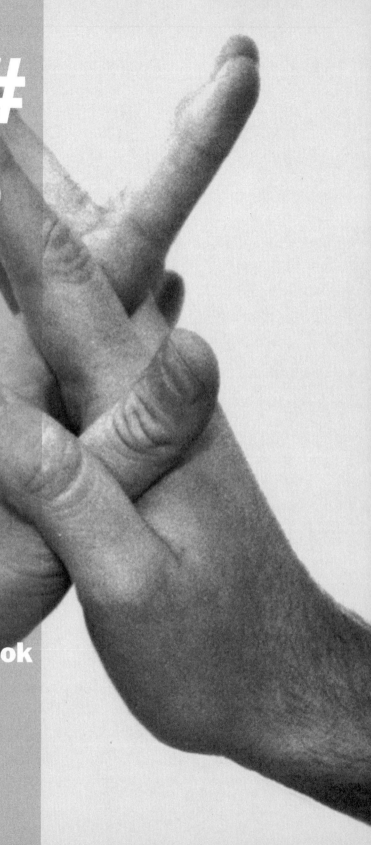

C#

Data Security

Handbook

6

6

Key and Certificate Management

Key management is one of the most important aspects of cryptography, yet it is often the least well understood. Unless the keys to encrypted information are safe, the information might as well be public in the first place. The same goes for signed data as well, because unless the private key is kept in a safe place, it is easy for the owner of it to disclaim responsibility regardless of digital signatures.

One word represents the core of this whole chapter, and that is the word **trust**. It is word loaded with significance and may be hard to interpret as it appears in different contexts, but it is nevertheless the most important word in this chapter. You implicitly trust the technology you use (unless you want to invent your own) and you (are assumed) to trust the content of this book. That's not what this chapter is about though; it is about how to use cryptographic technology to keep your keys safe, how it is possible to trust others, and how it possible for others to trust you by implementing cryptographic technology and issuing practice statements.

> **The cryptographic technology does not establish trust between two parties by itself; practice statements and human interaction are necessary as well.**

This chapter will help you to find out how keys are stored in Windows and how to access them using .NET environment. We'll also examine:

- ❑ The concepts behind digital certificates
- ❑ What certificates really are
- ❑ What to use certificates for
- ❑ How to manage certificates

Digital Certificates

The whole idea with digital certificates is to have a universal platform for all digital transactions where trust is an implied part of each transaction. A certificate includes information about the entity it represents, which doesn't have to be a human: information like who (or what) the owner is, to what organization the entity belongs, from where the certificate was issued, dates of validity, public key, key length, key usage etc. Although there is more than one certification specification, only one has reached global acceptance, the X.509 specification. The X.509 standard has evolved to version 3, which most certificates currently follow. Read more about the details in RFC 2459 at: http://www.ietf.org/rfc/rfc2459.txt

One very common usage of certificates is as server certificates; web servers use these to secure the channel between your browser and the web server. If you go to a site that has a server certificate, such as https://www.microsoft.com, using Internet Explorer you'll notice a little yellow lock icon in the status bar.

If you double-click the lock, you'll get a dialog that shows you information about the certificate.

This is the actual certificate that secures the communication between you and the server. Since all X.509 certificates are based on the public key cryptography principles, the certificate itself is only a public object where you can find the owner identity, the issuer, and the public key. Each certificate has a corresponding private key (as explained in the section about public key cryptography), which is not distributed along with the certificate; it is kept safe by the owner.

Figure 1

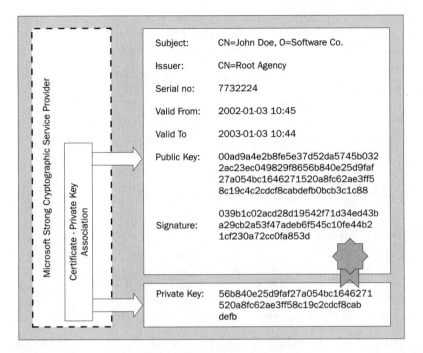

Even though there is a mathematical relation between the public and private keys, the association between the certificate and the private key is explicitly specified at the client, for example through the Microsoft Cryptographic Service Provider (CSP) interface. This association is normally hidden from the user.

The X.509 version 3 (X.509v3) specification includes a number of standard fields, but it also allows you to format the rest of the certificate pretty much as you like using extensions. This freedom is, as most things are, both a good and a bad thing. The good thing is that you may explore the full potential of PKI within a certain context, for example including an image of the owner. The bad side is that no one else can interpret your specific format. There are international efforts aimed at specifying an explicit significance of these fields (like RFC 2459, http://www.ietf.org/rfc/rfc2459.txt), and you may want to adopt to these specifications in your organization, at least if you plan to accept other certification roots than your own.

Typical Uses

When a certificate is created, the purpose of it is also defined. Not all certificates are created as server certificates, there are other purposes like securing mail (S/MIME), client authentication, signature (non-repudiation), and code signing to name but a few.

Secure E-mail Certificates

There is a standard called S/MIME that defines how certificates can be used to secure e-mails going over the Internet (RFC 2632, 2633, 2634) and many e-mail client vendors have already adapted to it, like Microsoft Outlook or Netscape Messenger.

You need an e-mail certificate for this to work and you can get one free from Thawte (http://www.thawte.com). After you have received and installed the certificate, you must configure you e-mail client to use it.

You can sign all outgoing mail with your new certificate, but that doesn't include secrecy. If you sign a message to Alice, she can then encrypt her messages to you since she has received your private key. For you to be able to encrypt messages to Alice, she has to get a certificate herself and sign a message to you, then you have her public key and the e-mail client will be able to encrypt all messages to her for you.

Client Authentication

This is typically used by web sites that want to increase the security by using two-way SSL, that is, both the server and the client have a certificate to secure the channel between them. It is for example possible for an Internet bank to issue certificates to its online customers, and configure its web site so that customers must present their certificates to gain access to the site.

It is possible to extract the identity from the client certificate at the server side, which makes it possible for the server to trust the client is a certain customer. However, if the issued certificate is stored in software without password protection of the private key (which is often the case since it is the least expensive implementation), it is likely the site will complement the certificate-based client authentication with an ID and PIN for example.

Non-repudiation Signature

These kinds of certificates are used to sign things with legal bearing, like agreements or contracts, and they require **strong** trust. Strong trust means that the certificate root is well known, well trusted, and that the policies and practices of the issuers include secure identification of the certificate subjects (the receivers of the certificates).

Nevertheless, the end-user certificate storage must also be trusted, and that typically means that these kinds of certificates must be stored on hardware tokens right now. Certificates stored in software do not provide enough protection in an open office for example, where many computers are left unattended for a few minutes every day, which is enough for anyone to misuse someone else's signature.

Code Signing

This usage of certificates is becoming increasingly popular, and no wonder since it protects the users from installing malicious software that they download from the Internet. By using code-signing certificates, it is possible for software vendors to simplify their software distribution since the end-users that download their software can install it without having to worry.

The software vendor simply signs the code with a trustworthy certificate, and the user can then verify the signature before it is installed.

Microsoft has been kind enough to implement this technique already in its browsers and software development kits, called Authenticode. It is for example possible for an Assembly to be automatically signed after it is built, and the Internet Explorer will automatically verify the signature of all downloaded software for you. It will even warn you if you have downloaded software without a signature that it may contain malicious software.

Practical PKI or Identity Management

The aims of most PKI working groups today are very ambitious, they intend to solve all kinds of identity issues raised by use of the Internet, like knowing for sure who sent you an e-mail or that it actually is Joe Smith from Joe's Software Emporium that ordered pizza for $200 from your pizza delivery web shop. Unfortunately, these efforts are tend to be a little nose-heavy, which means it is difficult for those not included in the inner circles of PKI to understand what the specifications actually mean. So, here follows a daring attempt at describing the most important aspects PKI:

> **The abbreviation PKI is becoming less and less popular; the buzzwords right now are *Identity Management*!**

Trust

Identity management is all about trust in different contexts. The technology makes it, for example, possible for you to trust the content of an agreement, or makes it possible for an Internet bank to know that all transactions on your account were made by you and no one else. It makes it possible to know the identity behind a certificate really is the real-world person it states it is. It makes it possible to trust a digital signature because you know that an agreement or commitment is made by the real person. The technology that provides such trust is interestingly enough the same regardless of context; it is the practices and policies of a trusted third party that determine the **strength** of the trust.

> **The technology doesn't determine the strength of the trust; it is the practices and policies of the trusted third parties!**

195

Technology

So, how does it work technically? Well, the trust is technically founded on something called a root certificate (or certificate root). This certificate is able to issue other certificates, like end-user certificates or authority certificates (also called CA certificates). CA certificates are able to issue certificates in turn, which creates a chain of trust. The end-user certificate is securely linked to the root, and as long as the root is trusted, all certificates in the chain can be trusted. This is why global brand certificate roots often are located in high-security facilities with armed guards outside, no joke!

The chain is established by the parent certificate-associated private key signing the child certificate, so a child certificate is verified against the parent certificate by verifying the signature included in the child certificate against the parent's public key. So, who signs the root certificate, which doesn't have a parent? Well, the root certificate is signed with its own private key, it's as simple as that.

Figure 2

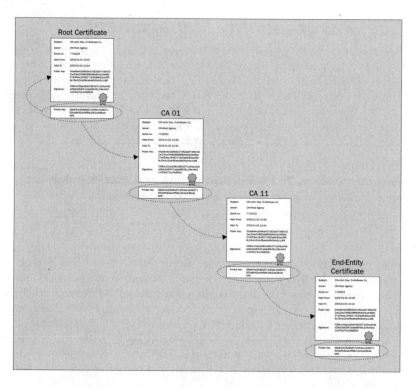

The names CA 01 and CA 11 doesn't signify anything in particular, they are just example names of intermediate Certification Authorities. In the real world, the end-user certificate could belong to you as an employee; CA 11 could be the department CA server, CA 01 the certificate server on corporate level, and the certificate root a well-known CA like Verisign or Thawte.

It is easy to verify the integrity of this chain by simply verifying the signature in each certificate against the public key in the issuing certificate. The last signature is verified against its own certificate since it is a root certificate and therefore self-signed. Normally, the verification procedure also includes verification of the dates of validity and sometimes key-usage as well.

Root Certificates

Understanding the aspects of certificate roots is very important, because they represent the technological foundation of trust. It is therefore important to have a separate storage for **trusted root certificates** that may not be altered as easily as other storages, otherwise you may end up with root certificates that look OK, but that are actually from some malicious source.

Windows already comes with quite a long list of trusted root certificates, which you can see for yourself using the command-line utility certmgr. Check the Trusted Root Certificate Authorities tab and you'll see names like Verisign, Thawte, Entrust, and Valicert.

Whenever a new trusted root certificate is added to your trusted root certificate store, Windows will ask you if you really want to add it as a precaution by presenting a dialog box like this:

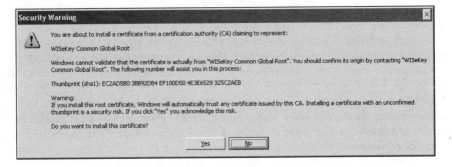

> **You should NEVER EVER accept a root certificate unless you are positively sure it really comes from a trustworthy source. The only way to know that is to manually verify the fingerprint against the source, preferably by calling a representative from the source.**

Consider this: it is technically possible for anyone to construct a root certificate of their own, which makes it possible for anyone to create a root certificate that looks the same as a Verisign root certificate for example, except for the signature or fingerprint (which is impossible to forge). However, the fingerprint is often presented as a large hexadecimal value that cannot possibly be remembered by anyone (there may exist exceptions of course), which also makes it extremely difficult for a normal human to visually determine whether or not a certificate comes from a trusted root.

It is therefore very important that all verifications include the certificate chain all the way into the trusted certificate root store, because if the root of the certificate chain in the signature you verify doesn't come from the trusted certificate root store, it may come from anyone and is practically worthless.

Practice and Policy

The technology itself cannot establish trust, since a certificate can be distributed to and used by anyone that has the right credentials to it. Having the right credentials is not the same as having the right identity, because an FTP account for example may be used by several users, which means they all have the right credentials, but that the FTP site doesn't know who uses it! It is therefore necessary to wrap the creation and distribution of certificates in policies and practices, so human rules can be set on how a certificate may be distributed and how the private key must be stored. The strength of the policies and practices also implies the strength of the trust in the certification. Weird? Then try thinking of it this way:

A root certificate may be created by anyone, and end-entity (end-user, server) certificates may be derived from it. It is simple to create a certificate in Bill Gates's name from such a root; and think of all the fun if it was possible to sign high-value transactions with a certificate like that; I'd be the first one with a brightly colored Ferrari on my driveway.

Serious certificate authorities therefore establish a number of policies and practice statements in order to guarantee the identity of a certificate holder. Often they also define how the private key must be stored. There is something called a 'qualified' certificate profile (RFC 3039), which mean it is distributed according to very strict rules about the identification of the holder. This profile also states that the private key must be kept very safe, such as on a smart card or other hardware token since software based cryptographic storage often isn't secure enough. These kinds of certificates are generally accepted as a true digital identity of the holder, and they can safely be used for any online transactions where this is required.

Issuing

A certificate is brought to life the first time by a number of actions. First, a certificate request, called CRQ, must be produced. Even though the creation process is well defined, some of the steps may be executed wherever practical whereas some must be performed at certain physical locations. The following example illustrates a preferred process for certificates stored in software where the key pair is generated on the client side (computer):

Figure 3

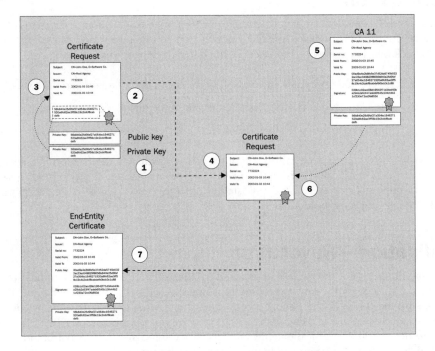

1. An asymmetric key pair is generated in the client computer.

2. A certificate request, a CRQ is compiled including both information about the requesting subject and the public key.

3. The CRQ is signed by the newly generated private key.

4. The CRQ is submitted to a CA.

5. A CA validation agent validates the content of the CRQ, including the subject information. If the certificate is intended to identify the subject, the agent or other authorized representative must manually validate the identity of the subject.

6. The CA signs the CRQ to produce a certificate.

7. The certificate is installed at the client and associated with the private key.

This is a simple example where no identification of the holder is performed. If the purpose of a certificate is to identify someone, additional actions must be taken before the certificate can be installed in the client computer. Such actions may be implemented using one-time PIN code activation for example. The PIN is given to the manually identified party who then can install the certificate, and will be useless once the certificate has been installed.

Verification

Certificate verification is a simple procedure to make a brief examination of the status of a certificate, for example to make sure that it comes from a trusted root, and that the validity dates check out. The following list describes the different steps to verify a certificate:

1. Before and after dates are verified. Certificates have a limited period of validity.

2. The signature is verified against the parent certificate (or itself if root).

3. This is repeated with the parent certificate until the root has been processed.

Obviously, the date and time in the computer that performs the verification is essential for the result. A certificate is preferably verified before a signature is performed to save time, but must still be verified and validated at the application that is interested in the signature in order to uphold an acceptable level of security.

Validation – Revocation

So, what happens if a private key is exposed to others than the owner? Naturally, the owner does not want the key to be used by someone without their authorization. The CA sets up the rules (before issuing a certificate) about what to do if you know (or even suspect) someone is using your private key without permission. Maybe you don't have to do anything at all if the certificate was issued internally, but global brands often require you to report a suspected key compromise (the private key is made public or otherwise available to others than the owner) to them as soon as possible, so they may revoke the certificate (mark it as not trustworthy). When a certificate is revoked, it is added to a certificate revocation list, a CRL. Since this action does not prevent the private key from being used, all applications that want to know the revocation status of certificate must download the CRL and check the certificate against to find out if it is revoked or not.

The CRL is normally published over the Internet, and therefore often included in each certificate is a specific field, called the CRL Distribution Point or CDP. The CDP is often an URL from which you can download the CRL manually if you want to, but as you will see, the CAPICOM library mentioned later includes this functionality, so you don't have to implement it yourself.

A CRL does not only list 'blocked' certificates, but also contains information about its distribution, for example:

❑ Issuer (CA)

❑ This update time

❑ Next update time (optional)

❑ Issuer signature

Validation is today usually conducted using CRLs, but there are online interfaces like Online Certificate Status Protocol that are becoming increasingly available, mostly as an alternative to CRLs. It is theoretically possible for the CA to be compromised as well (and thereby all certificates issued by that CA), and ARLs (Authority Revocation List) are published by the parent CA. The CA certificate must also be validated in order to be really sure that an end-user certificate is valid. This procedure is repeated all the way to the root certificate for which there is no revocation list.

Digital Identity

This section is intended to provide some insight in the complexity of digital identities. Here we will look at a few issues that you need to understand thoroughly in order to implement a high-security system and/or process.

What is a Digital Identity?

A digital identity may be one or all of many things, but there is a commonly accepted definition called a certificate. As we have already discussed, a certificate contains different values that constitute a digital representation of a person (or maybe of something like a server). The integrity and strength of the digital representation is secured by the technology itself together with a trusted third party. A TTP develops policies and practice statements in an attempt to make it impossible for anyone without the right credentials to use the private key.

What if the certificate is issued to you internally by your company IT administrator? Does that disqualify it as a digital identity because there aren't any company policies that state the rules for issuing certificates? Well, no! The certificate still represents you in this case, and it can definitely be used for internal identification. The problem is to clearly define the context where a certificate provides strong identification and where it does not. Although your company certificate sufficiently identifies you within your company, it doesn't necessarily mean anything for other companies.

Digital Signatures

The same goes for digital signatures as for digital identities. Although identifications and signatures are very similar technically, there are some 'soft' differences like purpose. A typical case would be distributing software over the Internet. The user who downloads the software cannot be sure it hasn't been tampered with by a virus for example unless the installation files are signed. The signed files makes it possible for the user to feel safe to install it as long as the certificate that signed the files comes from a trusted root (see Root Certificates section), but it doesn't prove a personal identity.

> **It is important to understand all the implications of a digital signature, not only the technical.**

It is easy to produce a digital signature with the tools available today, but you are advised to make sure you know what each digital signature actually means in each case and each context before you use them. What a signature means in a certain context cannot be described in this book; it must be analyzed case by case. There are a few points that might provide some guidance:

❑ Define context

❑ Evaluate available CAs

❑ Evaluate signing tools and formats

❑ Archive data

Define Context

This is probably the most important aspect of a digital signature and unless the contexts are clearly defined, your digital signatures may be pointless.

❑ What is the purpose of the signature; is it for example to prove the integrity of downloadable software or to prove a conscious action like contract agreement?

❑ How important is the signature; are there for example any costs like time or money related to the signature or are there any legal implications of it?

❑ Does the signature belong to an individual, role, or service?

You should also consider the necessity of informing the signer of the implications of the signature. If the context defines a signature to be equal to a manual signature and the document being signed implies high value responsibility, it is probably a good idea to inform the signer of that before they sign the document, and it is a good idea to mention it in the document being signed. It is a good idea to mention the implications of a digital signature in the data being signed, especially if the signature is intended to prove an action in the same way as a manual signature. For example, if you want another person's digital signature on a plain text agreement to mean the other person accepts the agreement, you should state that a signature also means acceptance in the agreement text, so it is clear to the other person.

> **It is possible to repudiate a digital signature, regardless of its strength, unless it is possible to prove that the signer was well informed beforehand.**

Evaluate the Available Certification Authorities

If you are using an external CA, it is important you evaluate the possible choice of CAs. Should you set up your own? Are you going for global brands? The choice is of course yours; just make sure the identity strength matches your needs. Also, remember that identity strength also comes from hardware tokens!

Another important aspect to choosing a CA is that the parties you are communicating with also must trust the CA of your choice. External parties are unlikely to accept your proprietary root, so even if you are fine with it within your own corporation, you are bound to have a certificate from a well-trusted external root like Verisign as well.

Evaluate Signing Tools and Formats

A signing tool is any application that presents whatever is to be signed for you, which means it is important that it shows you the content of whatever is to be signed in exactly the same way every time.

Because of techniques like steganography, it is important to evaluate the tools you want to use for signing. The more complex data formats you allow to be signed, the more problems you may have with proving the signer actually saw and understood what they signed. Even if you only allow plain text to be signed for safety reasons, it is possible for a signing tool to exclude important parts of that text.

> **Plain text is a good format to sign, Microsoft Word documents not necessarily so because VBA (Visual Basic for Applications) could be used to manipulate the information presented to view.**
>
> **For textual information, you shouldn't accept any scriptable formats if you want to be really sure of what is being signed.**

The signing tool should preferably also only accept read-only plaintext or at least make it 'read-only' if possible. Unless the signed data is protected bit wise or at least stored so that it can be restored to the same bit data as was signed, you will have difficulties verifying the signature.

Archive Everything

If you make a habit of archiving everything that's been signed, you will be well prepared for the event a signature must be verified. It is also a good idea to bundle the signature and the certificate chain together with a signed timestamp and sign that bundle before archiving it. If you save all this stuff, you have all the necessary evidence to prove someone signed certain data. The timestamp makes it valid evidence even if the original signer's private key is compromised afterwards. So, bundle and sign before stowing it away:

❏ Original data

❏ Signature

❏ Certificate chain

❏ Signed timestamp (from the time the data was signed)

Example: Intra-corporation Document Signature

This is an example where Alice and Bob both work at the same corporation, Alice in the buying department and Bob as manager for the service department. This corporation has its own certificate root, and all employees have personal certificates issued from this root via department CA certificates. Carol who works at Bob's office writes a purchase request for a new computer, which she signs with her certificate and then send the request to Bob for approval. Bob know she needs a new computer, and approves the request by signing it himself. Bob send the request to Alice who verifies Bob's signature and authenticates Bob's rights to make such requests. Alice buys the computer and signs all associated documents as well, which are bundled, time-stamped and signed by the administrative system before archived.

As Bob does have the correct rights, Carol will eventually get her new computer, and the accounting department will be overjoyed because of the efficient administration of this request. It works so well because they have paid attention to the following points when they designed the system:

❏ Define the context. The signatures represent individual requests and their respective authority. It also makes it very difficult for each person who has signed a document to deny that they have, to repudiate their actions. It is an intra-corporate exchange.

❏ Evaluate a CA. This is a very simple case since it is a corporation, because it is easy to establish **strong** trust in the identities of the certificate bearers since the certificates are always issued within the corporation, and can be validated by the line of management.

❏ Evaluate signing tools and formats. Again, it is easy to do this since all participants can use the same administrative system, so everyone will see the same things. It is also easy for the system to decide on simple formats that are easily presented correctly.

❏ Archive data. Since all data items are put into the system, it can easily bundle, timestamp, and sign all of it before it is archived.

Example: Extra-corporation Document Signature

This example extends the previous example by discussing the administration of the actual purchase. Alice works for the corporation that makes the purchase, and Bob works for the company that sells computers to Alice's corporation.

Alice writes a purchase order to Bob, signs it, and sends it. Since Bob doesn't work for the same corporation as Alice, and doesn't know anything about her corporate certificate root, he doesn't accept her corporate certificate for the signature. Alice must therefore use another certificate than her corporate one when she signs the order to Bob, and that certificate must come from a certificate root that Bob accepts. After Alice has procured a certificate that Bob accepts, she must also agree with him on a signing tool and format as well. Since both are using Outlook 2000, they agree it will sufficient to sign and encrypt all messages using S/MIME in Outlook 2000 as long as all messages are in plain text.

The only thing Alice needs to do additionally is to archive her correspondence with Bob in the corporate administration system. This all works out well because they have paid attention to the following points:

❑ Define the context – The signatures authorize orders from Alice and validate confirmations from Bob, this involves exchange between corporations.

❑ Evaluate a CA – Bob doesn't know anything about Alice's corporation certificate root, they must procure certificates from an external and well-trusted root, like Verisign. They don't have to have certificates from the same root as long as they both accept the others root.

❑ Evaluate signing tools and formats – Using the same tool to produce and verify signatures is a good idea; especially if the tool comes from a third party that can be trusted. They also choose plain text so that all content is presented, unlike HTML for example where it is possible to have comments in the content that aren't presented.

❑ Archive data – Outlook has its own archiving features, but it is still a good idea to time stamp the mails, sign them with a separate certificate, and record them in a secure archive.

Example: Code Signature

Alice work for a software company that distributes all its software over Internet, and chooses to sign it to prove the origin and integrity to the users. Bob is a dedicated user of Alice's software, and downloads it frequently. He knows the software can be installed safely because the Internet Explorer verifies the signature of the code and presents the code-signing certificate for Bob before he installs it.

It is possible for Bob to trust the certificate because it comes from a **trusted root** (the root certificate exists in his trusted certificate root storage), and he hasn't installed any other roots ever. This is yet another case that underlines the importance of not installing root certificates in the trusted certificate root store unless you are 100% sure that the root comes from a trusted source. Be paranoid about this to be safe.

This example also illustrate that the guidelines mentioned earlier are just guidelines, since the point about archiving data may not be interesting in this case. However, the other points are still more or less valid:

❑ Define the context – The signature represents the origin of the software and proof it hasn't changed since production. The code is downloaded by end users outside the company. The software targets Microsoft Windows systems only.

❑ Evaluate a CA – Alice must use a certificate from a root already in Bob's trusted certificate root storage since Bob doesn't know anything about other roots at all.

❑ Evaluate signing tools and formats – Since the targets are MS Windows systems, the obvious choice is Authenticode, which is automatically verified by Internet Explorer upon download.

Example: Archive

Alice is an attorney in this case, and uses a signing certificate from a trusted certificate root. She sign all legal documents handled by her with this certificate and then sends them to the corporate archiving system. This system first verifies all signatures, zips all documents and signatures together in a compressed file archive, adds a file including a time stamp (using a time from a trustworthy time source of course) and then signs the compressed file archive with a certificate that also comes from a trusted certificate root. The compressed file archive and system signature is then put into the system archive.

Since both Alice's and the system certificates come from a trusted certificate root, it is possible for anyone to verify the signatures. Since a time stamp was added using a trusted time source, the firm has secured the documentation very well.

Certificates in Windows

This is an important aspect of cryptography in general, and this section discusses how keys are handled in Windows. There are **stores**, **system store locations**, and **store providers**, which can be confusing!

A *store location* is simply a group of several related *stores*. There are system store locations associated with the Current User, Local Machine, and other common Windows roles. Each system store location is has at least four predefined stores that divide up the different contexts for that location MY (personal keys and certificates), Root (trusted root certificates), Trust (certificates of trusted third parties), and CA (Intermediate CA certificates). Stores (as of Windows 2000) are logical rather than physical, so each store is associated with one or more store providers. Store providers represent the actual implementation of a store, like a temporary in-memory store, System Registry located store, or hardware-based store. It is best not worry too much about where a key is actually located, as this can depend on the operating system version and configuration.

The relationship between stores, store locations, and store providers is complex and can be difficult to fully comprehend. The Web Services Enhancements for .NET (WSE) and CAPICOM libraries (which we cover later) have interfaces that simplify access to the most common stores made available by Microsoft, combining these three aspects in a more easily understandable way.

System Store Locations

A store location describes in which context the certificate stores are available, for example a typical store location is under the current user or the local machine context. The following is an example of typical store locations available in Crypto API:

❑   Current Service

❑   Current User

❑   Local Machine

❑   Services

All of these are available programmatically through the CryptoAPI (with the right credentials), but may also be managed manually using the MMC.exe (Microsoft Management Console) or CertMgr.exe.

System Store Locations in .NET

Few store locations are accessible from .NET through the existing libraries. The CryptoAPI has extensive support for accessing these locations and actually includes the possibility to add your own. CAPICOM and the WSE support a subset of the store locations available via the CryptoAPI.

The WSE library supports four store locations:

Store Location	Description
Current User	The current user's store location, this type of store may be a read/write store. If it is, changes to the contents of the store are persisted.
Local Machine	The Local machine store can be a read/write store only if the user has read/write permissions. If the user has read/write permissions and if the store is opened in read/write mode, then changes in the contents of the store are persisted.
Services	This is a store location for specified local service accounts used by applications such the Event Log.
Unknown	The store location is unknown.

The CAPICOM library supports the following store locations in version 2.0.0.1:

Store Location	Description
Memory	The store location is a temporary memory store location; any changes in the contents of the store are not persisted.
Current User	The current user's store location; this type of store may be a read/write store. If it is, changes to the contents of the store are persisted.
Local Machine	The Local machine store can be a read/write store only if the user has read/write permissions. If the user has read/write permissions and if the store is opened in read/write mode, then changes in the contents of the store are persisted.
Active Directory	The store location is an Active Directory store location. No error is generated if an Active Directory store is opened in read/write mode, but any changes to the store will not be persisted.
Smart Card User	This store location represents the group of present smart cards. Introduced in CAPICOM 2.0, this location is very secure since the key is located on removable hardware. Using a password to restrict access to the card's key further enhances security.

If you can't find the stores you are looking for in framework class library, WSE, or CAPICOM, have a look in the CryptoAPI reference first.

Certificate Stores

The stores used by the Microsoft cryptography libraries are oriented towards the context they appear in, such as My for your own personal keys (and certificates) and Root for Root public keys (mostly associated with certificates).

There are several standard system stores, My, CA, Trust and Root.

- ❑ My – contains your personal certificates and a reference to their respective private keys (wherever they are located physically).

- ❑ CA – also called the intermediate CA store, this is where all certificates that lie between the root and end entity certificates are located.

- ❑ Trust – this contains the keys associated with trusted third parties.

- ❑ Root – this is where all trusted root certificates are located. This store should be kept safe because it provides an important part in the trust chain. A malicious root may pretend to be some other root here since all visible fields can easily be copied.

Stores in .NET

As CAPICOM, .NET Framework and WSE cryptography libraries are built on it, the CryptoAPI library with the operations implemented in it represents the basic cryptography primitive in Microsoft Windows. These various libraries only offer access to some of the functionality provide by the CryptoAPI.

Symmetric keys cannot be persisted in the stores directly accessible from .NET, which is understandable since they are usually protected by asymmetric keys in enveloped data (described later) or are volatile session keys. It is possible to persistent symmetric keys, but to do so you will have to explore the low-level CryptoAPI.

The table below shows the various stores supported by WSE and CAPOICOM.

Store	WSE	CAPICOM
My	✓	✓
CA	✓	✓
Root	✓	✓
Other		✓

Manual System Store Management

The easiest way to look at certificates available for the current user is to either run the CertMgr command-line utility, Start | Run: certmgr or through the Tools menu in Internet Explorer, Tools | Internet Options... | Content | Certificates...

Another way that will show you all installed certificates for a store location is to use the certificate snap-in (available in W2K and XP) to the Management Console. This is done by starting the MMC application; one way is via Start | Run: mmc.exe then:

1. Select Add/Remove Snap-in... from the Console menu.

2. Click Add....

3. Select the Certificate snap-in.

4. Choose the store location you want to manage.

5. Repeat from step 2 if you want to include more than one store location.

6. Click OK.

7. Browse the stores, adding and removing certificates to your liking. You should of course be careful when you do this; if you remove a personal certificate you're likely to remove the private key as well, and then you cannot decrypt any information that was encrypted with the public key. You should also refrain from tampering with the trusted root certificates since they represent the foundation of all trust.

Here is an example showing the certificates associated with the EventLog service account on a Windows XP computer:

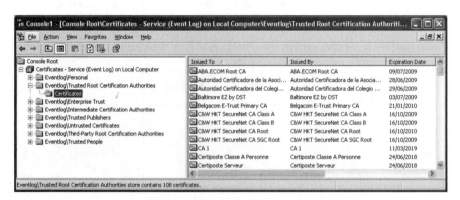

Obtaining a Certificate

There are several options available to you when creating a certificate; where you get the certificate from is primary driven by who you want to trust the certificate and what it is for. For instance, it is no good self-signing a certificate that you are going to use to establish your identify to unknown third parties.

Obtaining a Certificate from a Recognized CA

One way to find a recognized CA is to list the trusted certificate root store using one of the examples below, or using certmgr and looking in the Trusted Root Certification Authorities tab. This gives you a list of CA's that by default most Windows users trust. All other things being equal people are more likely to trust certificates issued by well-established certificate authorities:

Name	URL	Services
Verisign	http://www.verisign.com	Personal and server certificates
Thawte	http://www.thawte.com	Personal and server certificates
Entrust	http://www.entrust.com	Server certificates

Since they all have their own way of issuing the certificates, you must visit their web sites to find out how to procure one from them. Thawte issues free e-mail certificates for example, but they do not include your identity. If you want a certificate that includes identification of you as person, you have to present evidence that you are you and most probably pay for it as well.

If you get a personal certificate from a CA listed above, your digital signatures are likely to be accepted in most parts of the world, so it may be a worthwhile investment.

Obtaining a Certificate from an Internal Certificate Server

It is possible for you to set up a certificate root, and serve certificates to anyone you like. However, if you set up your own root, the certificates derived from it are unlikely to be accepted outside of the community you serve. It may be an excellent idea set your own root server for internal corporate identifications though. Giving individual certificates to all employees provides many new opportunities not possible using password authentication, such as non-repudiable recording of all actions and commitments made within the corporation.

Windows 2000 Server and Windows .NET Server both comes with a Certificate Server (this is only available if you are using Active Directory). The certificate server does, however, provide users with a simple web interface where they can apply for a certificate, and if you already use the Active Directory, this may be your preferred choice.

Another option is to set up a CA using OpenSSL, a free open source SSL toolkit. The drawback is that you must implement all user interfaces yourself. There is a section at the end of this chapter that discusses using OpenSSL.

All certificates are created by first creating a certificate request, a CRQ. Usually you generate the CRQ locally together with asymmetric key generation, and then submitted it to the certificate server for validation and approval.

There is an ActiveX component called xenroll in Windows (available to local VBScripts) that provide a simple interface for creating CRQs (also called PKCS10 objects, PKCS#10 being the specification of the CRQ format).

Here is a simple example of VBScript (scripted locally in the browser) that generates a CRQ:

```
<HTML>
<HEAD>
<TITLE>VBScript Certificate Enrollment Control Sample
</TITLE>
<OBJECT classid="clsid:43F8F289-7A20-11D0-8F06-00C04FC295E1"
        codebase="xenroll.dll"
```

```
          id=Enroll >
</OBJECT>
<OBJECT classid="clsid:98AFF3F0-5524-11D0-8812-00A0C903B83C"
        codebase="certcli.dll"
        id=Request >
</OBJECT>
<BR>
Certificate Enrollment Control Request Sample
<BR>
<BR>

<SCRIPT language="VBScript">
' Declare the distinguished name variable
Dim strDN

' Declare the request variable.
Dim strReq

' Declare a local variable for request disposition
Dim nDisp

' Enable error handling.
On Error Resume Next

' Declare consts used by CertRequest object
const CR_IN_BASE64 = &H1
const CR_IN_PKCS10 = &H100

' Build the DN.
strDN =   "CN=Erik Johansson" _
        & ",OU=Research & Development" _
        & ",O=DynaZon AB" _
        & ",L=Västerås" _
        & ",S=Västerås" _
        & ",C=SE"
' Attempt to use the control, in this case, to create a PKCS #10
MsgBox("Creating PKCS #10 " & strDN)
strReq = Enroll.createPKCS10( strDN, "1.3.6.1.5.5.7.3.2")
' If above line failed, Err.Number will not be 0.
if ( Err.Number <> 0 ) then
    MsgBox("Error in call to createPKCS10 " & Err.Number & _
        ", strReq=" & strReq)
    err.clear
else
    MsgBox("Submitting request " & strReq)
    nDisp = Request.Submit( CR_IN_BASE64 OR CR_IN_PKCS10, _
                            strReq, _
                            "", _
                            "Machine\CertAuth")
    ' If the preceding line failed, Err.Number will not be 0.
    if ( Err.Number <> 0 ) then
        MsgBox("Error in Request Submit " & Err.Number)
        err.clear
```

```
      else
          MsgBox("Submitted certificate; disposition = " & nDisp)
      end if

  end if
  </SCRIPT>
  <BR>
  </HEAD>
  </HTML>
```

Generating a Test Certificate

If you just need a certificate for testing purposes and don't want to go to the expense of buying a certificate or the trouble of setting up a certificate server you can generate you own by using the makecert command-line utility included with the .NET Framework. The makecert utility includes numerous options, including parameters to set an expiration date, company name, and encryption algorithm options. To generate a default certificate, however, you simply need to specify a filename:

```
> makecert c:\myCertFile.cer
```

This certificate will include some basic information about "Joe's Software Emporium". It will not be validatable through a certificate authority. You can view the certificate details by double-clicking on the certificate file in Windows Explorer.

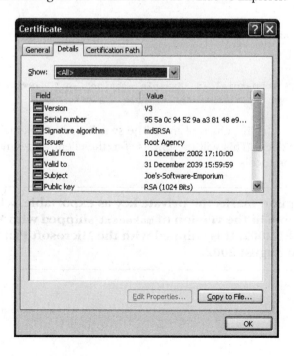

> You can also create a new certificate and install it into a key store on the current computer using additional `makecert` options, or the `certmgr` utility. Run `certmgr` with no parameters to start the GUI.

Unfortunately, the WSE classes require the private key to be exportable, and the makecert version shipped with the .NET Framework SDK does not mark them exportable. If you create test certificates using the makecert utility (version 5.131.2157.1) shipped with Visual Studio .NET 2002, you won't be able to use those in the WSE examples later on. However, the version of makecert included with the platform SDK from August 2002 (version 5.131.3639.0 or later) does! You should be able to download the latest version of the platform SDK from http://www.microsoft.com/msdownload/platformsdk/sdkupdate/.

Generating a Root Certificate

For testing purposes, you might want to simulate the entire trust chain. As we have already discussed root certificates are somewhat different from normal. Effectively you set yourself up as a certifying authority. Create a root certificate and its associated private key file.

```
> makecert -a sha1 -sv richard.pvk -n "CN=Richard" -d Richard -r
richard.cer
```

Then create another cert and import the self-signed certificate above as its root authority.

```
> makecert -$ commercial -d "Example website" -n "CN=www.example.org"
-iv richard.pvk -ic richard.cer example.org.cer -pe
```

This will create an effective chain of trust. The switches are explained in the documentation in detail. This will present itself to the client as genuine using application-level protocols.

> The -pe option marks the private key as exportable, which is not available in the version of makecert shipped with Visual Studio .NET 2002. It is shipped with the Microsoft Platform SDK from August 2002.

Certificates and WSE

Although there is an X509Certificates namespace in the standard Framework Class Library, System.Security.Cryptography.X509Certificates, it does not include any certificate store classes. The following examples use a namespace from the Web Services Enhancements 1.0 for Microsoft .NET package, (this is the released and supported version of the Web Services Development Kit Technology Preview) Microsoft.Web.Services.Security.X509.

Web Services Enhancements for .NET

Go to the link below for instructions on how to download and install the Web Services Enhancements for .NET (WSE). This distribution also comes with documentation and is available from http://msdn.microsoft.com/webservices/building/wse/. The System.Security.Cryptography namespace is used for all other cryptographic operations.

To include WSE in your C# project, select the Microsoft.Web.Services.dll from the .NET tab in the Add Reference dialog (after installing the WSE of course).

> **The .NET security namespaces (including WSE) are easy to use, but do not always support necessary operations to cover high security needs like smartcard-protected keys, at least not yet. Consider either complementing these operations with CAPICOM (described later on) or writing your whole implementation using CAPICOM from the beginning.**

List Your Own Store

As a first test drive of the store classes in the WSE, we look into your private certificate store to see if we can find anything. You are not likely to have a certificate with a corresponding private key at all unless you find it using the example below. They are normally put in the 'My' store in the default (CurrentUser) system store location.

Remember that all X509 classes come from the WSE library, and all other cryptographic classes from FCL.

```
// ListCertsWSE.cs
using System;
using System.Security.Cryptography;
using Microsoft.Web.Services.Security.X509;
```

Create a certificate store object representing the current user's personal certificates:

```
class ListCertsWSE{

  static void Main()
  {
    X509CertificateStore store =
      X509CertificateStore.CurrentUserStore(
                                     X509CertificateStore.MyStore);
```

Open it in read-only mode so we don't have to worry about trashing it:

```
    store.OpenRead();
```

List through all certificates in the store and print out the subject in a humanly readable format. Remember, the X509Certificate class comes from the WSE here, not FCL!

```
    foreach ( X509Certificate cert in store.Certificates )
        Console.WriteLine(cert.GetName());

store.Close();
  }
}
```

> **Remember that all X509 classes come from the WSE namespace Microsoft.Web.Services.Security.X509.**

The results from such a store listing might look like:

```
CN=Arne Anka, OU=Development, O=Software & Co, L=Västerås, C=SE
C=SE, OU=AddTrust2Mail, O=AddTrust, CN=Arne Anka, E=arne.anka@acme.com
```

The CN, OU, O, etc. tags are called distinguished names according to the OSI Directory also known as X.500. There are a few standard names still in use, see RFC 1779 (http://www.ietf.org/rfc/rfc1779.txt) for more details. If you are familiar with LDAP (Lightweight Directory Access Protocol), you will probably recognize the use of distinguished names from there.

Examine Your Certificates

The .NET Framework provides easy access to some of the certificate fields that may otherwise be relatively complex to extract. The values of these fields are unfortunately more or less arbitrary today since it has been difficult to unite around one specific meaning. This does not mean they don't contain important information though; you just have to know what to look for in different contexts (there you go again). For example, all individuals in Sweden have a unique number (actually invented before 1984), which makes it simple to identify people in many different contexts, not only digital. Anyway, a X.509 profile has been developed there, called eID, which includes this number and that makes it very simple to identify Swedes using certificates complying with this profile. The profile policies also define the strict identification process involved in the distribution of these certificates, which makes them safe to use on the Internet.

The problem is of course to know what to look for; how can we for example tell whether or not a certificate is following a certain profile so we know if there is a unique number to extract? Unfortunately, there aren't any simple ways of knowing. What we can do here is to have a closer look at the possibilities we have when examining the certificate content.

```
// ExamineCertsWSE.cs
using System;
using System.Security.Cryptography;
using Microsoft.Web.Services.Security.X509;

class ExamineCertsWSE{

  static void Main()
  {

    // Set up the personal certificate store and list the
    // certificates in it
    X509CertificateStore store =
      X509CertificateStore.CurrentUserStore(
                                X509CertificateStore.MyStore);
    store.OpenRead();

    foreach ( X509Certificate cert in store.Certificates )
    {
      // The issuer specifies the distinguished names of the CA
      // that produced this certificate (signed the CRQ)
      Console.WriteLine("issuer   : " + cert.GetIssuerName());

      // The subject is your own distinguished names
      Console.WriteLine("subject  : " + cert.GetName());

      // The serial number is unique within the issuer (CA)
      Console.WriteLine("serial   : " + cert.GetSerialNumberString());
```

```
        // A certificate isn't valid unless the current date is between
        // the notBefore and notAfter dates
        Console.WriteLine("notBefore: " +
          cert.GetEffectiveDateString());
        Console.WriteLine("notAfter : " +
                          cert.GetExpirationDateString());
```

The following fields are interesting in a more advanced context. There are fields called KeyUsage and ExtendedKeyUsage and they define the intended usage of the certificate, like identification, non-repudiation, and key encryption (there are many more). There are only two usage flags available through the framework, though that doesn't mean there aren't any others!

```
        Console.WriteLine("Data encryption  : " +
                        cert.SupportsDataEncryption);
        Console.WriteLine("Digital signature: " +
        cert.SupportsDigitalSignature);

        Console.WriteLine("----------------------------------------\n");
      }

      store.Close();

      Console.ReadLine();
    }
}
```

The output from this example might look like:

```
issuer    : CN=CA01, OU=Examples, O=Test CA, L=Västerås, C=SE
subject   : CN=Arne Anka, OU=MyDep, O=MyCompany, L=MyTown, C=US
serial    : A949CD0AEC00
notBefore: 2002-02-14 09:18:27
notAfter : 2003-02-14 09:18:27
Data encryption  : True
Digital signature: True
------------------------------------------

issuer    : C=SE, L=Stockholm, O=Another CA, OU=Test, CN=CA02
subject   : C=SE, L=Västerås, OU=1443 MyRoad, CN=Arne Anka
serial    : CA3912000100408B692A
notBefore: 2001-11-06 01:27:12
notAfter : 2002-11-06 01:37:12
Data encryption  : True
Digital signature: True
------------------------------------------
```

Sign Simple Plaintext

Let's see how a digital signature is produced from a certificate in the certificate store then. This example shows how a very simple text string is signed and what the signature may look like after being transformed into base64 encoding (a very common binary-to-text transform, used a great deal in MIME).

> **The private key of the certificate must be exportable for this example to work, and you'll receive a** `System.Security.Cryptography.CryptographicException` **exception if it isn't. Please read the *Obtaining a certificate* section in order to create a test certificate that allows export of the private key.**

Note that we select which certificate to use by changing the `Certificates[0]` index. You have as many certificates as were listed by the previous example.

```csharp
// SimpleSignWSE.cs
using System;
using System.Security.Cryptography;
using Microsoft.Web.Services.Security.X509;

class SimpleSignWSE.cs {

  static void Main()
  {
    // Create a certificate store object representing the
    // current users personal certificates
    X509CertificateStore store =
      X509CertificateStore.CurrentUserStore(
                                  X509CertificateStore.MyStore);

    store.OpenRead();

    // Pick out the first certificate we find in the store
    X509Certificate cert = (X509Certificate)store.Certificates[0];
    store.Close();

    // Get the private key from the certificate, specified by 'true'
    // as argument to ExportParameters
    RSAParameters privateKey = cert.Key.ExportParameters(true);

    // Set up a RSA provider and set the private key handle
    RSACryptoServiceProvider rsa = new RSACryptoServiceProvider();
    rsa.ImportParameters(privateKey);

    // Create a hash provider used for the signature
    SHA1CryptoServiceProvider sha1 = new SHA1CryptoServiceProvider();
```

Set up a utility encoder to have a specific format for the signature. Signature verification is less problematic if the signed data is saved in *exactly* the same format (you should keep the same character encoding for example), or if the original and the specific formats are known at the time of the verification. Consider treating all plaintext as binary to avoid unintended encoding transformations.

```
System.Text.UTF8Encoding utf8Encoder = new
    System.Text.UTF8Encoding();

byte[] plaintext = utf8Encoder.GetBytes("Sign this");
byte[] signature = rsa.SignData(plaintext, sha1);

Console.WriteLine(Convert.ToBase64String(signature));
    }
}
```

A typical output from this code snippet would be the signature in base64 encoding:

```
XX2pUsZa2s4yKws1MQIaZMwCFQl89gLfc/qwBrshr1rfW+Yl0NQnTHj9juL5XJwcWI+Cdq
bqf1zGoLDfoutd0rXgB4YSps5xRyZiKYztGxvawHGAVX4CCr1nUKlcVY4jSaBoq5KadVy6
D+7AnTQ9BBHWSF7uQKKEB6X5r0aFzuyTLwGqZbsYDYirof1f3oQFj/8DRfo0ACZEvubBOc
BtIBOM/OIYMelgeR4/lnDzbdFwWinEk+lBstC6dRiROzaTy4xm0Om7JUx7ypRmat5sfOoY
e6HlLm2fHbLAYIA8nZw77o/7OY2phGdr8+Pt2NzPhrAVJ4h0qm93coAOFo3UFA==
```

Verify a Signature

OK, so now we want to verify the signature against the public key of the certificate. The VerifyData() method only verifies the data against the certificate that signed it; it doesn't verify the certificate chain. It is a good idea to verify the chain as well to make sure the certificate that produced the signature really comes from a trusted root, but since FCL v1.0 doesn't have this support, you should consider using CAPICOM for this instead because it includes full verification features.

This example uses the previous snippet to save space; first pick out the public key handle from the same certificate as in the previous example, and set the RSA provider with it:

```
RSAParameters publicKey = cert.Key.ExportParameters(false);
rsa.ImportParameters(publicKey);
```

Then verify the signature against the plaintext produced in the previous example, using the same hash provider as well:

```
bool result = rsa.VerifyData(plaintext, sha1, signature);

Console.WriteLine("signature verified: " + result);
```

Unless the signature or plaintext data has changed (try that later, for fun), the signature will check out OK.

> **This signature verification is very simple and the `VerifyData()` method should not be used unless there is no doubt about the origin of the certificate.**
>
> **Consider using CAPICOM in any case since it supports full chain verification. See the CAPICOM section later in the chapter.**

The output in this case would be:

```
signature verified: True
```

Protect Another Key

This example illustrates how a symmetric (secret) key is used to encrypt a simple text string and how a public key of a certificate then encrypts that secret key (and thereby protects it). The encrypted key is decrypted with the private key associated with the certificate. This is a classic example of how to protect personal information in a safe way. This is also the most basic pattern used to share protected information as other people's public keys can encrypt the secret key as well. The terms sender and recipient in this example are meant to illustrate that possibility.

```
// ProtectKeyWSE.cs
using System;
using System.Security.Cryptography;
using Microsoft.Web.Services.Security.X509;

class ProtectKeyWSE{

  static void Main()
  {
    System.Text.UTF8Encoding utf8 = new System.Text.UTF8Encoding();
```

Set up the symmetric cipher for the sender. This is also the secret key used to encrypt the plaintext.

```
    SymmetricAlgorithm sCipher = SymmetricAlgorithm.Create();
    ICryptoTransform enc = sCipher.CreateEncryptor();

    // Set up a simple plaintext example and print it to the console
    byte[] sPlaintext = utf8.GetBytes(
      "The red fox jumps over the brown dog");
```

```
Console.WriteLine("Sender's plaintext   : " +
    utf8.GetString(sPlaintext));
```

Encrypt the plaintext to ciphertext and print the ciphertext as a UTF-8 encoded string to the console. This doesn't really make any sense; it is only provided to make a point:

```
byte[] ciphertext = enc.TransformFinalBlock(sPlaintext, 0,
    sPlaintext.GetLength(0));
Console.WriteLine("Ciphertext           : " +
    utf8.GetString(ciphertext));
```

Now we get a certificate from our personal store the same way as we did before (in previous examples). Pick up the public key and set up an RSA cipher object.

Remember, the `Certificates` collection contain all the certificates in the store, and the index 0 indicates the first enumerated certificate.

```
X509CertificateStore sStore =
    X509CertificateStore.CurrentUserStore(
        X509CertificateStore.MyStore);

sStore.OpenRead();
X509Certificate sCert = (X509Certificate)sStore.Certificates[0];
RSAParameters publicKey = sCert.Key.ExportParameters(false);
sStore.Close();

RSACryptoServiceProvider sRSA = new RSACryptoServiceProvider();
sRSA.ImportParameters(publicKey);
```

This is the fun part where we actually protect the secret key with the public key of the recipient. We have to save the IV as well, unless we use ECB mode.

```
byte[] eKey = sRSA.Encrypt(sCipher.Key, false);
byte[] iv = sCipher.IV;
```

This is where the protected secret key, key parameters (like IV), and ciphertext are sent to the recipient. The section below uses the symbols `eKey`, `iv`, and `ciphertext` from the section above. Now we do everything again but in the reverse order this time.

```
X509CertificateStore rStore =
    X509CertificateStore.CurrentUserStore(
        X509CertificateStore.MyStore);

rStore.OpenRead();
X509Certificate rCert = (X509Certificate)rStore.Certificates[0];
RSAParameters privateKey = rCert.Key.ExportParameters(true);
rStore.Close();
```

```
        RSACryptoServiceProvider rRSA = new RSACryptoServiceProvider();
        rRSA.ImportParameters(privateKey);
```

Decrypt the secret key and set up a default cipher again with the parameters we got from the sender (IV).

```
        byte[] sKey = rRSA.Decrypt(eKey, false);

        SymmetricAlgorithm rCipher = SymmetricAlgorithm.Create();
        rCipher.Key = sKey;
        rCipher.IV = iv;

        ICryptoTransform dec = rCipher.CreateDecryptor();
        byte[] rPlaintext = dec.TransformFinalBlock(ciphertext, 0,
            ciphertext.GetLength(0));

        Console.Write("Recipient's plaintext: " +
                    utf8.GetString(rPlaintext));

        Console.ReadLine();
    }
}
```

A typical output would be (note the nonsense ciphertext printout):

```
sender's plaintext    : The red fox jumps over the brown dog
ciphertext            : P$?lZLs)?ztI)H?ZW?|f?(_
recipient's plaintext: The red fox jumps over the brown dog
```

This particular example just demonstrates the basic principles behind a key exchange, but a number of other issues that must be understood. All symmetric cipher parameters are 'default' in this case and the possibility to defined default crypto parameters is almost unique to the .NET Framework. It does make it somewhat easier to accomplish simple cryptographic tasks, but it also hides important aspects like algorithm ID, mode, etc. which is vital to know if exchanging ciphertext between systems.

> **Beware of the interoperability risks involved in using default crypto configurations in .NET! Consider using specific ciphers and modes instead, to be able to exchange information between two computers with different default settings.**

Certificates and CAPICOM

CAPICOM is a COM wrapper for Microsoft Cryptography API, known as CryptoAPI or CAPI, hence the name CAPICOM. The CAPICOM interface differs a little from the System.Security.Cryptography namespace regarding the abstraction level. The CAPICOM interface almost exclusively implements interfaces that handle certificates, certificate stores and everything that has anything to do with certificates. The signing and verification operations for example are a little more specialized and handle standard formats such as Enveloped Data (PKCS#7, RFC 2315: http://www.ietf.org/rfc/rfc2315.txt), while the framework provides more primitive operations. CAPICOM also provides an EnvelopedData object in PKCS#7 format that takes care of both symmetric encryption and asymmetric protection of the secret key instead of forcing you to do that explicitly. This makes it more attractive in some aspects, but it also reduces the flexibility.

CAPICOM 2.0 is available for download from http://www.microsoft.com/downloads/search.asp? Choose Keyword Search and use CAPICOM as the keyword. The current version at the time of this writing was 2.0.0.1. Once you have downloaded this, extract CAPICOM.dll and place it in your system's Windows/Stystem32 directory, then register it as a COM server:

```
> regsvr32 CAPICOM.dll
```

If you are using Visual Studio .NET all you need to do to include CAPICOM in your C# project is select the CAPICOM v2.0 Type Library from the COM tab in the Add Reference dialog (after installing CAPICOM of course).

If you are developing just using the framework SDK, you will need to generate a runtime-callable wrapper yourself:

```
> tlbimp CAPICOM.dll /out:CAPICOM_RCW.dll /namescape:CAPICOM
```

List your Personal Store

Listing your personal store in CAPICOM is nearly as simple as with the WSE. There are more and longer parameter names in CAPICOM, which may be a little annoying at times, but it does give access to more advanced options, such as the possibility to select smartcard stores or full signature verification.

```
// ListCertCAPICOM.cs

using System;
using CAPICOM;
```

```
class ListCertCAPICOM
{
  static void Main()
  {
    Store store = new Store();
    store.Open(CAPICOM_STORE_LOCATION.CAPICOM_CURRENT_USER_STORE,
               "My",
               CAPICOM_STORE_OPEN_MODE.CAPICOM_STORE_OPEN_READ_ONLY);
    foreach ( Certificate cert in store.Certificates )
      Console.WriteLine(cert.SubjectName);
    Console.ReadLine();
  }
}
```

The output for the above example should look something like this:

```
C=SE, L=Västerås, O=Software & Ca, OU=Development, CN=Arne Anka
E=arne.anka@acme.com, CN=Arne Anka, O=AddTrust, OU=AddTrust2Mail, C=SE
```

This output should presumably look the same as for the WSE example, but that is not necessarily true. There are no rules detailing how to display the distinguished names, and is entirely up to the operation that parses and translates the certificate fields.

Examine your Certificates

As already stated in the WSE example, the .NET Framework only directly supports analysis of a few of the fields in a certificate, limiting its usefulness in serious security applications. Unless the FCL is extended in this area, you will be forced to use CAPICOM or CAPI directly.

```
// ExamineCertCAPICOM.cs

using System;
using CAPICOM;

class ExamineCertCAPICOM
{
  static void Main()
  {
    Store store = new Store();
    store.Open(CAPICOM_STORE_LOCATION.CAPICOM_CURRENT_USER_STORE,
    "My",
    CAPICOM_STORE_OPEN_MODE.CAPICOM_STORE_OPEN_READ_ONLY);

    foreach ( Certificate cert in store.Certificates )
    {
    // The issuer specifies the unique names of the CA
    // that produced this certificate (signed the CRQ)
    Console.WriteLine("issuer   : " + cert.IssuerName);
```

```
// The subject is your own distinguished names
Console.WriteLine("subject  : " + cert.SubjectName);

// The serial number is unique within the issuer (CA)
Console.WriteLine("serial   : " + cert.SerialNumber.ToString());

// A certificate isn't valid unless the current date is between
// the notBefore and notAfter dates
Console.WriteLine("notBefore: " + cert.ValidFromDate.ToString());
Console.WriteLine("notAfter : " + cert.ValidToDate.ToString());
```

The following fields are interesting in a more advanced context. There are fields called KeyUsage and ExtendedKeyUsage and they define the intended usage of the certificate, like identification, non-repudiation, code signing, and key encryption to name but a few. The standard fields are mentioned in the standards specifications RFC 2459 and 3280, which can be found at http://www.ietf.com/rfc.html. You should read the CAPICOM reference manual if you want to know more about the available fields in CAPICOM: http://msdn.microsoft.com/library/en-us/security/security/capicom_oid.asp.

```
KeyUsage ku = cert.KeyUsage();
Console.WriteLine("\nKey usage +++++++++++++++++++++++++++++++");
Console.WriteLine("Critical               : " + ku.IsCritical);
Console.WriteLine("May sign CRL:s         : " +
                  ku.IsCRLSignEnabled);
Console.WriteLine("May sign certificates: " +
                  ku.IsKeyCertSignEnabled);
Console.WriteLine("Digital signature     : " +
                  ku.IsDigitalSignatureEnabled);
Console.WriteLine("Data encryption       : " +
                  ku.IsDataEnciphermentEnabled);
Console.WriteLine("Encryption only       : " +
                  ku.IsEncipherOnlyEnabled);
Console.WriteLine("Decryption only       : " +
                  ku.IsDecipherOnlyEnabled);
Console.WriteLine("Key agreement         : " +
                  ku.IsKeyAgreementEnabled);
Console.WriteLine("Key encryption        : " +
                  ku.IsKeyEnciphermentEnabled);
Console.WriteLine("Non-repudiation       : " +
                  ku.IsNonRepudiationEnabled);

ExtendedKeyUsage ekus = cert.ExtendedKeyUsage();
Console.WriteLine("\nExtended Key usage  +++++++++++++++++++++");
foreach ( EKU eku in ekus.EKUs )
{
   Console.WriteLine(eku.Name + " : " + eku.OID);
}
Console.WriteLine("\nCertificate extensions +++++++++++++++++");
foreach (Extension ex in cert.Extensions())
{
   Console.WriteLine(ex.OID.Name + " : " + ex.OID.Value);
```

```
      }
      Console.WriteLine("\nExtended properties +++++++++++++++++++++");
      foreach (ExtendedProperty ep in cert.ExtendedProperties())
      {
        Console.WriteLine(ep.PropID + " : " +
          ep.get_Value(CAPICOM_ENCODING_TYPE.CAPICOM_ENCODE_ANY));
      }
      Console.WriteLine("------------------------------------------\n");
    }
    Console.ReadLine();
  }
}
```

Output from this example should look something like this:

```
issuer   : C=SE, L=Västerås, O=Test CA, OU=Examples, CN=CA01
subject  : C=SE, L=MyTown, O=MyCompany, OU=MyDep, CN=Arne Anka
serial   : 00EC0ACD49A9
notBefore: 2002-02-14 19:18:27
notAfter : 2003-02-14 19:18:27

Key usage +++++++++++++++++++++++++++++++
Critical              : True
May sign CRL:s        : False
May sign certificates: False
Digital signature     : True
Data encryption       : True
Encryption only       : False
Decryption only       : True
Key agreement         : False
Key encryption        : True
Non-repudiation       : False

Extended Key usage +++++++++++++++++++++

Certificate extensions +++++++++++++++++++
CAPICOM_OID_SUBJECT_KEY_IDENTIFIER_EXTENSION : 2.5.29.14
CAPICOM_OID_KEY_USAGE_EXTENSION : 2.5.29.15

Extended properties +++++++++++++++++++++
CAPICOM_PROPID_KEY_PROV_INFO :
pDEXAL4xFwABAAAAAAAAAAAAAAAAAAAAAQAAAEgAbQBoAHgAYwBrAFoAUgBaADkAUgBzAA
AATQBpAGMAcgBvAHMAbwBmAHQAIABFAG4AaABhAG4AYwBlAGQAIABDAHIAeQBwAHQAbwBn
AHIAYQBwAGgAaQBjACAAUAByAG8AdgBpAGQAQQZQByACAAdgAxAC4AMAAAAAA==

CAPICOM_PROPID_HASH_PROP : 1DRuiYoYHeMR4Svq9rQOWe9DiX0=

CAPICOM_PROPID_MD5_HASH : xWAoDekixcTkVIpCOq6GJg==

CAPICOM_PROPID_KEY_IDENTIFIER : j7e2j5BGwTt87Q4dVHnJy0rsPUc=

------------------------------------------
```

As you can understand from these simple examples, it can be a tough job to handle certificates as each library has its own way of presenting the content in readable form. If you must compare fields between certificates, you are well advised to learn more about the actual content format before you make any assumptions.

As you see in the example output, there are many different fields in a certificate and it can be difficult to get a hold of which fields are relevant for you. The most common fields are published through user-friendly interfaces, but there are others that may be interesting to examine:

Certificate Extensions

Field	Comment
CAPICOM_OID_CRL_DIST_POINTS_EXTENSION	Specifies the location (normally a URL) where the CA CRL is published. This field must be present in a certificate in order to check the revocation status.
CAPICOM_OID_CLIENT_AUTH_EKU	An EKU (Extended Key Usage) that isn't available through the user-friendly FCL interface. This field tells you that one of the certificate's purposes is to act as a client-side SSL certificate (Client Authentication).
CAPICOM_OID_SERVER_AUTH_EKU	Another EKU that should be present in all server certificates used to for SSL.
*_EKU	Several other EKU values may be interesting to examine. Read more about CAPICOM_OID at the MSDN site.

If you want to learn more about the available extensions, you should visit the following MSDN web site: http://msdn.microsoft.com/library/en-us/security/security/capicom_oid.asp.

Sign Simple Plaintext

In the WSE example, we managed to produce a simple signature as a single object. We had to provide certificate and plaintext in order to verify it. CAPICOM, however, produces a PKCS#7 formatted object at the Sign() operation, including the plaintext (optional), the signature, and the certificate chain. This object is a little more inflexible in that you cannot extract the signature entity directly, but it supports other operations like co-signing and full verification.

```
// SimpleSignCAPICOM.cs
using System;
using CAPICOM;

class SimpleSignCAPICOM
{

  static void Main()
  {
    // Open the personal store as usual
    Store store = new Store();
    store.Open(CAPICOM_STORE_LOCATION.CAPICOM_CURRENT_USER_STORE,
               "My",
               CAPICOM_STORE_OPEN_MODE.CAPICOM_STORE_OPEN_READ_ONLY);

    // Pick out the first certificate (one based array)
    ICertificate cert = (Certificate)store.Certificates[1];

    // Create a Signer class as holder of the certificate
    Signer signer = new SignerClass();
    signer.Certificate = cert;

    // Create a SignedData class including the original message
    SignedData sd = new SignedDataClass();
    sd.Content = "The red fox jumped over the brown dog";
```

Sign the data using the `Signer` object that hold the certificate. Base64 is a neat format to handle, so we ask for the signature in that encoding. The result is PKCS#7 formatted.

```
    string signedMessage = sd.Sign(signer, false,
      CAPICOM_ENCODING_TYPE.CAPICOM_ENCODE_BASE64);

    Console.WriteLine(signedMessage);
    Console.ReadLine();
  }
}
```

This output is considerably larger than the signature from the WSE example, mainly because the certificate chain is included (not optional), that is, the end-user certificate as well as all ancestor certificates are included. If the content is chosen to be included as well, it may be extracted from this lump of data by using the `VerifyData()` operation and then examining the `Content` property. Here is some (truncated) output from the above program.

```
MIIJPQYJKoZIhvcNAQcCoIIJLjCCCSoCAQExCzAJBgUrDgMCGgUAMFkGCSqGSIb3DQEHAa
BMBEpUAGgAZQAgAHIAZQBkACAAZgBvAHgAIABqAHUAbQBwAGUAZAAv6cZjo+zyewuLTcW2
...
8AhLa5S0e5lzxuP7F3zULLfUTbxjl2ew3Yeh8nXgA7WjJvm3FbfRBGzTE/4y1HHUofjvZw
IONj772N4E5QTZe7p/lkKXV8Lqpvi5+vrfKMgf7+82Xc=
```

Verify Signature

In order to save some space, assume that the signedMessage object is already set with the data listed above. It is very simple to verify the signed message including verification of the certificate. The VerifyData() operation does not return any value, but always throws an exception if the verification fails for some reason.

Set up a new SignedData object, and verify the signedMessage content. After a successful verification, the Content property contain the original message that was signed (unless the plaintext was excluded in the Sign() method.

```
SignedData verifyThis = new SignedDataClass();
verifyThis.Verify(signedMessage, false,
   CAPICOM_SIGNED_DATA_VERIFY_FLAG.CAPICOM_VERIFY_SIGNATURE
   _AND_CERTIFICATE);

Console.WriteLine("content = " + verifyThis.Content);

Console.ReadLine();
```

The output from this example would be the plaintext of the original signature:

```
content = The red fox jumped over the brown dog
```

Validate a Certificate

As mentioned in a previous section, a certificate validation often includes more than a verification of the certificate chain, such as a certificate revocation check. Such a check can be complicated to perform, but the CAPICOM interface includes operations to handle this for you, by downloading the available CRLs and caching them locally. The following is a table of possible validation flags:

Flag	Comment
CAPICOM_CHECK_NONE	No validation is made at all
CAPICOM_CHECK_TRUSTED_ROOT	Make sure the root certificate is trusted
CAPICOM_CHECK_TIME_VALIDITY	Check the date validity of all certificates in the chain
CAPICOM_CHECK_SIGNATURE_VALIDITY	Check the signatures of all certificates in the chain

Flag	Comment
CAPICOM_CHECK_ONLINE_REVOCATION_STATUS	Check the certificate against the CA CRL. This requires a CRL Distribution Point (CDP) field in the certificate, which URL must be available. Check for the CDP extension in the certificate.
CAPICOM_CHECK_OFFLINE_REVOCATION_STATUS	Checks the local CRL cache first, if not found in the offline cache, it tries to get it online.
CAPICOM_CHECK_COMPLETE_CHAIN	Checks the complete chain.
CAPICOM_CHECK_NAME_CONSTRAINTS	Checks the name constraints, see RFC 2459 for details.
CAPICOM_CHECK_BASIC_CONSTRAINTS	Checks the basic constraints like path length, see RFC 2459 for details.
CAPICOM_CHECK_NESTED_VALIDITY_PERIOD	This checks nested validity dates if present in any of the certificates in the chain.
CAPICOM_CHECK_ONLINE_ALL	Checks the revocation status of all certificates in the chain except the root certificate online.
CAPICOM_CHECK_OFFLINE_ALL	Checks the revocation status of all certificates in the chain except the root certificate offline.

This example lists the certificates in your personal store and checks the revocation status online for all certificates with a CDP (CRL Distribution Point) extension; otherwise, a simple validation is performed.

```
// ValidateCertCAPICOM.cs

using System;
using CAPICOM;

class ValidateCertCAPICOM
{
   static void Main()
   {
      Store store = new StoreClass();
```

```
store.Open(CAPICOM_STORE_LOCATION.CAPICOM_CURRENT_USER_STORE,
           "My",
           CAPICOM_STORE_OPEN_MODE.CAPICOM_STORE_OPEN_READ_ONLY);

foreach (Certificate cert in store.Certificates)
{
  CertificateStatus cs = (CertificateStatus)cert.IsValid();
```

The code above opens the personal store in read-only mode as usual then loops through all certificates in the store and checks the validity depending on the presence of a CDP entry or not.

This part is a little backwards, but the IsValid() method sets up the CertificateStatus object, which is then used to check the status again if other than the default flag is wanted. The Result value is updated after each update of the CheckFlag property!

Here we find out if the CRL Distribution Point field is present in the certificate.

```
bool cdpPresent = false;
foreach ( Extension e in cert.Extensions() )
{
  if ( e.OID.Name ==
    CAPICOM_OID.CAPICOM_OID_CRL_DIST_POINTS_EXTENSION )
  {
    cdpPresent = true;
    break;
  }
}

if ( cdpPresent )
{
```

If there is a CDP field present, we ask for the online revocation status of all certificates in the chain (including CA certificates).

```
cs.CheckFlag = CAPICOM_CHECK_FLAG.CAPICOM_CHECK_ONLINE_ALL;

if ( cs.Result == false )
   Console.WriteLine("online check failed: " +
                        cert.SubjectName);
}
else
{
```

If no CDP is present, we check only the available fields in each certificate and the integrity of the chain.

```
            cs.CheckFlag =
                CAPICOM_CHECK_FLAG.CAPICOM_CHECK_COMPLETE_CHAIN;

            if ( cs.Result == false )
                Console.WriteLine("complete check failed: " +
                                    cert.SubjectName);
        }
    }
    Console.WriteLine("Done!");
    Console.ReadLine();
    }
}
```

Managing Certificate Chains

There is also a Chain class, which helps you examine and operate on a certificate chain, if you want for example to find out more information about the CA and root certificates. The Chain class provides you with a simple interface to access all certificates in the chain. If you have initialized a CertificateStatus object by a call to IsValid(), the Chain.Build() method will execute all validations specified in that status object.

```
// CertChainCAPICOM.cs

using System;
using CAPICOM;

class CertChainCAPICOM
{

    static void Main(string[] args)
    {
        Store store = new StoreClass();
        store.Open(CAPICOM_STORE_LOCATION.CAPICOM_CURRENT_USER_STORE,
        "My",
        CAPICOM_STORE_OPEN_MODE.CAPICOM_STORE_OPEN_READ_ONLY);
```

Loop through all the certificates in the store and build a Chain object for all of them. The Build() method validates all certificates in the chain according to the CertificateStatus of the end certificate.

```
        foreach ( Certificate cert in store.Certificates )
        {
            Chain chain = new ChainClass();
            bool result = chain.Build(cert);
            if ( result == false )
                Console.WriteLine("\nValidation failed for certificate: " +
                    cert.SubjectName);

            Console.WriteLine("\nListing certificates in chain:");
```

Since the chain.Certificates collection is ordered, we get a listing that represents the correct order in the chain, starting with the end certificate.

```
        int c = 1;
        foreach ( Certificate parent in chain.Certificates )
            Console.WriteLine("chain[" + c++ + "]: " +
                                parent.SubjectName);
    }
    Console.ReadLine();
  }
}
```

If other validation flags are wanted, you have to get a CertificateStatus object using cert.IsValid() and set the new flags using the CheckFlag property before building the chain. In this run, all certificates checked out OK with the default validation flags set.

```
Listing certificates in chain:
chain[1]: C=SE, L=Västerås, O=MyCompany, OU=MyDep, CN=Arne Anka
chain[2]: C=SE, L=Västerås, O=SomeCA, OU=Class 1 Domain, CN=CA01
chain[3]: C=SE, L=Västerås, O=SomeRoot, OU=Class 1 Domain, CN=Root CA

Listing certificates in chain:
chain[1]: E=arne.anka@acme.com, CN=Arne Anka, O=AddTrust,
OU=AddTrust2Mail, C=SE
chain[2]: CN=AddTrust2Mail CA, OU=AddTrust TTP Network, O=AddTrust AB,
C=SE
chain[3]: E=info@valicert.com, CN=http://www.valicert.com/,
OU=ValiCert Class 1
Policy Validation Authority, O="ValiCert, Inc.", L=ValiCert Validation
Network
```

Enveloped Data

The PKCS#7 format also includes something called enveloped data, meaning data that is encrypted with a secret key that in turn is protected with the public key of the recipient's. As mentioned before, this is a common pattern (used for example in S/MIME, the secure e-mail standard) for protecting data, and there is an object in CAPICOM that handles all these operations for you.

> **Consider using this class instead of implementing a key protection scheme yourself, when you exchange messages with someone for example.**

This example is similar to the previous example but all in one object.

```
// EnvelopedCAPICOM.cs

using System;
using CAPICOM;

class EnvelopedCAPICOM
{
  static void Main(string[] args)
  {
    StoreClass store = new StoreClass();
    store.Open(CAPICOM_STORE_LOCATION.CAPICOM_CURRENT_USER_STORE,
    "My",
    CAPICOM_STORE_OPEN_MODE.CAPICOM_STORE_OPEN_READ_ONLY);

    // Create an object for enveloped data and fill in the content
    EnvelopedDataClass ed = new EnvelopedDataClass();
    ed.Content = "This is the actual content";

    // Set secret key parameters
    ed.Algorithm.Name =
      CAPICOM_ENCRYPTION_ALGORITHM.CAPICOM_ENCRYPTION_ALGORITHM_3DES;
    ed.Algorithm.KeyLength =
      CAPICOM_ENCRYPTION_KEY_LENGTH.CAPICOM_ENCRYPTION_KEY
        _LENGTH_MAXIMUM;
```

Add the first certificate as recipient of the encrypted message. The public key is used to encrypt the secret key. First, encrypt the content with the secret key and then the secret key with the public key of each recipient (it is possible to have more than one recipient).

Remember, the Certificates collection contains all the certificates in the store, and the index 0 indicates the first enumerated certificate.

```
    ed.Recipients.Add( (Certificate)store.Certificates[1]);

    string eContent = ed.Encrypt(
      CAPICOM_ENCODING_TYPE.CAPICOM_ENCODE_BASE64);

    // Print out the encrypted result and secret key information
    Console.WriteLine("Key algorithm = " + ed.Algorithm.Name);
    Console.WriteLine("Key length    = " + ed.Algorithm.KeyLength);
    Console.WriteLine(eContent + "\n");
```

Set up a 'recipient' site where only the encrypted content is inherited from the code above:

```
    EnvelopedDataClass rEd = new EnvelopedDataClass();
```

Decrypt the envelope. This operation tries to find a match between your stored certificates and the ones in the envelope. The stored certificate must have a corresponding private key.

```
rEd.Decrypt(eContent);

// Print out the original plaintext and secret key information
Console.WriteLine("Key algorithm = " + rEd.Algorithm.Name);
Console.WriteLine("Key length   = " + rEd.Algorithm.KeyLength);
Console.WriteLine(rEd.Content);

Console.ReadLine();

    }
}
```

A typical output would look like:

```
Key algorithm = CAPICOM_ENCRYPTION_ALGORITHM_3DES
Key length    = CAPICOM_ENCRYPTION_KEY_LENGTH_MAXIMUM
MIICEAYJKoZIhvcNAQcDoIICATCCAf0CAQAxggGZMIIBlQIBADB9MHMxETAPBgNVBAMTCE
RUUyBDQTAxMRwwGgYDVQQLExNEb21haW4gVHJ1c3QgU2VydmVyMSAwHgYDVQQKExdJbmZy
YXRydXN0IFRlY2hub2xvZ2llczERMA8GA1UEBxMIVmFzdGVyYXMxCzAJBgNVBAYTAlNFAg
YA7ArNSakwDQYJKoZIhvcNAQEBBQAEggEALJTUTRa0wpNCelfTyY6TLbWz40ucw9HcmGhn
xy+LRFrm+wn78BdTi8tacBqOPRfsS0qR21bpyzRowP9dulN3S7ML3oYwcLIXV9Q3+VM22c
DK/CzVuZ3wWhCTY66EVElsXVdho4WJpaX0y91UwdJq3amCW7tdcqWOjDDZAzlRB9WAfqDM
EQqOJ7CToX05Cbi+mbAKOBCV0D1gMNHt9awi5P9E7We7ESWHgeOsg8LEfXq2GsyQ8lX90j
9JTpj06r3u6yv8uQeWQuQE/kduwEJgw183ZGwFJOXaGI4UKxMqKP8eernSKbYzeM2U3yQL
kSPLPwK1/M/nLijasdG2zrEo0jBbBgkqhkiG9w0BBwEwFAYIKoZIhvcNAwcECBMLp2+Mdv
NsgDidBPzChHblEHyZW7Xt6vxneNCOoo5rVITAASeo43oLPb321ZE42mDf/p3zcHfCPS2E
Dh5SRgUnvg==

Key algorithm = CAPICOM_ENCRYPTION_ALGORITHM_3DES
Key length    = CAPICOM_ENCRYPTION_KEY_LENGTH_MAXIMUM
This is the actual content
```

Interoperability

Now you have learned a lot about how to keep data safe within a well-defined environment and the aspects around it. If you have other systems in your configuration or even want to exchange information and trust over Internet, you have to consider a couple of other issues as well. The status of cryptography as such may have reached a certain level of maturity, but the crypto libraries have not always kept up. There are even interoperability issues regarding standard formats, so do not assume there won't be any problems after you've outwitted the .NET Framework security. You might want to have a look at Microsoft's own thoughts on PKI in its W2K PKI whitepaper:
http://www.microsoft.com/windows2000/techinfo/howitworks/security/pkiintro.asp.

There is also an attempt at a very abstract level to describe what PKI or Identification Management outside Microsoft is all about and how it should be implemented in a global context; find out more at: http://www.ietf.org/internet-drafts/draft-ietf-pkix-roadmap-09.txt.

The examples in this section use OpenSSL applications (included in the OpenSSL distributions) to help illustrate certain things. OpenSSL is a freeware C library available at the following link: http://www.openssl.org. This site only makes available the C source code so you need to compile this yourself. Alternatively, binary Windows distributions of OpenSSL are available on the Web at locations such as http://www.stunnel.org/download/binaries.html.

ASN.1, DER, and PEM

Many public-key cryptographic formats are described in ASN.1 (Abstract Syntax Notation 1), which is similar to other abstract syntax definition notations or languages like the EBNF (Extended Backus-Naur Form). As ASN.1 doesn't specify how the notation is translated into bits and bytes, there are encoding specifications like DER (Distinguished Encoding Rules) to describe that.

Most X.509 certificate, signature, and PKCS objects are DER encoded. Since DER content is binary, it may be difficult to handle in some situations and is therefore often encoded in BASE64 in turn to have a textual representation (not readable) of the object.

The PEM (Privacy Enhanced Mail) format adds a header and footer to a BASE64-encoded DER entity in order to identify it (among other things). Typical headers are:

```
-----BEGIN CERTIFICATE-----
-----END CERTIFICATE-----

-----BEGIN PRIVATE KEY-----
-----END PRIVATE KEY-----

-----BEGIN PKCS7-----
-----END PKCS7-----
```

Therefore, if you get a file in PEM format, remove the header and footer, and decode the BASE64 content you will have the actual DER-encoded object.

As X.509 certificates are described with ASN.1, it is possible to exchange an X.509 certificate between any computer systems. Because binary content doesn't print very well, all objects in this example are PEM formatted, like this certificate for example:

```
-----BEGIN CERTIFICATE-----
MIIDPDCCAqWgAwIBAgIBAjANBgkqhkiG9w0BAQQFADBYMQswCQYDVQQGEwJTRTER
MA8GA1UEBxMIVmFzdGVyYXMxDTALBgNVBAoTBENBMDExEDAOBgNVBAsTB0V4YW1w
bGUxFTATBgNVBAMTDEV4YW1wbGUgQ0EwMTAeFw0wMjEwMjIxNzM5MTRaFw0wMzEw
MjIxNzM5MTRaMHsxCzAJBgNVBAYTAlNFMREwDwYDVQQHEwhWYXN0ZXJhczESMBAG
A1UEChMJTX1Db21wYW55MQ4wDAYDVQQLEwVNeURlcDESMBAGA1UEAxMJQXJuZSBB
bmthMSEwHwYJKoZIhvcNAQkBFhJhcm5lLmFua2FAYWNtZS5jb20wgZ8wDQYJKoZI
hvcNAQEBBQADgY0AMIGJAoGBAK7ak4gZAn7CkMF+Ug6ngxunSKQJpYhWELI/ERwx
sJtRN7rqdhRIQzIv7AR8IeowsJZJU/AccaKpU02rSQI/m8VD7nZqLuRE+4PuzMuB
vpSuzkVhrnSL63+epuW08DHxNXK0iM1BuzodQ0roAumxQdN/mKROVHoZozHEB1pD
X5KVAgMBAAGjgfIwge8wCQYDVR0TBAIwADALBgNVHQ8EBAMCBeAwMwYJYIZIAYb4
QgENBCYWJEMjIERhdGEgU2VjdXJpdHkgRXhhbXBBsZSBDZXJ0aWZpY2F0ZTAdBgNV
HQ4EFgQULXVjsdz2pW3VPbi/roqr6VBc4RcwgYAGA1UdIwR5MHeAFHul/pbZI7T7
GvLHCmYOjdyV6FEnoVykWjBYMQswCQYDVQQGEwJTRTERMA8GA1UEBxMIVmFzdGVy
YXMxDTALBgNVBAoTBFJvb3QxEDAOBgNVBAsTB0V4YW1wbGUxFTATBgNVBAMTDEV4
YW1wbGUgUm9vdIIBATANBgkqhkiG9w0BAQQFAAOBgQBZMi+uzlqleb7jbydfcvn2
8PVksdFMMNHf/ZEkr+KlEEruztAd3sibKBW5P8rAf3u13TSIGLDgInvw5veG3SPE
EhQzYLQDlV7gv1YfGDK1FCfrburpEWolvTxX+96KNlNe8wUTsJSJ0gPrik0Qagx5
EwzuZ/Qk1PTnOLUdmR8sRA==
-----END CERTIFICATE-----
```

There are detailed instructions in the OpenSSL distribution about how to create your
own test certificates, including root and intermediate CA certificates. The certificates in
these examples were created in the OpenSSL environment. Some of the examples
assume the following files on your file system:

❑   arneanka.pem – A simple PEM-formatted end-user certificate with no
     private key.

❑   arneanka.cer – The same certificate but in the binary DER format; this
     type of file may be opened with the certmgr.exe application.

❑   arneanka.pfx – The same certificate again but as exported from your
     certificate store including all certificates in the chain and the private key (in
     PKCS#12 format). The password used in this example is: hemligt

If you have a certificate including the private key in your certificate store, it is possible
for you to create these files using the certmgr.exe application. Use the certmgr or
mmc application to list your certificate stores.

Display Certificate Content

The easiest way to print information about a certificate in OpenSSL is to use the
openssl x509 command. The x509 argument doesn't work for the .pfx file because
it is in formatted differently (PKCS#12).

The following two statements result in the same output using the command-line utility openssl that comes with the OpenSSL distribution:

```
openssl> x509 < arneanka.pem -text -noout
```

```
openssl> x509 < arneanka.der -inform DER -text -noout
```

prints the certificate in as readable format as possible:

```
Certificate:
  Data:
    Version: 3 (0x2)
    Serial Number: 2 (0x2)
    Signature Algorithm: md5WithRSAEncryption
    Issuer: C=SE, L=Vasteras, O=CA01, OU=Example, CN=Example CA01
    Validity
      Not Before: Oct 22 17:39:14 2002 GMT
      Not After : Oct 22 17:39:14 2003 GMT
    Subject: C=SE, L=Vasteras, O=MyCompany, OU=MyDep, CN=Arne
     Anka/Email=arne.anka@acme.com
    Subject Public Key Info:
      Public Key Algorithm: rsaEncryption
      RSA Public Key: (1024 bit)
        Modulus (1024 bit):
          00:ae:da:93:88:19:02:7e:c2:90:c1:7e:52:0e:a7:
          83:1b:a7:48:a4:09:a5:88:56:10:b2:3f:11:1c:31:
          b0:9b:51:37:ba:ea:76:14:48:43:32:2f:ec:04:7c:
          21:ea:30:b0:96:49:53:f0:1c:71:a2:a9:53:4d:ab:
          49:02:3f:9b:c5:43:ee:76:6a:2e:e4:44:fb:83:ee:
          cc:cb:81:be:94:ae:ce:45:61:ae:74:8b:eb:7f:9e:
          a6:e5:b4:f0:31:f1:35:72:b4:88:cd:41:bb:3a:1d:
          43:4a:e8:02:e9:b1:41:d3:7f:98:a4:4e:54:7a:19:
          a3:31:c4:07:5a:43:5f:92:95
        Exponent: 65537 (0x10001)
    X509v3 extensions:
      X509v3 Basic Constraints:
        CA:FALSE
      X509v3 Key Usage:
        Digital Signature, Non Repudiation, Key Encipherment
      Netscape Comment:
        C# Data Security Example Certificate
      X509v3 Subject Key Identifier:
        2D:75:63:B1:DC:F6:A5:6D:D5:3D:B8:BF:AE:8A:AB:E9:50:5C:E1:17
      X509v3 Authority Key Identifier:
        keyid:7B
          :A5:FE:96:D9:23:B4:FB:1A:F2:C7:0A:66:0E:8D:DC:95:E8:51:27
        DirName:/C=SE/L=Vasteras/O=Root/OU=Example/CN=Example Root
        serial:01
```

```
Signature Algorithm: md5WithRSAEncryption
   59:32:2f:ae:ce:5a:a5:79:be:e3:6f:27:5f:72:f9:f6:f0:f5:
   64:b1:d1:4c:30:d1:df:fd:91:24:af:e2:a5:10:4a:ee:ce:d0:
   1d:de:c8:9b:28:15:b9:3f:ca:c0:7f:7b:b5:dd:34:88:18:b0:
   e0:22:7b:f0:e6:f7:86:dd:23:c4:12:14:33:60:b4:03:95:5e:
   e0:bf:56:1f:18:32:b5:14:27:eb:6e:ea:e9:11:6a:35:bd:3c:
   57:fb:de:8a:36:53:5e:f3:05:13:b0:94:89:d2:03:eb:8a:4d:
   10:6a:0c:79:13:0c:ee:67:f4:24:d4:f4:e7:38:b5:1d:99:1f:
   2c:44
```

To display a .pfx file (PKCS#12 formatted file), which often includes the private key; you have to know the password with which the .pfx file is protected. The file in this example is protected with the password hemligt.

```
openssl> pkcs12 < arneanka.pfx -clcerts
Enter Import Password:
MAC verified OK
Bag Attributes
   localKeyID: 01 00 00 00
   friendlyName: {AA941D8C-EC07-4891-B71B-C8360CD320E5}
   1.3.6.1.4.1.311.17.1: Microsoft Enhanced Cryptographic Provider v1.0
Key Attributes
   X509v3 Key Usage: 10
Enter PEM pass phrase:
Verifying password - Enter PEM pass phrase:
-----BEGIN RSA PRIVATE KEY-----
Proc-Type: 4,ENCRYPTED
DEK-Info: DES-EDE3-CBC,749161BB4C214F29

Yg1OHMFz0YYWTuouaWGhFG48sG/fiwptKSq3HrYHC3vGxqpSXei7xx0eLFoKBmul
pubFIZJE/2pfhglWQBTWw+LqhA5nZYZmestTJ0LcY4f2eG965vj0H550sxPcjH9G
cqe3IwODcX4mXvaApMPhBU0NaO+ph885hjo1EpacgpMDmjWXIaTbu0rIg1Ke75No
z65ujoFFWmfC0+lc1sYIhUMwq8b/G2xd+TjGZ5P6J+6r3+0QcwjGFEYOZDdGHnIc
g6bdI6NdEbmGOIpFKZ3MSPFvsLTMB8LOD1ncavoH7GVE1WT6XCLb2Sz4qNcO1qFM
G6JbEspTkivLEziEEfRzbKLFPoGN795C01QgDmhPtdb2eIgNvwLTAzHs/VgulXN6
KswR0tUDZp1r2SQilRStT25QhmEPy6g4hPyOugh7wek59tVsFca/5MOOYPkyBomT
Kxs1vYcUZ9CdpPEMsUQUmbE/KrG1EZ29RMKM3PNE2UiGGY6D4p2LdZUnBuHdK401
ab4NeC+GR2fQHsgcwqcifGSYjV2SNw0JX1CIq7NPTRjBzQp1b6wBOPx8hdRj4Bb6
xQ70WTa9gd+5QJvbkPYAJkqujFNLtFQvBqIvdz7imzizbYPTuQUEDKtZkKDB/l1q
ocK7QQ3cVemI0vizSJxOicCp/W1ChaUjMnH0CB9B7f15e79uw+9aYFPaYVHG45OH
0ZwgFjZsGoZ09mT7GwWVlQV+XNpGcyGULDt3H954B/Jx5GPAZOS6HP8S2hB95f8y
iObxaGl9cVOas6alBRUd1gBrVEqxyklkCdlfVOv4/ywfgrqsjR6++A==
-----END RSA PRIVATE KEY-----
Bag Attributes
   localKeyID: 01 00 00 00
   friendlyName: My Certificate
subject=/C=SE/L=Vasteras/O=MyCompany/OU=MyDep/CN=Arne
Anka/Email=arne.anka@acme.com
issuer= /C=SE/L=Vasteras/O=CA01/OU=Example/CN=Example CA01
```

```
-----BEGIN CERTIFICATE-----
MIIDPDCCAqWgAwIBAgIBAjANBgkqhkiG9w0BAQQFADBYMQswCQYDVQQGEwJTRTERMA8GA1
UEBxMIVmFzdGVyYXMxDTALBgNVBAoTBENBMDExEDAOBgNVBAsTB0V4YW1wbGUxFTATBgNV
BAMTDEV4YW1wbGUgQ0EwMTAeFw0wMjEwMjIxNzM5MTRaFw0wMzEwMjIxNzM5MTRaMHsxCz
AJBgNVBAYTAlNFMREwDwYDVQQHEwhWYXN0ZXJhczESMBAGA1UEChMJTXlDb21wYW55MQ4w
DAYDVQQLEwVNeURlcESMBAGA1UEAxMJQXJuZSBBbmthMSEwHwYJKoZIhvcNAQkBFhJhcm
5lLmFua2FAYWNtZS5jb20wgZ8wDQYJKoZIhvcNAQEBBQADgY0AMIGJAoGBAK7ak4gZAn7C
kMF+Ug6ngxunSKQJpYhWELI/ERwxsJtRN7rqdhRIQzIv7AR8IeowsJZJU/AccaKpU02rSQ
I/m8VD7nZqLuRE+4PuzMuBvpSuzkVhrnSL63+epuW08DHxNXK0iM1BuzodQ0roAumxQdN/
mKROVHoZozHEB1pDX5KVAgMBAAGjgfIwge8wCQYDVR0TBAIwADALBgNVHQ8EBAMCBeAwMw
YJYIZIAYb4QgENBCYWJEMjIERhdGEgU2VjdXJpdHkgRXhhbXBsZSBDZXJ0aWZpY2F0ZTAd
BgNVHQ4EFgQULXVjsdz2pW3VPbi/roqr6VBc4RcwgYAGA1UdIwR5MHeAFHul/pbZI7T7Gv
LHCmYOjdyV6FEnoVykWjBYMQswCQYDVQQGEwJTRTERMA8GA1UEBxMIVmFzdGVyYXMxDTAL
BgNVBAoTBFJvb3QxEDAOBgNVBAsTB0V4YW1wbGUxFTATBgNVBAMTDEV4YW1wbGUgUm9vdI
IBATANBgkqhkiG9w0BAQQFAAOBgQBZMi+uzlqleb7jbydfcvn28PVksdFMMNHf/ZEkr+Kl
EEruztAd3sibKBW5P8rAf3u13TSIGLDgInvw5veG3SPEEhQzYLQDlV7gv1YfGDK1FCfrbu
rpEWo1vTxX+96KNlNe8wUTsJSJ0gPrik0Qagx5EwzuZ/Qk1PTnOLUdmR8sRA==
-----END CERTIFICATE-----
```

Convert between PEM and DER

Although it isn't very hard to write a program that make a DER-PEM converter for X.509 certificates, you can as well use openssl if you have gone through the trouble to install it.

To convert from PEM to DER:

```
openssl> x509 < arneanka.pem > arneanka.der -outform DER
```

To convert from DER to PEM:

```
openssl> x509 < arneanka.der > arneanka.pem -outform PEM
```

Summary

This chapter focused a lot on certificates and how they can help you protect both data and secret keys. The public key encryption scheme is suitable for exactly that and in combination with certificates it gives you a tool that can help establish trust with others electronically, over the Internet.

The public key encryption scheme is easy to use, and there are several suitable tools available for you to explore. What you must be aware of is not only how much trust you can put in the safekeeping of the private key the intended recipients have, but also how sure you can be that the holder of the private key actually is the right person; how much trust can you put in the certificate content?

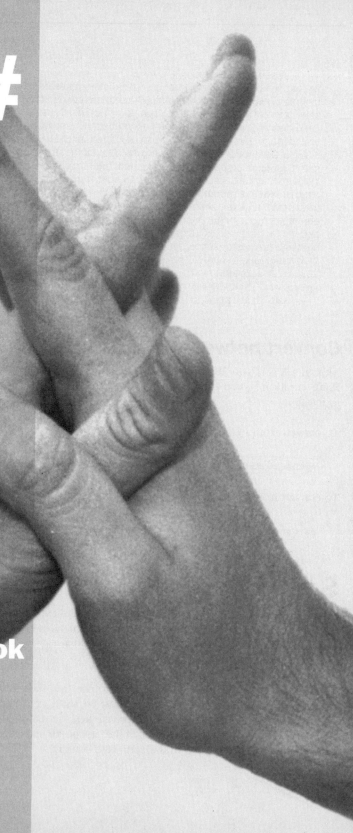

C#

Data Security

Handbook

7

7

Cryptography – Best and Worst Practices

Writing secure code is hard. It requires a different mindset from ordinary programming, which usually places the emphasis on goals like economy, efficiency, reusability, and performance. To create secure code, the developer not only needs to understand cryptography theory and the concepts presented throughout this book, but must also be able to anticipate weaknesses in working code and close the gaps that could allow a malicious user to launch an attack.

The thoroughness and attention to detail that secure programming demands challenges even experienced programmers. Microsoft, in pursuing its new security initiatives, now sends newly hired developers to a special in-house security class, and even monitors attendance!

Some of the characteristics that make it difficult to write secure code include:

❑ Security considerations stretch across all areas of code. They include logic to authenticate users and authorize their requests, mask sensitive data, and verify data authenticity. In addition, code-access security and machine-level settings can be used to prevent viruses and luring attacks.

❑ Security considerations stretch across all stages of the programming process, from development to deployment. They include coding issues like hiding secrets in code (always a bad idea), design issues like system architecture (which will determine the type of information that needs to be exchanged over the network), and deployment issues (like licensing and locking down the server environment).

❏	There are widely different types of security risks. Attackers may attempt to steal sensitive information, eavesdrop on communication so they can learn enough for a later attack, harm other user sessions, or simply attempt to temporarily bring your web server to its knees.

❏	It's difficult to assess the security risks exposed in a given piece of code. Many insecure applications appeared to be completely solid until challenged by the right attacker.

In this chapter, we'll consider the most common types of attacks, and how you should plan for them. We'll also consider some of the best decisions and worst mistakes you can make while coding an application, and provide some canonical examples.

Types of Attacks

To design secure code, you must understand the repertoire of tools and techniques that attackers can use. Often, code that is well protected against one type of attack can be alarmingly susceptible to another. A common mistake that even large organizations make is assuming that attackers will only be interested in stealing information. In reality, attackers might be just as likely to try to damage your application by submitting corrupted information, or content to simply overload your servers with redundant requests.

There are numerous types of attacks. The susceptibility of your code and the likelihood of a given type of attack depend on the type of application (for example, desktop versus distributed), the service it provides (for example, financial versus recreational), and the motivation of an attacker. Some attacks are passive, meaning information is monitored. Others are active, meaning that information is produced or altered with the goal of compromising the application or its environment.

There are essentially four categories of attacks:

❏	Unauthorized use, where the attacker uses the resources of the target without permission.

❏	Data trespass, where the attacker steals data from the target, or from an illicitly monitored message.

❏	Data corruption, where the attacker attempts to compromise the system by tricking it into accepting and storing invalid information (and possibly overwriting the correct data).

❏	Denial of Service (DoS), where the attacker tries to slow, impede, or prevent the operations of the target (usually a server hosting an application).

The following sections explain some specific attacks that fall into these categories, and are often used against an enterprise application. Generally, network-based exploits like sniffing and the replay attack are more difficult for the hacker, less common, and may require some access to a privileged part of a company network. However, when successful they are often devastating, and they are becoming more common with wireless network technology. Attacks that exploit the human fallibility of the user, network administrator, or programmer (like social engineering, third-party exploits, or brute force attacks against weak passwords) are much more common. Finally, it's worth noting that many of these attacks have at least some help or privileged information from a trusted employee (or former employee).

Sniffing or Snooping

This is the process where an attacker eavesdrops on network communication between components in an application. This might be communication between a client and a server-side component (like a web server), or between two back-end components (like a web service that routes a message to a task scheduler through a message queue). Usually, a sniffing attack is used to steal some piece of information (like a user password) that could be used later to launch another attack. However, a sniffing attack could simply be used to study network traffic, providing the information an attacker would need to eventually cause your network to crash or become corrupted.

To defend against sniffing, you must use ncryption. In some controlled internal environments, you may be able to use a transport-level technology, like IPSec (IP Security), which is described in Appendix A. However, in most cases you will need to use SSL or application-level encryption using the .NET classes, as explored in earlier chapters.

It's important to remember that to an attacker, *all types of information are interesting.* In other words, simply encrypting passwords and other sensitive information may not be enough. The attacker may still be able to see enough other information to determine who is using the application, and infer what tasks they are performing. In this case, it may be a tradeoff between performance and security, because encrypting all data will take time. Finally, even if all the data is encrypted, the attacker may still be able to determine the computers involved, the frequency of communication, and possibly infer other details to use when planning their next attack. For example, traffic analysis was used in one notable example to determine the movement of the secret service before presidential appearances. In this case, the sudden flurry of pager data was useful enough, without needing to break the encryption used for the messages.

Impersonation or Spoofing

This common attack occurs when an attacker pretends to be a valid user. This is a two-stage attack. First, the attacker steals the required authentication information (like a password and user name combination). Once the information is acquired, the attacker accesses the system under that identity, or exploits a security bug in your platform software (for example, IIS or the Windows operating system) to gain elevated privileges.

To retrieve the authentication information, the attacker may use a sniffer program, as described above, or something else. These other approaches can include a malicious client-side application that can transparently monitor keystrokes, a password Trojan that masquerades as the front-end for the client application, or a rewired network that allows the attacker to come between the client and the server. This last approach, known as a *man-in-the-middle* attack, is particularly devious, because the client application believes it is communicating with the server application, but is actually interacting with a malicious application that will record sensitive information sent from the user. Man-in-the-middle attacks can be quite difficult to defend against correctly, and many modern-day applications suffer from them in one way or another.

Most security code attempts to protect against impersonation by thwarting the first the first stage of this attack. For example, communication is encrypted so passwords are not visible in clear text, database passwords are stored in encrypted or hashed format, and the user table is made not accessible to non-administrator users. However, these steps do not resolve some of the most common risks, including the possibility that a user will store information about a password (for example, on paper or in a clear text file on a personal computer), or that an internal user with the required access rights will divulge user information.

Unfortunately, there is no way to determine if a password has been compromised, or if the user submitting a password is really the correct user. However, there are some techniques you can use to reduce the risk:

- ❑ Force users to user cryptographically strong passwords, and counsel them not to store this information anywhere else but in their memory. Strong passwords are long, do not correspond to words in any language, and contain a mixture of lowercase, uppercase, digit and other characters.

- ❑ Periodically expire passwords, and force users to switch to new values. Of course, this could be taken too far. If you expire passwords too frequently, users will have added incentive to choose weak, easy-to-remember (and thus easy-to-guess) values.

- ❑ Use logs to track user actions, and review them regularly for suspicious patterns (for example, a user accessing the system outside of business hours) that might indicate compromised security.

- ❑ Introduce some basic security checks into your application. For example, if you are designing a session-based web service, you can check a user's IP address using the `Request.UserHostAddress` property. If the same user attempts to access your system from two different IP addresses in a single session it makes sense to assume that an impersonation attack may have taken place, refuse the request, expire the session, and log the incident to a security log.

❑   Consider user authentication devices that depend on hardware (like a smart card) or an installed certificate. This way, the user won't become involved in the process, and won't be able to compromise the password. However, a new risk is exposed – the system might be compromised if an attacker gains physical access to the computer where the hardware or certificate is installed. Hence, this system also becomes more complex and expensive to maintain.

Finally, if server security is ever breached, expect that all passwords have been compromised, and force all users to create new passwords.

> **The examples above focus on application-level impersonation; however, attackers can also use IP impersonation to try to impersonate your computer during a session. You can thwart this type of attack using a protocol like IPSec, or with application-level encryption (which prevents the user from understanding the intercepted information).**

Replay

A more devious form of impersonation is accomplished through a replay attacks. In a replay attack, a hacker uses some sort of protocol analyzer to monitor and copy packets as they flow across the network. However, unlike the sniffing attack, the hacker doesn't attempt to find and decrypt a user password. Instead, the hacker simply keeps a copy of the packets. At a later time, the attacker resends the packets to the server to become authenticated.

The replay attack works because the attacker doesn't need to decode the message in order to reuse it. Assuming every user session starts with essentially the same login sequence, the attacker can mimic this by sending the same packets as used by an authenticated user.

To protect against a replay attack, you have several low-level choices. In a Windows 2000 network, you could use IPSec, which uses (and validates) a sequence number to prevent this type of attack. You could also use Windows authentication, which uses a challenge/response authentication system. Because the challenge is always different, a past response can't be reused. You could also use SSL, in which case the packets are encrypted using a dynamically generated session key.

At the application level, there are several techniques to ensure that the authentication packets are always different.

❑ Allow the client to periodically create new session keys. Strictly speaking, this doesn't prevent replay attacks, but it limits their ability because keys are exploitable for a shorter window of time.

❑ Use a challenge/response system. For example, at the beginning of an interaction, the server can start by sending some random bytes to the client. The client then adds these bytes to the password, and hashes the result. This response isn't subject to a replay attack, because every challenge (the random bytes) will differ.

❑ Use security auditing. For example, the client could generate a statistically unique GUID, encrypt it along with a password hash, and send it to the server. The server would then decrypt the message and store the GUID in a database. If the GUID ever shows up in a future login request, the server then knows that a replay attack has just happened.

As an example, a client might use the pattern shown below to combine a date string with both a user name and a password before encrypting them, and thereby thwart most replay attacks.

```
// Instantiate a cryptographic object using the web service key.
EncryptionTest.SecureService proxy =
    new EncryptionTest.SecureService();
RSACryptoServiceProvider crypt = new RSACryptoServiceProvider();
crypt.FromXmlString(proxy.GetPublicKey());

// Create the login authentication information.
string userName = "testuser";
string password = "opensesame";

// Note that the following method uses UTC (universal time) to ensure
// that the code is independent of the client's time zone.
string now = DateTime.UtcNow.ToString("yyyy-dd-MM-HH-mm-ss-tt");

// Convert the authentication information to bytes.
UTF8Encoding enc = new UTF8Encoding();
byte[] userNameBytes, passwordBytes;
userNameBytes = enc.GetBytes(userName + now);
passwordBytes = enc.GetBytes(password + now);

// Encrypt the authentication information.
userNameBytes = crypt.Encrypt(userNameBytes, true);
passwordBytes = crypt.Encrypt(passwordBytes, true);

// Log in.
proxy.Login(userNameBytes, passwordBytes);
```

The web service would decrypt this information, and verify that the time was reasonable (perhaps within five minutes of the current time) before processing the request. Note that it is extremely important that you agree on a canonical date format in order for this to work. Otherwise, the web service could snip off the wrong portion of the string and fail to validate a correct message. To enforce this, the web service code uses the `DateTime.ParseExact()` method instead of `DateTime.Parse()`.

```
[WebMethod()]
public string Login(byte[] encryptedUserName,
                     byte[] encryptedPassword)
{
   // Retrieve the server key (using a private function).
   RSACryptoServiceProvider serverKey = GetKeyFromState();

   // Decrypt the user name and password.
   byte[] userNameBytes, passwordBytes;
   userNameBytes = serverKey.Decrypt(encryptedUserName, false);
   passwordBytes = serverKey.Decrypt(encryptedPassword, false);

   // Convert the authentication information into strings
   string userName, password;
   UTF8Encoding enc = new UTF8Encoding();
   userName = enc.GetString(userNameBytes);
   password = enc.GetString(passwordBytes);

   // Verify that both dates match.
   string dateString = userName.Substring(userName.Length, 22);
   if (dateString != password.Substring(password.Length, 22))
   {
     throw new SecurityException("Cannot start session.");
   }

   // Verify that the date is not in the future,
   // and is not more than five minutes in the past.
   DateTime date = DateTime.ParseExact(dateString,
     "yyyy-dd-MM-HH-mm-ss-tt", null);
   if (date.AddMinutes(5) < DateTime.UtcNow ||
     date > DateTime.UtcNow)
   {
     throw new SecurityException("Cannot start session.");
   }

   // Verify that the user name and password are in the database
   // using a private function.
   if (!ValidateUser(decryptedUserName, decryptedPassword))
   {
     throw new SecurityException("Cannot start session.");
   }
```

```
    // (Only an authenticated user will reach this point.)
    // (Register the user and issue a ticket here.)
}
```

The only weakness in the approach shown above is the fact that it gives a five minute window for an attacker. You can defend against this by giving each message a unique, randomly generated identifier. The web service would then cache these identifiers for six minutes (one minute longer than the message expiration date), and check the cache every time it receives a request. Duplicate requests would be rejected. This identifier is called a **nonce**.

The WS-Security standard for SOAP-based web services defines a standard method for defeating replay attacks, which will likely be built into the .NET Framework in a future release. It creates a password hash using the password, nonce, and date, and adds it to the message as a SOAP header.

Here is an example:

```
<wsse:UsernameToken
        xmlns:wsse="http://schemas.xmlsoap.org/ws/2002/07/secext"
        xmlns:wsu="http://schemas.xmlsoap.org/ws/2002/07/utility">
    <wsse:Username>NNK</wsse:Username>
    <wsse:Password Type="wsse:PasswordDigest ">FEdR...</wsse:Password>
    <wsse:Nonce>FKJh...</wsse:Nonce>
    <wsu:Created>2001-10-13T09:00:00Z </wsu:Created>
</wsse:UsernameToken>
```

Microsoft have released an implementation of WS-Security called *Web Service Enhancements for Microsoft .NET*, this is available from, http://msdn.microsoft.com/webservices/building/wse/. Remember, the WS-Security standard is in draft only, and may change before it is fully incorporated into programming frameworks like .NET.

Session Replay or Session Hijack

A session replay is a special type of replay attack that works against web services that use ticket-based authentication. It allows a hacker to hijack a user's session by stealing a user's session ticket. Usually, this ticket is easy to find because it is added to every message as a SOAP header. If a message is intercepted, the hacker can steal this ticket and apply it to other messages.

The damage of a session replay is much more limited than that of the authentication replay attack, because a session typically has a finite lifetime. Once the ticket expires, it is worthless. To defend against session replay attacks, use cryptographically secure tickets. GUID values are much better than simple sequence numbers or timestamps, because an attacker could easily guess these values without needing to intercept a packet. However, GUID values are not guaranteed to be cryptographically secure, and it's not clear how they are created by the .NET framework (and if the algorithm could be exploited to predict a "random" GUID that a computer might generate). Thus, for the strongest possible tickets, use a sequence of random bytes derived from RNGCryptoServiceProvider, or sign the GUID ticket with the web server's private key. We'll explore this technique in the next chapter.

Finally, you should enforce a strict expiration policy to limit the usefulness of tickets, and include a logout feature that allows users to end their sessions at will. You may also want to record a client's IP address with the session information, and validate it on subsequent requests to ensure that the same session cannot be used from other computers (unless the attacker is sophisticated enough to combine an IP spoofing attack with a ticket-theft).

Brute Force

In a brute force attack, an attacker does not have any special information or technique. Instead, the attacker simply tries every possible combination of actions until the goal is achieved. In the world of cryptography, a brute force attack usually means attempting to decipher communication or user logon information by guessing a secret key. With most cryptographic algorithms, a brute force attack will take far too much time to be feasible. By the time it succeeds, the data may no longer be valuable. However, processing power is continually increasing, along with advances in distributed computing that allow large networks of computers to work together. (In this fashion, the DES-encrypted data can be cracked in a modest 3 hours or so.) You can increase security by increasing the bit length of your encryption algorithm.

> **Remember, the goal of cryptography is not to make a system completely impervious to attack, but make it costly enough (in terms of time or required resources) that it just isn't practical for the attacker. Certain types of data have relatively short lifetimes, and thus don't need the same degree of protection.**

A successful brute force attack is almost always one that can narrow the list of possibilities based on assumptions about the user or other information. For example, a brute force attempt to break an encrypted message using every possible sequence of bytes for a key will almost always take far too long to be practical. However, a brute force attack that tries to crack an encrypted message using every known word in the dictionary (known as a dictionary attack) is much faster. Always remember, your encryption is only as strong as your secret value.

Often, it is extremely easy to guess user passwords, which makes brute force attacks one of the most common types of attacks. To make it difficult to break encryption, use passwords for user authentication *only*. If you want to encrypt persisted data or exchanged messages, use a randomly generated key. This key can be encrypted with a server-side key or the user's password when it is stored along with the encrypted information.

You also need to give careful thought to user passwords, which are one of the most common weaknesses of any large system. Force users to use cryptographically strong passwords. For example, reject words from the dictionary, advise against easily guessed values (like names and dates), impose a minimum length, or mandate the inclusion of one or more numbers or mixed case. This vastly increases the number of possibilities that will need to be tried to break a key. For example, a good password cracking dictionary might have millions of entries, but the number of possible non-dictionary-word passwords of ten characters is trillions of trillions times larger. Optionally, you might simply want to assign a pre-generated random password (although the more complex the password, the more likely the user will record in some insecure fashion, like on a scrap of paper).

You should also use good auditing practices to track login failures. This allows you to spot suspicious patterns (like the same user attempting to log in dozens of times and failing).

Denial of Service

Denial of service (DoS) attacks are one of the most common attacks against servers in the web-enabled world, largely because they are easy. Denial of service attacks typically require little work and no special access to the network or proprietary information. With a denial of service attack, an attacker attempts to overtax a server (usually with spurious requests), and eventually force it offline. Sometimes, the term "distributed denial of service" attack (DDoS) is used to denote a denial of service attack launched from more than one external computer against the same server. Conceptually, a denial of service attack is equivalent to shouting at a victim until the victim becomes disoriented.

Many denial of service attacks do not take place at the application level. Some don't even take place against computers, but target routers, printers, or other parts of your network infrastructure. Here are some common examples (although there are many more):

- Ping of Death floods the server with ping requests that request information about its status. The pings come at such a rate that the server cannot perform any other tasks. (Turning off ICMP 13 and 18 at the router level can stop most ping attacks.)

- Smurf Attack is similar to the ping of death, but uses an intermediary network and broadcast messages.

- SYN Flooding attack tricks the server into opening TCP connections that cannot be completed, because the requesting system does not complete the TCP handshake. Router control software can be used to limit the effect of this from a single source.

- Teardrop attack fragments IP data into extremely small packets that can bypass many routers and intrusion detection systems. When the packets are reassembled, they cause a buffer overflow.

- FTP Bounce Back uses FTP to upload a time-consuming script, and then requests that it be transferred to a web server where it can do its damage.

The attacker will usually combine these attacks with some sort of IP spoofing, so that the packets cannot be blocked by IP address. To protect against these attacks, you need to know the vulnerabilities of your software, and install the necessary patches and security software. This is the domain of the network administrator.

What's less obvious to many programmers is that there are many other possible avenues for a denial of service attack in the application layer. For example, if your web service includes a time-consuming login method that verifies a user against the database, an attacker can call this method in quick succession thousands of times, tying up your database. To defend against this type of attack is not always easy. One way is to use some sort of hash validation technique.

For example, in Microsoft's Favorite Service (a platform sample described on MSDN), all tickets are created using a GUID and an additional segment with the hash of the GUID. The hash is signed using the server's private key, and thus can't be tampered with. Before querying the database to examine if a ticket is valid, the service verifies that the hash code is correct. Thus, spurious requests that don't correspond to authenticated users can be rejected more quickly, lessening the risk of a denial of service attack. Put simply, the goal is to minimize the amount of resources that can be consumed by a non-authenticated user.

> **For many organizations, a denial of service attack is not as significant as an intrusion or information theft. The only effect it will have it temporarily putting your web server offline. However, in a mission-critical environment, the consequences of an extended period of downtime can be quite expensive.**

Social Engineering

Social engineering is simply fooling a user to perform an action or reveal information. It's probably the oldest form of attack, and it has thousands of variations. One example is an attacker sending an e-mail to user pretending to be an administrator and instructing them to change or reveal their password. Another example is an e-mail virus that contains malicious code masquerading a humorous story or an interesting application.

Social engineering attacks are impossible to defend against in code, and require ongoing user education. However, preventing social engineering attacks is still partly the responsibility of the developers, and you must consider the possibilities for a social engineering attack when designing an application. For example, many social engineering attacks are made possible by a poorly designed client interface. Default settings that grant the user too many privileges (in the case of an e-mail program, enough to run an executable mail attachment), or simply forcing the user to make decisions that they aren't qualified to evaluate (such as ActiveX control downloading in a web page). Asking users to make a trust decision is always a bad idea, because users lack the information they need to make a decision, and are more aware of the task they need to complete than the risks they may be exposed to. Users will quickly learn that they only way they can carry out their work is by accepting all code, and will click Yes or OK at common security dialogs by force of habit.

Third-Party Exploits

Third-party exploits depend on weaknesses in the software that runs your application or other applications on the same computer. These include operating system vulnerabilities, or security holes in programs like IIS. These exploits are fairly common because security risks in a popular application or operating system are widely known and discussed. For example, consider a proprietary web service. Though it is quite possible that the web service has more security flaws than the IIS software it runs on, the IIS limitations are more widely known, whereas the application bugs take time to discover.

Defending against third-party exploits is simply a matter of staying informed, and always applying to appropriate patches. If a security bulletin from Microsoft advises of a potential problem, assume that the entire hacker community now knows about the problem, and how to exploit it. The Internet includes many excellent sources for security information, including the CERT Coordination Center (http://www.cert.org) and NTBugTrack (http://www.ntbugtraq.com). In addition, it can't hurt to keep up with the latest cryptography news, in case a mathematical exploit is every discovered for an algorithm you use.

Application-Layer Exploits

An application-layer attack makes use of a security hole or limitation in your software. Application layer attacks are common because most software has flaws that can be exploited. Some examples include:

❑ Coding errors that allow a user to perform actions beyond what that user should be allowed. These are often errors in properly formatting and validating user input (known as canonicalization errors).

❑ Insecure coding practices that allow an attacker to discover enough information about your service to attack, simply by causing different types of errors.

❑ Insecure paths in your code ("back doors") that fail to carry out the appropriate authentication steps.

There is no generic way to solve an application-layer problem; each error requires a different type of correction. We'll consider these common mistakes (and how to fix them) in the *Best and Worst Practices* section later in this chapter.

Viruses and Luring Attacks

One of the most pervasive client-side security problems is viruses – essentially miniature programs installed on the computer that wreak havoc. Viruses can't be easily defended against because operating systems lack methods to distinguish between good and bad code. If a virus is installed on a system, it often gains complete control to perform any action it wants.

To prevent viruses, you need some form of sandboxing, which can limit the abilities of code based on certain criteria. For example, when you load a Java applet in your browser, you assume that it doesn't have the ability to perform a harmful action like modifying the system registry. However, you are often still exposed to luring attacks, where a malicious piece of code tricks a more trusted piece of utility code into performing a malicious action. The utility code allows the action because it doesn't recognize the possible security problem, and the malicious code gains the ability to perform an action it otherwise could not. These problems are extremely difficult to guard against, and are some of the principle motivational factors behind the creation of code-access security in the .NET Framework.

Best and Worst Practices

In this section, we'll consider some of the best and worst practices developers follow when trying to create secure code. The focus of these examples is on cryptography, not on other issues like code access security, or authorization and authentication. However, many of these practices stretch into these other areas, because security touches all aspects of code development.

Of course, this only means that there are important areas of security that we won't tackle, namely code-access security and trust models. Strictly speaking, these issues don't relate to cryptography. However, it's important to realize that there are a number of ways for malicious code to interact with your application code. For example, if you are using one of the "adaptable application" designs that are currently in vogue, such as Windows Forms applications that download components from the Internet or dynamically instantiate types using reflection, you are opening vast new areas for potential security breaches. The user, however, will not realize the change in the underlying technology, and will expect you to ensure the security of any add-ins, pluggable components, downloadable updates, and so on.

> *For more information about code-access security, you may want to consult* Visual Basic .NET Code Security Handbook *(Wrox Press, 2002, ISBN 1-86100-747-7). For a more general tutorial about writing secure code, you may want to consider Microsoft's own in-house security manual,* Writing Secure Code *(Microsoft Press), which is being updated; the second edition will includes more .NET specific information.*

Worst Practice: Expect Security through Obscurity

In a client application, assume that an attacker knows everything about how your application works. In a distributed application, assume that an attacker knows everything about the encryption algorithms and key length you use, and the techniques you use for generating random numbers, tickets, and random symmetric keys.

> **Cryptography depends on the strength of the algorithm and the secrecy of the keys, not the secrecy of the algorithm. Good cryptography ensures that an attacker cannot decrypt a message, even if they know how it is encrypted.**

There are a number of good reasons that you should assume that you couldn't keep these sorts of secrets. First, higher-level information about the architecture of a system may be stolen from an organization (physically or electronically), or it may be publicly available in white papers or other resources without you even realizing. Or, an attacker may be able to infer this information from another part of the application that is accessible (like a client front-end), or an attacker may simply be able to make an educated guess. If your security depends on a secret operation, you need to be able to replace your entire application with a new version if the secret is ever discovered. Not only is this impractical, it's unlikely that you'll know when an attacker acquires this sort of information.

In a client application, it's even easier to gain information about your code. .NET code can be easily viewed as MSIL, which is a much higher-level language than the native code used in a typical Windows executable. Even programmers who aren't familiar with IL will be able to easily recognize this "hello world" application from its IL code. The `WriteLine()` and `ReadLine()` method calls are highlighted, along with the string that will be displayed.

```
.namespace HelloWorld
{
.class private auto ansi beforefieldinit Class1
    extends [mscorlib] System.Object
{
  .method private hidebysig static void
      Main(string[] args) cil managed
  {
   .entrypoint
   .custom instance void
    [mscorlib] System.STAThreadAttribute::.ctor() = ( 01 00 00 00 )

   .maxstack 1

    IL_0000: ldstr    "Hello World"
    IL_0005: call     void
                [mscorlib] System.Console::WriteLine(string)
    IL_000a: call     string [mscorlib] System.Console::ReadLine()
    IL_000f: pop
    IL_0010: ret
  } // end of method Class1::Main
 } // end of class Class1
} // end of namespace RandomTest
```

To generate this code, all that's needed is the ILDasm (IL Disassembler) utility included with the .NET Framework. You can load a GUI that allows you to look at an assembly type by type, or you can write out debugging information at the command-line as shown here:

```
> ildasm HelloWorld.exe /TEXT
```

The methods and properties used for .NET Framework classes are clearly visible, as is all hard-coded information (like strings). Even more interesting is what a user can do with a more sophisticated disassembler. One proof-of-concept example is Exemplar, which is freely available at http://www.saurik.com/net/exemplar/. When using Exemplar with the Console application above, the full code is retrieved, with some trivial formatting changes and semantic differences (for example, all class member names are fully qualified).

```
namespace HelloWorld {
  class Class1 {

    private static void Main(string[] args) {
      System.Console.WriteLine("Hello World");
      System.Console.ReadLine();
    }

    public Class1() : base() {
    }
  }
}
```

Of course, obscurity isn't necessarily a bad thing. You shouldn't feel the need to divulge any extra information about your application that could allow a user to devise an attack strategy. However, don't *rely* on that obscurity, because it will be woefully insufficient in a production environment. In fact, you should always assume that your code could be disassembled. It's remarkably easy in .NET, but *possible* in any language.

Best Practice: Don't Store Secrets in Code

All this reinforces the fact that you should never rely on secret operations or embedded secrets in a client application. The worst mistake you could make is to hard-code a secret value like a symmetric key, password, or database connection string. Storing this information backward, in binary form, or using any one of a dozen other possible tricks to try to mask a stored secret in your code is futile, because an attacker who can access the assembly file will see information about both data and operations.

Some third-party obfuscators are available, which attempt to make code more difficult to understand by renaming methods and variable names, and possibly rearranging certain logic (including one that is bundled with version 1.1 of the .NET Framework). These obfuscators will do very little to deter a dedicated hacker, and could even introduce problems if an obfuscator bug results in a non-compatible rearrangement of code.

The bottom line is that there is no foolproof way for a software program to hide a secret from the individual that uses it. This of true of any code, but in the world of .NET, the disassembling process is alarmingly easy. One option for storing secrets may be dedicated hardware like a smartcard, but this is typically much more expensive (and still not completely impervious to attack).

Worst Practice: Store User Secrets as Preferences

Code isn't the only insecure place you can store information. Many applications use a professional encryption system to protect passwords in the database and over the wire, only to add a convenience feature that allows it to be easily compromised. Common examples are the automatic log-on feature, or the "save this password" checkbox on a dialog. Often, when these features are used a secret is stored in an insecure location like a file, the Windows registry or a cookie. Some well-behaved applications such as Windows Messenger will properly secure this information so that it cannot be retrieved without knowledge of the user's password, but unfortunately, no managed classes wrap this functionality.

There is no excuse for these features; programmers simply have to refuse to implement dangerous features. It won't be the only time you encounter the conflict between security and additional features.

Worst Practice: Use ad hoc Encryption Algorithms

Many programming textbooks present off-the-cuff encryption techniques in order to introduce concepts. One popular example is XOR "encryption" which performs a bitwise XOR operation between characters in a string and values in a secret key. These algorithms are interesting learning examples, but they are not suitable for a professional environment. For example, WordPerfect uses XOR encryption to encrypt password-protected files. At least one third-party provides a utility that can decrypt any WordPerfect file by brute force, which works particularly quickly if the key used to encrypt the document is ten characters or less.

Unless you are a highly schooled cryptanalyst, your encryption system will likely be vulnerable to attacks like frequency analysis. You'll also need to worry about highly complex mathematical issues like weak keys, chaining modes, and so on. In fact, most brute force attacks on an encryption algorithm make use of flaws in an implementation of a particular algorithm, not weaknesses in the algorithm itself (which has probably been scrutinized by hundreds of cryptography experts). You should also never assume that encoding issues (like converting a string to bytes or concatenating several pieces of data into a larger structure) will make your data any harder to read. They won't.

Remember, .NET provides a robust support for production-level encryption algorithms. Use them.

Best Practice: Use Cipher Block Chaining

CBC chaining mode is the default for symmetric key algorithms, but it's worth emphasizing. With CBC, before a block is encrypted, it is combined with the ciphertext of the previous block by a bitwise exclusive OR operation. This ensures that even if the previous block contains many similarities, the encrypted data will differ. Although this does require some additional processor work, it dramatically reduces the effectiveness of some analysis attacks. For example, at least one attack works by encrypting a common data segment (possibly a block of all zeroes) with all possible keys. The attacker then scans communication looking for any blocks that match one of the generated blocks. If a match is made, the attacker can then decode the rest of the communication using the same key. This attack is rendered much more difficult with CBC.

To use cipher block chaining, set the `SymmetricAlgorithm.CipherMode` property to `CipherMode.CBC`.

Worst Practice: Use System.Random

The `Random` class is a pseudo-random number generator that chooses "random" numbers from a finite set of numbers, using a mathematical algorithm. These numbers are statistically random enough for many applications (for example, generating sample data), but they are not cryptographically secure. They have the following problems:

❑ If an attacker knows the algorithm used to create a random number, the attacker can predict the random numbers you will generate. This information can easily be snooped out in IL code.

❑ The attacker doesn't even need to understand the algorithm, if they monitor enough of the random numbers that you generate. Eventually, they can correlate the random numbers to commonly used seed values (like the current millisecond value of the time).

❑ From time to time, certain sequences of random numbers will reoccur. If this is identified, subsequent "random" numbers can be predicted, even though these numbers are statistically random.

❑ The default constructor for the `Random` class uses the millisecond value of the time as a seed. Unfortunately, this means that if you attempt to generate multiple random numbers with duplicate instances of this class at the same time, you will receive the same number. This flaw is easily reproducible (and demonstrated in *Appendix B*).

Fortunately, .NET provides a cryptographically secure random number generated in the `System.Security.Cryptography` namespace named `RNGCryptoServiceProvider`. For more information about this class, refer to Appendix B.

Worst Practice: Use Asymmetric Encryption for Large Data

You can use asymmetric encryption to securely encode a large amount of data, like a large message or data file. However, performance will be terrible (on the order of 100-1000 times slower then using symmetric encription), and the encrypted data will be much larger than necessary. Fortunately, there is an easy solution. If you need to deal with large amounts of data and you only have an asymmetric key available, follow these three steps:

1. Randomly generate a new symmetric key. You can do this implicitly by simply instantiating a new `SymmetricAlgorithm` object.

2. Store this key with the message or file, encrypted using the asymmetric public key. The only user who will be able to decrypt the symmetric key is the user who owns the corresponding private key from the key pair.

3. Encrypt the remainder of the data using the symmetric key.

Examples of this technique are provided in Chapter 4 (with persisted data) and Chapter 5 (with a key exchange in a distributed system).

Best Practice: Design in Layers

Secure code doesn't just mean making a security breach more difficult, it also means limiting the damage that a breach can cause. One of the best ways to do this is to design your security infrastructure in layers, so that the most important information is protected by several different security mechanisms. Here are a few good examples of a layered security design:

❑   Encrypting any sensitive data that is stored in a database, so that if a user gains access to the database, they won't have access it. For some types of data (like passwords), you may only need to store a hash of the data.

❑   Using network technologies like IPSec in internal networks or SSL to make it more difficult for network monitoring and sniffing, while still encrypting payloads at the application level.

❑   Using randomly generated keys to secure messages and large amounts of data. That way a user who obtains one symmetric secret key won't be able to decrypt more than one document.

❑   Using EFS (Windows Encrypting File System) to mask data files on server computers to non-administrator users. To the application, this additional layer of encryption is transparent, but if a malicious user gains access to the internal network or physical computer, this extra layer of protection can prevent the attacker from retrieving data.

In short, never rely on just a single defense.

Worst Practice: Return Sensitive Information

One of the tools hackers use when inspecting a system for exploitable application-level flaws is *discovery*. With discovery, the attacker is able to derive a significant amount of information about your system by causing different errors to occur. With enough time, a significant amount of information can be gathered, and this information can be used to launch a future attack.

Here's an example of one the worst possible ways to write a Login() method:

```
public bool Login(string userName, string password)
{
  SqlConnection con = new SqlConnection(connectionString);

  // Define command for checking the user.
  string SQL = "SELECT Password From Users " +
    "WHERE UserName='" + userName;

  SqlCommand GetUser = new SqlCommand(SQL, con);

  try
  {
    con.Open();
    SqlDataReader r = GetUser.ExecuteReader();

    if (!r.Read())
    {
      throw new ApplicationException("User does not exist.");
    }
    else if (password != r["Password"].ToString())
    {
      throw new ApplicationException("Invalid password.");
    }
  }
  finally
  {
    con.Close();
  }

  // (Register logged in user here.)
  return true;
}
```

Now, with at little effort and some brute force guessing the attacker will be able to determine a list of users on your system. (One possible approach is to generate a list of possible names, try them all one by one with an automated tool, and check what type of error message is returned.) That information makes an excellent basis for a more targeted attack that tries to guess the passwords for particular users. By leaking privileged information, this code makes the attacker's work much easier. Unfortunately, it's not at all rare to see this worst practice in use in production-level code.

A better approach is shown here:

```
public void Login(string userName, string password)
{
  SqlConnection con = new SqlConnection(connectionString);

  // Define command for checking the user.
  string SQL = "SELECT Password From Users " +
    "WHERE UserName='" + userName +
    "' AND Password='" + password + "'";

  SqlCommand getUser = new SqlCommand(SQL, con);

  bool isAuthenticated = false;
  try
  {
    con.Open();
    SqlDataReader r = getUser.ExecuteReader();

    if (r.Read())
    {
      if (password == r["Password"].ToString())
      {
        isAuthenticated = true;
      }
    }
  }
  finally
  {
    con.Close();
  }
  if (isAuthenticated == true)
  {
    // (Register logged in user here.)
  }
  else
  {
    throw new SecurityException("User could not be logged in.");
  }
}
```

This code could still be improved significantly by encapsulating the database code in a separate component. In addition, it uses a dynamically constructed SQL string, which makes it subject to SQL injection attacks. A stored procedure or parameterized command would be an ever better approach, as you'll see in the next section.

Best Practice: Canonicalize User Input

Canonicalization errors are a specific type of application error that can occur when your code assumes that user-supplied values will always be in a standardized form. Canonicalization errors are low-tech but quite serious, and they usually have the result of allowing a user to perform an action that should be restricted.

One infamous type of canonicalization error is SQL injection, where a user submits incorrectly formatted values to "trick" your application in to executing a modified SQL command. For example, consider a case where your code is used to validate a user. You might use a query like this:

```
string SQL = "SELECT Password From Users " +
   "WHERE UserName='" + userName +
   "' AND Password='" + password + "'";
```

An attacker can exploit this query by submitting a password in the form "InvalidPassword OR '1'='1'". The dynamic query will then look like this:

```
SELECT Password From Users WHERE UserName='InvalidUser'
   AND Password='InvalidPassword' Or '1'='1';
```

The final portion of this query ('1''='1') will always evaluate to true, and thus the query will return a table with all user passwords! If the authentication code simply verifies that there is at least one record in the returned resultset (for example, by calling r.Read() and verifying that it returns true), authentication will succeed.

In this case, SQL injection is used to exploit user authentication code, but the same approach could be used to manipulate a query so that it returns sensitive information. In some cases, the user may be able to add a semicolon to create a batch query, and tack on an arbitrary SQL statement to the end of the query. Given that SQL Server includes an xp_cmdshell stored procedure that runs command-line programs will full rights, this can be extremely serious.

To prevent SQL injection, you can sanitize your input, by checking for illegal characters like apostrophes and removing them. You can also use parameterized commands, which automatically perform the required escaping. Here's an example of an equivalent parameterized command with SQL Server:

```
// Define the SQL string with named parameters.
string SQL = "SELECT Password From Users WHERE UserName=@UserName " +
   "AND Password=@Password";
SqlCommand getUser = new SqlCommand(SQL, con);
```

```
// Add the parameter values to the command.
SqlParameter param;
param = getUser.Parameters.Add("@UserName", SqlDbType.NChar, 25);
param.Value = userName;
param = getUser.Parameters.Add("@Password", SqlDbType.NChar, 25);
param.Value = password;
```

Now, if a malicious user submits the same invalid values, the query will be escaped as shown here:

```
SQL = "SELECT * FROM Users WHERE UserID='InvalidUser'
   AND Password='InvalidPassword'' OR ''1''=''1'
```

This will return no records, because no password will match the supplied string (`InvalidPassword'' OR ''1''=''1`).

Other forms of canonicalization problems can occur with file paths and URLs. For example, consider the following web method that returns file data from a fixed document directory:

```
[WebMethod()]
public byte[] DownloadFile(string filename)
{
  FileInfo f;
  f = new FileInfo(Server.MapPath("Documents\\" + filename));
  FileStream fs = f.OpenRead();

  // Create the byte array.
  byte[] bytes = new byte[fs.Length];

  // Read the file into the byte array.
  fs.Read(bytes, 0, (int)fs.Length);
  fs.Close();

  return bytes;
}
```

This code looks simple enough. It concatenates the user-supplied filename with the `Documents` path, allowing the user to retrieve data from any file in this directory.

The problem is that filenames can be represented in multiple formats. Instead of submitting a valid file name, an attacker can submit a qualified file name like "`..\filename`". The concatenated path of "`WebApp\Documents\..\filename`" will actually retrieve a file from the parent of the `Documents` directory (`WebApp`). A similar approach will allow the user to specify any filename on the web application drive. Because the web service is only limited according to the restrictions of the ASP.NET worker process, the user may be allowed to download a sensitive server-side file.

The fix for this code is fairly easy. You can use the `Path` class (provided in the `System.IO` directory) to remove only the final filename portion of the string.

```
[WebMethod()]
public byte[] DownloadFile(string filename)
{
   filename = Path.GetFileName(filename);

   FileInfo f;
   f = new FileInfo(Server.MapPath("Documents\\" + filename));
   FileStream fs = f.OpenRead();

   // Create the byte array.
   byte[] bytes = new byte[fs.Length];

   // Read the file into the byte array.
   fs.Read(bytes, 0, (int)fs.Length);
   fs.Close();

   return bytes;
}
```

This ensures that the user is constrained to the correct directory. If you are dealing with URLs, you can work similar magic with the `System.Uri` type. For example, here's how you might remove query string arguments from a URI, and make sure it refers to a given server and virtual directory:

```
string uriString = "http://www.wrongsite.com/page.aspx?cmd=run";

Uri uri = new Uri(uriString);
string page = System.IO.Path.GetFileName(uri.AbsolutePath);
// page is now just "page.aspx"

Uri baseUri = new Uri("http://www.rightsite.com");
uri = new Uri(baseUri, page);
// uri now stores the path "http://www.rightsite.com/page.aspx"
```

Best Practice: Fail Early

Path discovery often works with server-side components that don't mask their exceptions. For example, a malicious user may invoke a server-side method with invalid parameters and insufficient credentials to be authorized for the action. However, if the method is poorly written, it may return an exception that indicates additional information about the database or file system, before it attempts to authenticate the user. Not only is this information of no use to the client, it can help a malicious user plan an attack.

For example, consider the following code that returns the contents of a file as a string:

```
public string GetFile(string filename, TicketInfo ticket)
{
  if File.Exists(filename)
  {
    throw new ApplicationException("File does not exist");
  }
  else
  {
    // Validate the user using the ticket.
    if ! ValidateTicker(ticket)
    {
      throw new SecurityException("Invalid user");
    }
    // Open the file and return the contents.
  }
}
```

This problem allows path discovery of the file system. By using different paths, an attacker can enumerate your entire directory structure, and learn something that may assist in a future attack (such as the location of sensitive files, installed application versions, etc.). In this example, it's easy to solve the problem by rearranging the code:

```
public string GetFile(string filename, TicketInfo ticket)
{
  // Validate the user using the ticket.
  if (!ValidateTicker(ticket))
  {
    throw new SecurityException("Invalid user.");
  }

  if (File.Exists(filename))
  {
    throw new ApplicationException("File does not exist.");
  }
  else
  {
    // Open the file and return the contents.
  }
}
```

However, in many cases the problem may not be as obvious because sensitive information may be leaked from an exception you don't expect. For example, consider this pattern:

```
public string GetFile(string filename, TicketInfo ticket)
{
  // 1. Acquire file.
  // 2. Authenticate user.
  // 3. Open file.
}
```

In this example, the code you use in Step 1 may lead to a `FileNotFoundException`. Thus, you will unwittingly return information about the file system to the attacker, without realizing it.

To combat these problems, ensure that user authentication always occurs first. Furthermore, use exception-handling code to trap any errors, and then throw a more generic exception. Even if a user is authenticated, there is no reason to give them explicit details about an invalid database operation, unless the user has some way of correcting the problem. Here's an example of how you might handle a database access problem:

```
try
{
   con.Open();

   // (Perform database tasks.)
}
catch
{
   throw new ApplicationException("Data access error.");
}
finally
{
   con.Close();
}
```

Better yet, log the exception on the server so you can review it if needed, and include contact information in your `ApplicationException` error string so the user has a valid option to deal with the problem. Add exception handling wherever an error like this could occur – in other words, whenever you access an external resource like a file, database, registry, or piece of hardware. Don't feel the need to give any low-level information that may expose the inner workings of your code.

> **What is appropriate for development testing is not appropriate for a production environment. While development testing, it may be important to return raw exceptions. However, when performing release testing, this exception handling code must be modified. To assist, you can use conditional compilation to ensure that some code is left out of the release version altogether.**

There is another reason that it's always a good idea to fail early: It helps to reduce the opportunity for a denial of service attack, where a malicious user ties up your server handling spurious requests. If you can fail before you perform a time-consuming task like connecting to the database, it will be much more difficult to tie up your server.

Best Practice: Log Exceptions

A typical brute force attack requires a lot of work. For example, a hacker may send millions of requests to your web server before finding a user name and password combination that works. If you have an early alert system to identify this sort of suspicious behavior, you may find evidence of an attack in progress before it does any damage.

One best practice is to log security exceptions. This information can be stored in a centralized database, or in the computer-specific event log. The event log is often used because of its simplicity. Though each computer has its own event log, you can easily inspect the event log of a remote computer using trivial .NET code. Here's how you might log a failed attempt to login:

```
// Create the log if needed.
if (!EventLog.Exists("MyAppLog"))
{
    EventLog.CreateEventSource("MyWebService", "MyAppLog");
}

EventLog log = new EventLog("MyAppLog");
log.Source = "MyWebService";
```

Note that we don't store the attempted password. This might help track down the cause of the problem, but it would also provide a security risk if another user read the log:

```
log.WriteEntry("Attempt to login for user " + userName + " failed.",
    EventLogEntryType.FailureAudit);
```

Some companies use automated tools to scan the event log looking for suspicious patterns, but it may be easier for an administrator to quickly review this information and identify potential problems at a glance. Part of the challenge with logging and auditing is that some trivial events may indicate problems that are more serious when they occur repeatedly (like a login failure). Getting this notification logic right can be difficult. If in doubt, store it somewhere durable so it can be reviewed later.

> **Do not use exception-logging code that sends e-mail about a problem to an administrator, unless a problem is very rare and very serious. Otherwise, the mail account you use for these notifications will probably become flooded with trivial errors, and important messages will eventually be ignored.**

If a security breach does occur, you must be properly prepared in order to limit its damage. This means that you must develop an incident response plan and brief all involved, including network engineers, web masters, and your ISP. You should have some basic network tools on hand like a packet sniffer. These details are outside the scope of this book. Instead, consult a dedicated book about network security (see Appendix C).

Best Practice: Use Hashes to Avoid the Database

To prevent a denial of service, you should not perform any time-consuming tasks before authenticating the user. If possible, you should always avoid the database, because database connections are a finite resource, and require some basic overhead to establish.

Unfortunately, it is not always possible to avoid the database. For example, when first authenticating a user, you probably need to compare credentials against a users table. However, in a ticket-based authentication, you can avoid the database on subsequent requests using hash codes.

Here's how ticket-based authentication works without hash codes:

1. A user logs in and receives a ticket. The ticket is a dynamically generated GUID.

2. The ticket information is stored in the database and the cache, and returned to the user.

3. The user presents the ticket on a subsequent request. The server-side code looks for this ticket in the cache.

4. If the ticket is not found in the cache, the server-side code checks the database.

The potential problem here is the fourth, and most time-consuming step. If an invalid ticket is submitted, the server will still waste time checking the database, which opens the possibility for a denial of service attack. To reduce this opportunity, the server needs a way to recognize if it generated the supplied ticket. Hash codes present an easy solution.

Here's how ticket-based authentication works *with* hash codes:

1. A user logs in and receives a ticket. The ticket is a dynamically generated GUID, with a short sequence of bytes appended on the end. These bytes are a digital signature generated using a hash of the GUID signed by the server's private key.

2. The ticket information is stored in the database and the cache, and returned to the user.

3. The user presents the ticket on a subsequent request. The server-side code authenticates the ticket by validating the signature and checking the expiration date.

4. Assuming the ticket is valid, the server-side code looks for this ticket in the cache.

5. If the ticket is not found in the cache, the server-side code checks the database.

> **Remember, an ordinary hash is not enough for a message authentication code, because a malicious user can easily generate a new message and a new hash. Instead, you must use a keyed hash or a signed hash.**

Worst Practice: Try to Compress Encrypted Data

Compression after encryption will not produce much data savings. If an encryption algorithm is good, it will produce output that is statistically indistinguishable from a series of random numbers. Because compression software works by identifying patterns, no compression algorithm can work with data that appears to be random. (Conversely, if you find it possible to significantly compress a large block of encrypted data, the encryption algorithm is flawed.)

Compression before encryption makes more sense provided it doesn't shorten the data to less than one block size in total. Compressed data is smaller, so it takes less CPU time to encrypt. Furthermore, compressed data is less redundant, which makes it more difficult to break the encryption using certain attacks.

Worst Practice: Fail to Protect All Messaging Protocols

Remember, when protecting data on the wire you need to consider all the methods you use to communicate between parts of your system. For example, it's all too easy to develop an encryption system that guards communication between a client and a web service, but forget to secure information that's sent to a back-end component through a message queue. Systems like Microsoft Message Queuing will provide encryption services, but it's up to you to use them.

Also, in cases where your data is routed through multiple components, you need to make sure that none of these components stores or exposes any sensitive information. As a general rule of thumb, a component should not decrypt the data unless it needs to use it. The most secure model for a multilayered application is to route an encrypted object through several components and only decrypt it at the very end.

Best Practice: Store Password Hashes, Not Passwords

When creating a custom authentication system, there's no need to store unencrypted passwords in the database. If you do, you're just creating a high-value target for attackers. Instead, store a password hash. For best resilience against a dictionary attack in the worst case scenario that an attacker gains unlimited access to your database, use salted hashes. This technique was described in detail in Chapter 4, and is applied in an end-to-end example in Chapter 8.

Worst Practice: Profile without Encryption

Encryption has an overhead. When you profile your application, you must take this into account in order to determine the necessary hardware and potential throughput. If cryptography is identified as a bottleneck, you may be able to lessen the burden by reducing the use of SSL (which may not be required for all interactions), or installing dedicated cryptography hardware; for instance many web servers, use SSL accelerator cards. Microsoft's MSDN website provides some interesting performance comparisons for different cryptographic algorithms at http://msdn.microsoft.com/en-us/dnbda/html/bdadotnetarch15.asp.

Best Practice: Standardize Encoding and Extraneous Details

As you introduce application-level encryption, your code becomes more complex. Handling details like string encoding, buffer copying, and streams can be awkward. Unfortunately, the more complex your code becomes, the more likely you are to introduce an error that could compromise security under the right circumstances.

To reduce this possibility, you should standardize on these details, document your standards, and, wherever possible, encapsulate cryptographic tasks in a dedicated component that can be used by both the client and server. An example of this design was introduced in Chapter 5.

Worst Practice: Encrypt Valuable Data and Then Loose the Key

Of course, your first consideration must be to prevent a malicious user from accessing a key. But what if the key is somehow destroyed, perhaps through a catastrophic drive failure or the malfunction of a hardware device? There's not much that you can do after the fact, but you may want to consider storing valuable keys with a trusted third party to prevent this possibility. In addition, in some cases you can reduce the reliance on a single key. For example, in the virtual web drive developed in Chapter 8, each user's individual key is used to encrypt the data. The server's key is only used to establish a secure session.

Best Practice: Keep a Log of Digitally Signed Documents

As discussed in Chapter 3 with XML signatures, digital signatures aren't just used to prevent malicious users from impersonating authenticated users. They also establish non-repudiation. In other words, if you have a digitally signed stock quote order, the requesting client can't deny making the trade. A log of digitally signed documents is thus extremely useful in dispute resolution.

Best Practice: Reduce Sensitive Information in Memory

If a hacker gains physical access to the computers that run your software, then there are a number of possible attacks. One approach is to cause an unhandled exception, and then catch the current memory contents with a debugger. The hacker can search through this information later, looking for stored secrets and other valuable pieces of information.

This type of attack should be very rare, because it assumes that a malicious user has privileged access to the most important parts of your system. However, it is still possible to limit the amount of information that can be recovered in a memory dump attack with the following best practices:

❑ After using a cryptographic object, immediately call the `Dispose()` method. This method is overloaded in cryptographic classes so that it not only releases the memory resources; it also overwrites the portion of memory that contained key data.

❑ Limit the use of strings or byte arrays with key data or passwords. Even if you try to overwrite this information after the fact, the information may remain in .NET. When retrieving this information, place it directly into the appropriate property of a cryptographic object.

❑ When accessing a database, retrieve connection strings directly into a `Connection` object rather than into an intermediate string variable. In the .NET Framework version 1.1 and later, this information is lightly encrypted in memory.

❑ Don't attempt to trigger garbage collection directly. Garbage collection simply marks memory as available; it does not actually change its contents. That means it's of little help for removing sensitive information.

❑ Always use `Dispose()` if it is available. Don't waste time trying to overwrite data with garbage values – this often won't have the intended effect because .NET can dynamically relocated memory (leaving copies of data long after the originals are gone) and reference types like strings are immutable, which means trying to modify them will simply release the object so it can be disposed.

In an ASP.NET application, be extremely careful about what you store in the cache. This information is accessible to any other page or web service in the same web application. An attacker that accesses the web server could easily create a malicious page that enumerates the contents of the cache and accesses all your sensitive data:

```
string itemList = "";

foreach(DictionaryEntry item in Context.Cache)
{
    Response.Write(item.Key.ToString());
    Response.Write(Context.Cache[item.Key].ToString());
}
```

The same attack is possible against information in application state. Unfortunately, there is no direct way to restrict access to Cache or Application collections. You may need to balance the benefit of increased performance versus the likelihood that your web server will become compromised in this way. Session state, on the other hand, is more difficult to access because it is indexed using a randomly generated GUID ticket that identifies the client.

Summary

This chapter looked at the types of attacks your code can be subjected to, and the types of errors that will make it susceptible. Though most of these examples appear straightforward, they can be quite difficult to spot in real-world code, which is much longer and more complex. Most security flaws are interwoven with business code and extraneous details that easily camouflage them. Unfortunately, the damage of a security flaw can only be truly determined after a hacker discovers it.

Remember, writing code is easy, but creating truly secure code is always difficult, and it takes time. Security cannot be implemented after the fact. Instead, a project should include security milestones at every stage of completion, from design to deployment (starting with threat modeling). Ensuring a proper process is the only way to ensure that secure code can be created. That means you should schedule in-house security audits, and develop a detailed incident response plan. You might even want to publish all security code, which will allow as many people as possible help you spot flaws.

Finally, remember that sensitive information doesn't always need to be made available to users. If you have serious security concerns about sending certain data over the network, consider how you might exclude some portion of it, and reduce the number of times it is transmitted.

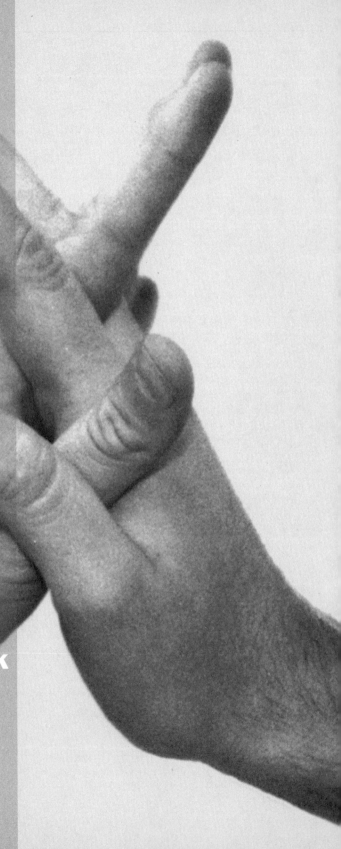

C#

Data Security

Handbook

8

8

Designing Secure Applications

Over the past six chapters, you've learned about key data security concepts and how to implement them using the tools provided with .NET. But making the jump to a complete application takes a little more work. One of the challenges that you'll face is managing the sheer number of details, like key sizes, algorithms, and byte encoding. You'll probably also need to combine several different cryptographic techniques in the same application. For example, you might need to blend encryption and validation, or use different forms of encryption to secure persisted data and data sent over the network. Finally, you'll also need to combine cryptography and data security techniques with other types of application-level security, like user authentication and authorization.

This chapter presents an end-to-end example that pulls together multiple techniques from the earlier chapters. It demonstrates a "virtual hard drive" web service that allows users to securely store and retrieve any type of data on a remote server. Some of the security concepts it addresses include:

- ❑ Ticket-based user authentication against a database, with "unguessable" tickets
- ❑ Encryption of data (both in transit over the network and when persisted)
- ❑ Authentication using salted password hashes, instead of encrypted passwords
- ❑ Date stamps to prevent replay attacks
- ❑ Message authentication codes to prevent tampered messages
- ❑ Validation of persisted data to ensure it hasn't been tampered with
- ❑ Canonicalization of user-supplied values to prevent security holes

In order to show all the code needed, this example won't use Windows Encrypting File System (EFS), SSL, or any other type of "automatic" encryption or authentication service, although these options are completely valid when they are available. Instead, this chapter develops the complete example with custom cryptography code. This allows us to explore the full capabilities of the .NET cryptographic system, learn about the challenges faced in architecting a secure end-to-end application, and be better prepared to evaluate third-party cryptography and off-the-shelf components. These techniques will also be useful if you need to design an application in an environment where prebuilt security services aren't available, or you need to create a highly customized solution. At the end of this chapter, we'll review some possible attacks against the application, and consider where it's secure – and where it could still be improved.

> **In most cases, the best security choice is to use prebuilt security services like Kerberos for authentication, SSL and IP/Sec for data transmission, and Windows Encrypting File System (EFS) for long-term storage. If you write your own cryptography code in a production application, you *must* have it carefully reviewed by cryptography experts – there are just too many possible vulnerabilities that the non-specialist may miss.**

Overview of the VirtualWebDrive Service

This example presents a web service (called VirtualWebDrive) that allows documents to be uploaded and retrieved. Data is encrypted on the server so that it can't be read, and a database keeps tracks of users and the files they created.

Conceptually, the VirtualWebDrive is a virtual safety deposit box service. Each client receives a box (the client program), in which they can lock items (data). They then send this box to the web service, which places the box in a protected location. On request, a client can find out how many boxes they've submitted, and request one back. However, the web service itself doesn't take part in encrypting or decrypting the client's data (although it will need to use encryption to protect message communication). The real challenge in this scenario isn't creating the locks on the client data or the secure server-side storage – it's recognizing the clients, verifying that they aren't impersonators, and ensuring that they can't accidentally receive another user's box.

The VirtualWebDrive web service includes six methods in total:

- ❑ The first method, `GetKey()`, is used to retrieve the web service's public key.

- ❑ Two methods, `Login()` and `Logout()`, are used to start and end a client session.

- ❑ The remaining three web methods, `GetFileInfo()`, `GetFile()`, and `SaveFile()`, are used to retrieve information about currently stored files, and upload or download an individual file.

In a more complex system, you would probably add additional web methods to manage stored files (for example, you might allow users to delete a stored file), and you might include a mechanism to automatically create user records. Currently, these need to be added manually by the administrator, using a separate utility.

User information is stored in a back-end database that includes two tables. The first table, `Users`, contains a list of users, and their passwords. The second table, `Files`, lists the files that have been uploaded, their file path on the server, and the user that owns them. The actual content of the uploaded files is not stored in the database, but on the server hard drive. This ensures that database queries and administrative operations can always be performed quickly.

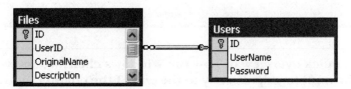

In order to ensure that filenames are random, GUID values are created by the server and used transparently. You could use some other approach, like sequence numbers, but GUIDs are useful in secure programming because they are more difficult to guess. For example, a given user will know the GUIDs that identify their files. This won't make it any easier to guess what GUID values are used for other users' files, which makes some types of attacks much more difficult. Sequence numbers, or some sort of timestamp with a random number added are much easier to reverse engineer.

The encryption logic is encapsulated in a dedicated component assembly that is used by both the client and the server. It's an elegant example of how you can perform application-level encryption without having to intermingle encryption code with your business logic, although it does mean that the code is tightly coupled to the .NET Framework, and therefore more difficult to use with cross-platform clients. This is a key tradeoff between ease-of-use and interoperability. Strictly speaking, the client doesn't *need* to use the custom component, but it will be difficult to replicate the encryption steps in the correct order without it.

The VirtualWebDrive example also includes a dedicated Windows client that works with the web service. It provides the user interface for uploading and retrieving files, and performs some of the cryptography work. Both the Windows client and the web service share the same component, which they use at a high level for all cryptographic tasks.

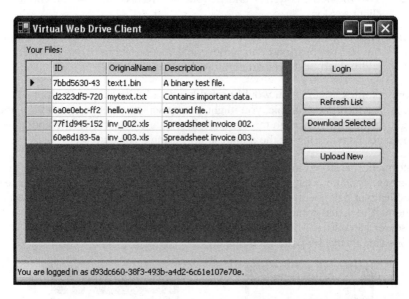

For a quick overview of how the Windows client works, you might want to skip directly to the end of the chapter, which demonstrates the client. You can download the complete code (and a script to install the database) from http://www.prosetech.com or http://www.wrox.com/books/1861008015.htm.

Security Analysis

The VirtualWebDrive has the following security requirements:

❑ It must not be possible for non-authenticated users to perform any operation (aside from retrieving the public key and attempting to log in).

❑ It must not be possible for users to retrieve files or information about files they did not upload.

❑ Data transmitted between the client and web service should be encrypted in such a way that secret keys and other information should not be decipherable. In addition, replay attacks should not be possible.

❏ The stored data should be encrypted in such a way that the data is not visible to attackers, even if they gain access to the server. Ideally, the server component will not have the ability to decipher a file, because it does not need to inspect the data it contains. Thus, even if the server is compromised (or even stolen!) the attacker will only be able to retrieve password hashes and fully encrypted data.

❏ Some measure of security should be implemented to verify that files are not tampered with between the time they are uploaded and the time they are downloaded. In the VirtualWebDrive service, these checks are performed by the server.

The first requirement is easy to implement using a ticket-based authentication system. Under this system, the program must call the web service Login() method to receive a ticket before attempting any other operation. At the same time, it makes sense to perform a key exchange, as demonstrated in Chapter 5. The client creates a random symmetric key, which is used to encrypt data for the remainder of the interaction.

The persisted data is pre-encrypted by the client, and stored in encrypted form on the server's hard drive. The key used to encrypt this data is separate from the server's key and the key used in the session, which ensures that the data cannot be read, either in transit or on the server side. To encrypt the file, a random symmetric key is generated and used. The symmetric key is encrypted using the client's public key, and stored at the beginning of the file data. The client's asymmetric key can be provided through some secure mechanism (such as a client certificate). In the VirtualWebDrive example, it is simply hard-coded.

Figure 1

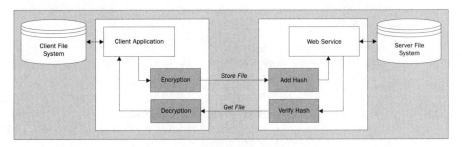

The VirtualWebDrive Component

The first set of classes we're going to look at belong to the component used by the service and the client. This component contains the encryption logic itself. We can subdivide the functionality contained in this component into sub-components, one containing the security-related logic and another containing the database-related logic. Let's take a look at each of these in turn.

The Security Component

The security component is a set of classes compiled into a separate DLL assembly, which is distributed to the client and server. The goal of the security component is to hide the low-level cryptography details and replace them with higher-level cryptography "tasks". Ideally, the client will call a method like "EncryptDataForServer" without worrying about the format, the keys, the use of streams, and so on.

The security component consists of two core parts: classes for encrypting data before it is sent over the wire and decrypting it when it is received, and classes for encrypting files (which is performed at the client end).

The File Encryption Class

The file encryption class is the most straightforward. It requires an asymmetric key, which it will use to encrypt a dynamically generated symmetric key. Here is the skeleton of the class:

```
public sealed class FileEncryptor
{
    private RSACryptoServiceProvider asymmetricKey;

    public FileEncryptor()
    {
        this.asymmetricKey = new RSACryptoServiceProvider ();

        // You can load the key from some source with the
        // RSACryptoServiceProvider.FromXmlString() method.
        // In the following implementation, the key is retrieved
        // from the user's certificate store.
        // This requires WSE (as explained in Chapter 2).
        X509CertificateStore store =
          X509CertificateStore.CurrentUserStore(
          X509CertificateStore.MyStore);
        store.OpenRead();

        // Read the key from the first certificate.
        X509Certificate c = (X509Certificate)store.Certificates[0];
        this.asymmetricKey.ImportParameters(
          c1.Key.ExportParameters(true));
    }

    public byte[] EncryptFile(byte[] fileContent)
    { ... }

    public byte[] DecryptFile(byte[] fileContent)
    { ... }
}
```

Note that in secure programming you should always declare classes as sealed, because this makes it impossible for malicious code to inherit from your classes, and override its functionality.

The full code for the EncryptFile() method is shown below. In this case, we use the Rijndael algorithm, which provides the strongest key sizes available in the .NET platform. The initialization vector is simply set to an empty byte array, because the security provided by the randomly generated key is deemed strong enough. However, for even greater defense against brute force attacks, you would use a non-zero IV and store this in the file along with the symmetric key data. Both pieces of data would be encrypted using the client's asymmetric key.

```
public byte[] EncryptFile(byte[] fileContent)
{
    // Create the random key.
    SymmetricAlgorithm key =  Rijndael.Create ();
    key.IV = new byte[key.IV.Length];
    byte[] keyData = asymmetricKey.Encrypt(key.Key, false);

    // Write the random key data (which has been encrypted using
    // the asymmetric key) and key size information
    // to the beginning of the file.
    MemoryStream ms = new MemoryStream();
    byte[] keyDataLength = BitConverter.GetBytes(keyData.Length);
    ms.Write(keyDataLength, 0, keyDataLength.Length);
    ms.Write(keyData, 0, keyData.Length);

    // Now encrypt and write the file data with the symmetric key.
    CryptoStream cs = new CryptoStream(ms,
    key.CreateEncryptor(), CryptoStreamMode.Write);
    cs.Write(fileContent, 0, fileContent.Length);
    cs.FlushFinalBlock();

    // Return all the data.
    return ms.ToArray();
}
```

Note that the EncryptFile() method prepends two pieces of information before the file content: the encrypted key size in bytes, and the encrypted key data, in that order. It's also important to realize that encryption classes are created in an algorithm-specific fashion (not by using the base SymmetricAlgorithm.Create() method). This is to make sure that the same algorithm is always used. Otherwise, the client could theoretically create a different encryption algorithm using the same method if the machine-specific configuration settings had been changed.

Here is the corresponding `DecryptFile()` method:

```
public byte[] DecryptFile(byte[] fileContent)
{
    // Retrieve the key size information.
    // This is the only unencrypted part of the file.
    byte[] keyDataLength = new byte[4];
    Buffer.BlockCopy(fileContent, 0, keyDataLength,
        0, keyDataLength.Length);
    int keyLength = BitConverter.ToInt32(keyDataLength, 0);

    // Check that the keyLength makes sense.
    // Otherwise a hacked file could conceivably trick the client
    // into allocating a huge amount of memory, and crashing.
    if (keyLength > fileContent.Length)
    {
        throw new ApplicationException("Invalid file data.");
    }

    // Retrieve the random symmetric key that was used,
    // and decrypt it.
    byte[] keyData = new byte[keyLength];
    Buffer.BlockCopy(fileContent, keyDataLength.Length,
                     keyData, 0, keyLength);
    SymmetricAlgorithm key = Rijndael.Create();
    key.IV = new byte[key.IV.Length];
    key.Key = asymmetricKey.Decrypt(keyData, false);

    // Decrypt the remaining file contents with the symmetric key.
    MemoryStream ms = new MemoryStream();
    CryptoStream cs = new CryptoStream(ms,
            key.CreateDecryptor(), CryptoStreamMode.Write);
    cs.Write(fileContent, keyDataLength.Length + keyLength,
            fileContent.Length - keyDataLength.Length - keyLength);
    cs.FlushFinalBlock();

    // Return the decrypted data.
    return ms.ToArray();
}
```

The primary advantage of this class is that it encapsulates the rules for finding the dynamically encrypted file key. There is no standard for this task, so different implementations may store the key at the beginning of the file or the end, with a variable number of bytes, and with or without the key length information. It's also possible to use the emerging XML Encryption standard to separate data from key information, although you will need to create the XML document programmatically (as .NET does not currently provide a XML Encryption API).

The Session Encryption Classes

The session encryption classes are used to encrypt any other type of data that needs to be sent over the wire. This information will be encrypted using a dynamically generated session key.

The session encryption classes are a little more involved than the file encryption classes, because they operate slightly differently on the client versus the server, and because they need to work with different types of data. To allow for this design, the VirtualWebDrive uses three classes. Core functionality is contained in an abstract base class called SecureSession. Two other classes, SecureClientSession and SecureServerSession, build on this to provide higher-level encryption tasks.

The Base SecureSession Class

Below is the bare skeleton of the abstract SecureSession class. It defines core functionality that can symmetrically or asymmetrically encrypt any serializable object. You'll notice that it also includes a reference for an asymmetric server key (provided by the web service) and a symmetric client key (used for the session, and generated by the client dynamically).

```
public abstract class SecureSession
{
    protected RSACryptoServiceProvider serverKey;
    protected SymmetricAlgorithm clientKey;

    protected byte[] EncryptSymmetric(object objectToEncrypt)
    { ... }

    protected object DecryptSymmetric(byte[] dataToDecrypt)
    { ... }

    protected byte[] EncryptAsymmetric(object objectToEncrypt)
    { ... }

    protected object DecryptAsymmetric(byte[] dataToDecrypt)
    { ... }

    protected bool CompareByteArray(byte[] array1, byte[] array2)
    { ... }
}
```

> **Using object serialization makes it easy to encrypt a broad range of serializable objects without writing custom code for each class. However, if you serialize a .NET Framework object, and the version of the framework running the web service differs from the version running the client, a serialization problem could occur. The solution is to serialize only your own custom objects, which you can version and control.**

The `SecureSession` code is somewhat lengthy. On the symmetric side, you run into the requirement that all symmetric encryption must be stream-based. Therefore, to symmetrically encrypt data, you need to first convert it to a stream.

In addition, the `EncryptSymmetric()` method uses a message authentication code, which it calculates using the client key, and appends to the end of the message data.

```
protected byte[] EncryptSymmetric(object objectToEncrypt)
{
    MemoryStream ms = new MemoryStream();
    CryptoStream cs = new CryptoStream(ms,
    clientKey.CreateEncryptor(), CryptoStreamMode.Write);

    BinaryFormatter f = new BinaryFormatter();
    f.Serialize(cs, objectToEncrypt);
    cs.FlushFinalBlock();

    // Create hash code.
    KeyedHashAlgorithm hash = HMACSHA1.Create();
    hash.Key = clientKey.Key;
    ms.Position = 0;
    hash.ComputeHash(ms);

    // Write the hash code to the end of the message.
    // Because it is a keyed hash code, it does not need further
    // encryption.
    ms.Write(hash.Hash, 0, hash.Hash.Length);

    return ms.ToArray();
}
```

The `DecryptSymmetric()` method begins by validating the message authentication code, to ensure that the data hasn't been tampered with. It then deserializes the object.

```
protected object DecryptSymmetric(byte[] dataToDecrypt)
{
    // Extract the hash from the data.
    byte[] data = new byte[dataToDecrypt.Length - hash.HashSize / 8];
    Buffer.BlockCopy(dataToDecrypt, 0, data, 0, data.Length);
    byte[] MAC = new byte[hash.HashSize / 8];
    Buffer.BlockCopy(dataToDecrypt, data.Length, MAC, 0, MAC.Length);

    // Recalculate the keyed hash code.
    KeyedHashAlgorithm hash = HMACSHA1.Create();
    hash.Key = clientKey.Key;
    hash.ComputeHash(data, 0, data.Length);

    // Verify the calculated hash with the hash on the message.
    if (!this.CompareByteArray(hash.Hash, MAC))
    {
        throw new ApplicationException("Invalid data.");
    }

    MemoryStream ms = new MemoryStream();
    CryptoStream cs = new CryptoStream(ms,
                                clientKey.CreateDecryptor(),
                                CryptoStreamMode.Write);

    cs.Write(data, 0, data.Length);
    cs.FlushFinalBlock();

    // Now deserialize the decrypted memory stream.
    ms.Position = 0;
    BinaryFormatter f = new BinaryFormatter();
    return f.Deserialize(ms);
}
```

The asymmetric encryption methods are more involved. The consideration here is that asymmetric encryption only works with one block at a time. That's fine for our earlier file encryption example, where a single block of data (the key information) is encrypted. Longer data, however, needs to be encrypted block by block and patched together. The code shown below is very similar to the asymmetric examples presented in Chapter 2, and it is described in more detail there. Bear in mind that the VirtualWebDrive service will only use asymmetric encryption at the very beginning of the interaction, to negotiate a key exchange.

```
protected byte[] EncryptAsymmetric(object objectToEncrypt)
{
    // Create the memory streams.
    MemoryStream msRaw = new MemoryStream();
    MemoryStream msEncrypted = new MemoryStream();
```

```
        BinaryFormatter f = new BinaryFormatter();
        f.Serialize(msRaw, objectToEncrypt);

        byte[] bytes = msRaw.ToArray();

        // Determine the optimum block size for encryption.
        int blockSize = 0;
        if (serverKey.KeySize == 1024)
        {
            blockSize = 16;
        }
        else
        {
            blockSize = 5;
        }

        // Move through the data one block at a time.
        byte[] rawBlock, encryptedBlock;
        for (int i = 0; i < bytes.Length; i += blockSize)
        {
            if ((bytes.Length - i) > blockSize)
            {
                rawBlock = new byte[blockSize];
            }
            else
            {
                rawBlock = new byte[bytes.Length - i];
            }

            // Copy a block of data.
            Buffer.BlockCopy(bytes, i, rawBlock, 0, rawBlock.Length);

            // Encrypt the block of data.
            encryptedBlock = serverKey.Encrypt(rawBlock, false);

            // Write the block of data.
            msEncrypted.Write(encryptedBlock, 0, encryptedBlock.Length);
        }

        return msEncrypted.ToArray();
}

protected object DecryptAsymmetric(byte[] dataToDecrypt)
{
        // Create the memory stream where the decrypted data
        // will be stored.
        MemoryStream msDecrypted = new MemoryStream();

        // Determine the block size for decrypting.
        int keySize = serverKey.KeySize / 8;
```

```
// Move through the data one block at a time.
byte[] decryptedBlock, rawBlock;
for (int i = 0; i < dataToDecrypt.Length; i += keySize)
{
    if ((dataToDecrypt.Length - i) > keySize)
    {
        rawBlock = new byte[keySize];
    }
    else
    {
        rawBlock = new byte[dataToDecrypt.Length - i];
    }

    // Copy a block of data.
    Buffer.BlockCopy(dataToDecrypt, i, rawBlock, 0,
                     rawBlock.Length);

    // Decrypt a block of data.
    decryptedBlock = serverKey.Decrypt(rawBlock, false);

    // Write the decrypted data to the in-memory stream.
    msDecrypted.Write(decryptedBlock, 0, decryptedBlock.Length);
}

msDecrypted.Position = 0;
BinaryFormatter f = new BinaryFormatter();
return f.Deserialize(msDecrypted);
}
```

The final `SecureSession` method is `CompareByteArray()`, which is useful for testing hash values:

```
protected bool CompareByteArray(byte[] array1, byte[] array2)
{
    if (array1.Length != array2.Length)
        return false;
    for (int i = 0; i < array1.Length; i++)
    {
        if (array1[i] != array2[i])
            return false;
    }
    return true;
}
```

This code is generic enough that you might consider implementing it in a separate utility class and using it for multiple cryptographic components. However, in practice it's often easier to separate this logic, so that you can tailor it later for different tasks without breaking some dependent parts of your application. Note that all these methods are protected, which means they are not available to any other classes except for those derived from `SecureSession`.

From `SecureSession`, we derive two specialized classes: one for the server, and one for the client.

```
public class SecureClientSession : SecureSession
{ ... }

public class SecureServerSession : SecureSession
{ ... }
```

These classes wrap specific encryption tasks on the server and client, and are described in more detail in the next section.

The Login Process

To understand how the `SecureClientSession` and `SecureServerSession` classes work, it's helpful to follow through the process a client will take when accessing the VirtualWebDrive service. First they attempt to log in. To perform this login attempt, the client must submit some credentials, which are encapsulated by the `LoginInfo` class:

```
[Serializable()]
public class LoginInfo
{
    public string UserName;
    public byte[] Password;
    public DateTime CreatedTime;
    public byte[] ClientKey;

    public LoginInfo(string userName, string password,
                     byte[] clientKey, DateTime serverDate)
    {
        this.UserName = userName;
        this.Password = password;
        this.CreatedTime = serverDate;
        this.ClientKey = clientKey;
    }

    public LoginInfo()
    {
        // Required for deserialization.
    }
}
```

Along with the user name and password, the `LoginInfo` class also includes a `CreatedTime` field. This is because the data in the `LoginInfo` object will be serialized and encrypted into a single byte array. By including a date and time, the server can reject old login packages, preventing a hacker from reusing an old intercepted network communication (known as a replay attack). In addition, `LoginInfo` includes a randomly generated symmetric key, which will be used for all future communication (assuming the login attempt succeeds).

290

In order to avoid time zone issues (or simple time discrepancies), the client must use the server's time. The web service provides a `GetServerDate()` method for this purpose. The client will call this method, and use the returned time for the `LoginInfo` package.

The process of creating, submitting, and then validating the login information is shown below. This diagram also shows the database validation step, which we won't consider until the next section.

Figure 2

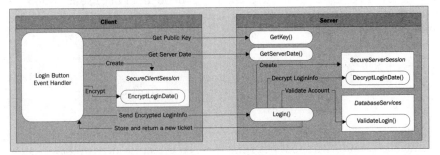

The client begins its use of `SecureClientSession` by creating an instance of the class. At this point, it needs to supply the public part of the server's key as an XML string. This information is required by the `SecureClientSession` constructor.

```
public SecureClientSession(string serverKeyXml)
{
    this.serverKey = new RSACryptoServiceProvider();
    this.serverKey.FromXmlString(serverKeyXml);
}
```

Now, the client calls the `EncryptLoginData()` method of the `SecureClientSession` class with a user name and password. This method creates a `LoginInfo` object with the client information and a randomly generated key, and encrypts it into a byte array using the server's asymmetric key. It then returns the resulting byte array.

```
public byte[] EncryptLoginData(string userName, string password)
{
    this.clientKey = (SymmetricAlgorithm)(new RijndaelManaged());
    this.clientKey.IV = new byte[this.clientKey.IV.Length];

    LoginInfo loginInfo = new LoginInfo(userName, password,
                                        clientKey.Key);
    return this.EncryptAsymmetric(loginInfo);
}
```

When we examine the Windows client, you'll see how this makes the client code extremely simple.

The SecureServerSession class is similar, but customized for the tasks the web service needs to perform. Its constructor requires the asymmetric key object:

```
public SecureServerSession(RSACryptoServiceProvider serverKey)
{
    this.serverKey = serverKey;
}
```

A DecryptLoginData() method of the SecureServerSession class retrieves the original LoginInfo object. As in the client, EncryptObjectForClient() and DecryptObjectFromClient() allow the SecureServerSesion object to deal with symmetrically-encrypted data.

```
public LoginInfo DecryptLoginData(byte[] loginData)
{
    return (LoginInfo)this.DecryptAsymmetric(loginData);
}
```

For all other methods, the interaction between client and server is governed by symmetric encryption. The SecureClientSession class provides two other methods for this task, which encrypt and decrypt objects using the base SecureSession methods:

```
public byte[] EncryptObjectForServer(object objectToEncrypt)
{
    return this.EncryptSymmetric(objectToEncrypt);
}

public object DecryptObjectFromServer(byte[] dataToDecrypt)
{
    return this.DecryptSymmetric(dataToDecrypt);
}
```

The SecureServerSession class uses the following two complementary methods:

```
public byte[] EncryptObjectForClient(object objectToEncrypt)
{
    return this.EncryptSymmetric(objectToEncrypt);
}

public object DecryptObjectFromClient(byte[] dataToDecrypt)
{
    return this.DecryptSymmetric(dataToDecrypt);
}
```

Remember, web services are stateless, and may interact with hundreds of clients at a time. At the beginning of every client interaction, the web service therefore needs to retrieve the appropriate client key, and apply it to the `SecureServerSession` class. This is accomplished through the `SetClientKey()` method of this class.

```
public void SetClientKey(byte[] keyData)
{
    this.clientKey = Rijndael.Create();
    this.clientKey.Key = keyData;
    this.clientKey.IV = new byte[this.clientKey.IV.Length];
}
```

Finally, two additional helper methods allow the web service to create and verify file hashes. As with the encryption classes, a specific hash algorithm implementation class is created directly to prevent errors from varying configuration. The hashes are tested for equality using the base `SecureSession.CompareByteArray()` method.

```
public byte[] CalculateHash(byte[] data)
{
    HashAlgorithm hash =
      (HashAlgorithm)SHA1CryptoServiceProvider.Create();
    return hash.ComputeHash(data, 0, data.Length);
}

public bool VerifyHash(byte[] data, byte[] storedHash)
{
    HashAlgorithm hash = SHA1CryptoServiceProvider.Create();

    return this.CompareByteArray(hash.ComputeHash(data, 0,
      data.Length), storedHash);
}
```

This completes the cryptographic code used to secure communication in the VirtualWebDrive system.

The Database Component

It's also important to identify the database operations that your code needs to perform early in the development cycle. In the VirtualWebDrive example, these operations include adding file records, retrieving file information, and validating login information. Ideally, all of these tasks would be performed through stored procedures. In this example, we'll use parameterized commands, which protect against SQL injection attacks and provide an easy code migration path to stored procedures.

First of all, a serializable `FileInfo` structure is defined, which bundles together the information that describes a file record. Note that this doesn't include the actual file data, which is stored separately. Like all of our serializable classes, this class is used to send information to the web service.

```
[Serializable()]
public class FileInfo
{
    public Guid ID;
    public int UserID;
    public string OriginalName;
    public string Description;
    public string ServerPath;
    public byte[] Hash;

    public FileInfo(string originalName, string description)
    {
        this.OriginalName = originalName;
        this.Description = description;
    }

    public FileInfo()
    {
        // Required for deserialization.
    }
}
```

The database code is encapsulated in a single class named `DatabaseServices`. When the class is created, the database connection string is read from a configuration file (in this case, the `web.config` file for the virtual directory where the web service is located). This connection string should grant *only* the permissions required to modify the `Files` table and access the `Users`.

```
public class DatabaseServices
{
    private string connectionString;

    public DatabaseServices()
    {
        connectionString =
            ConfigurationSettings.AppSettings["DatabaseConnection"];
    }

    // (Other code omitted.)
}
```

The `DatabaseServices` class provides four methods, all of which use parameterized commands and follow much the same approach (one of the best ways to write secure code is to write boring code!) The `AddUser()` method creates a new user record, and automatically hashes and salts the password before storing it in the database. To support this technique, the `HashHelper` class introduced in Chapter 4 is used.

```
public void AddUser(string userName, string password)
{
    // Define the SQL string with named parameters.
    string SQL = "INSERT Users (UserName, Password) VALUES " +
        "(@UserName, @Password)";
    SqlConnection con = new SqlConnection(connectionString);
    SqlCommand cmd = new SqlCommand(SQL, con);

    // Add the parameter values to the command.
    SqlParameter param;
    param = cmd.Parameters.Add("@UserName", SqlDbType.VarChar, 50);
    param.Value = userName;
    param = cmd.Parameters.Add("@Password", SqlDbType.VarBinary, 24);
    // Compute the salted password hash.
    HashHelper hashUtil = new HashHelper();
    param.Value = hashUtil.CreateDBPassword(password);

    // Add the record to the database.
    try
    {
        con.Open();
        cmd.ExecuteNonQuery();
    }
    catch (Exception err)
    {
        System.Diagnostics.Debug.WriteLine(err.ToString());
        throw new ApplicationException("Database error.");
    }
    finally
    {
        con.Close();
    }
}
```

Note that the web service does not use the `AddUser()` method directly. Instead, this method is used by a dedicated administrative utility that quickly allows you to add user records to the database. This utility is included with the downloadable code, but isn't shown here.

The `ValidateLogin()` method searches for a user in the database, and returns the corresponding user ID number and password hash. The password hash is then verified with the help of the `HashHelper` class. `ValidateLogin()` throws an exception if no user matches the supplied information, the password hash does not match, or the date stamp is invalid.

```
public int ValidateLogin(LoginInfo loginInfo)
{
    if (loginInfo.CreatedTime.AddMinutes(5) < DateTime.Now ||
        loginInfo.CreatedTime > DateTime.Now)
    {
        throw new ApplicationException("Invalid login attempt.");
    }

    // Define the SQL string with named parameters.
    string SQL = "SELECT ID, UserName, Password From Users WHERE " +
      "UserName=@UserName";
    SqlConnection con = new SqlConnection(connectionString);
    SqlCommand cmd = new SqlCommand(SQL, con);

    // Add the parameter values to the command.
    SqlParameter param;
    param = cmd.Parameters.Add("@UserName", SqlDbType.NChar, 50);
    param.Value = loginInfo.UserName;

    int userID = null;
    byte[] passwordHash = null;
    try
    {
        con.Open();
        SqlDataReader r = cmd.ExecuteReader();

        if (r.Read())
        {
            userID = (int)r["ID"];
            passwordHash = (byte[])r["Password"];
        }
    }
    catch (Exception err)
    {
        System.Diagnostics.Debug.WriteLine(err.ToString());

        throw new ApplicationException("Database error.");
    }
    finally
    {
        if (r!=null) r.Close();
        con.Close();
    }

    // Verify the password hash.
    HashHelper hashUtil = new HashHelper();
    if (hashUtil.ComparePasswords(passwordHash,
        loginInfo.PasswordHash))
    {
        return userID;
    }
```

```
        else
        {
            throw new ApplicationException("Invalid login attempt.");
        }
}
```

Note how any exceptions that occur are replaced with a non-committal
ApplicationException that won't reveal any information to would-be attackers.
While testing this code, you will probably want to comment out this logic to simplify
the identification of bugs (although you can rely on logging instead).

The GetFilesForUser() method takes a user ID, and returns the list of related files
as a DataSet with one DataTable. Alternatively, information could be returned as an
array of FileInfo objects, although the DataSet approach simplifies the client-side
data binding.

```
public DataSet GetFilesForUser(int userID)
{
    // Define the SQL string with named parameters.
    string SQL = "SELECT ID, OriginalName, Description FROM " +
        "Files WHERE UserID=@UserID ORDER BY CreateTime";
    SqlConnection con = new SqlConnection(connectionString);
    SqlCommand cmd = new SqlCommand(SQL, con);

    // Add the parameter values to the command.
    SqlParameter param;
    param = cmd.Parameters.Add("@UserID", SqlDbType.Int);
    param.Value = userID;

    SqlDataAdapter adapter = new SqlDataAdapter(cmd);
    DataSet ds = new DataSet("Virtual Web Drive");
    try
    {
        con.Open();
        adapter.Fill(ds);
    }
    catch (Exception err)
    {
        // Log error here.

        System.Diagnostics.Debug.WriteLine(err.ToString());
        throw new ApplicationException("Database error.");
    }
    finally
    {
        con.Close();
    }
    return ds;
}
```

Note that the GetFilesForUser() method only returns the three pieces of information that will interest the user. Information about the actual server path, hash code, and so on, is not returned. The GetFileInfo() method, on the other hand, returns the information that the web service will require to find and validate a file before returning it to the user. It's possible to create more generic methods that return all the information and manually strip out the unimportant details afterwards, but this approach is more efficient in this example.

```
public FileInfo GetFileInfo(Guid fileID)
{
    // Define the SQL string with named parameters.
    string SQL = "SELECT ServerPath, Hash, UserID FROM " +
      "Files WHERE ID=@ID";
    SqlConnection con = new SqlConnection(connectionString);
    SqlCommand cmd = new SqlCommand(SQL, con);

    // Add the parameter values to the command.
    SqlParameter param;
    param = cmd.Parameters.Add("@ID", SqlDbType.UniqueIdentifier);
    param.Value = fileID;

    FileInfo file = null;
    try
    {
        con.Open();
        SqlDataReader r = cmd.ExecuteReader();

        if (r.Read())
        {
            file = new FileInfo();
            file.UserID = (int)r["UserID"];
            file.ServerPath = r["ServerPath"].ToString();
            file.Hash = (byte[])r["Hash"];
        }

        r.Close();
    }
    catch (Exception err)
    {
        // Log error here.
        System.Diagnostics.Debug.WriteLine(err.ToString());

        throw new ApplicationException("Database error.");
    }
    finally
    {
        con.Close();
    }
    return file;
}
```

Finally, the AddFile() method inserts a new file record based on the information in a FileInfo object. This method does not generate the identifying GUID, which will be supplied by the web service (and used for the filename).

```
public void AddFile(FileInfo fileInfo)
{
    // Define the SQL string with named parameters.
    string SQL = "INSERT INTO Files (ID, UserID, OriginalName, " +
        "ServerPath, Hash, Description) VALUES (@ID, @UserID, " +
        "@OriginalName, @ServerPath, @Hash, @Description)";
    SqlConnection con = new SqlConnection(connectionString);
    SqlCommand cmd = new SqlCommand(SQL, con);

    // Add the parameter values to the command.
    SqlParameter param;
    param = cmd.Parameters.Add("@ID", SqlDbType.UniqueIdentifier);
    param.Value = fileInfo.ID;
    param = cmd.Parameters.Add("@UserID", SqlDbType.Int);
    param.Value = fileInfo.UserID;
    param = cmd.Parameters.Add("@OriginalName", SqlDbType.VarChar,
                              50);
    param.Value = fileInfo.OriginalName;
    param = cmd.Parameters.Add("@ServerPath", SqlDbType.VarChar, 100);
    param.Value = fileInfo.ServerPath;
    param = cmd.Parameters.Add("@Hash", SqlDbType.Binary, 20);
    param.Value = fileInfo.Hash;
    param = cmd.Parameters.Add("@Description", SqlDbType.VarChar,
                              200);
    param.Value = fileInfo.Description;

    try
    {
        con.Open();
        cmd.ExecuteNonQuery();
    }
    catch (Exception err)
    {
        // Log error here.

        System.Diagnostics.Debug.WriteLine(err.ToString());
        throw new ApplicationException("Database error.");
    }
    finally
    {
        con.Close();
    }
}
```

The VirtualWebDrive Service

Now that the security and database infrastructure is in place, it's actually fairly straightforward to build the client and web service. The first step is to create a web.config file that stores the file path and database connection string. Below is an example (although you will need to adjust the file path and database connection string depending on the test system you use).

```xml
<?xml version="1.0" encoding="utf-8" ?>
<configuration>

  <appSettings>
    <add key="DatabaseConnection"
     value="Initial Catalog=Wrox;Data Source=localhost;
     Integrated Security=SSPI" />
    <add key="FilePath" value="f:\VirtualWeb\UserFiles\" />
  </appSettings>

  <system.web>
    <!-- Other web application settings go here. -->
  </system.web>
</configuration>
```

The VirtualWebDriveService class defines three private member variables. One stores the asymmetric encryption key, while the other two reference an instance of the SecureServerSession and DatabaseServices classes, respectively.

```csharp
public class VirtualWebDriveService : System.Web.Services.WebService
{
    private RSACryptoServiceProvider crypt;
    private VirtualWebDriveComponent.SecureServerSession session;
    private VirtualWebDriveComponent.DatabaseServices DB;

    // (Code omitted.)
}
```

The web service constructor initializes these values:

```csharp
public VirtualWebDriveService()
{
    InitializeComponent();
    this.crypt = GetKeyFromState();
    this.session = new
      VirtualWebDriveComponent.SecureServerSession(crypt);
    this.DB = new VirtualWebDriveComponent.DatabaseServices();
}
```

Remember, web services are entirely stateless. Therefore this constructor is called at the beginning of each client request. Because each client receives a new VirtualWebDriveService instance, there is no possibility for synchronization conflicts with the member variables.

A private helper method retrieves the asymmetric web service key pair from application state. This ensures that all instances of the web service access the same key.

```
private RSACryptoServiceProvider GetKeyFromState()
{
    RSACryptoServiceProvider crypt = null;

    // Check if the key has been created yet.
    // This ensures that the key is only created once,
    // the first time this web service is accessed.
    // Alternatively, this key could be retrieved from a secure
    // storage location.
    if (Application["Key"] == null)
    {
        // Create a key for RSA encryption.
        CspParameters param = new CspParameters();
        param.Flags = CspProviderFlags.UseMachineKeyStore;
        crypt = new RSACryptoServiceProvider(param);

        // Store the key in the server memory.
        Application["Key"] = crypt;
    }
    else
    {
        crypt = (RSACryptoServiceProvider)Application["Key"];
    }
    return crypt;
}
```

The GetKey() web method allows the client to retrieve the public portion of this key:

```
// Return the public portion of the key only.
[WebMethod()]
public string GetKey()
{
    return crypt.ToXmlString(false);
}
```

Ticket-Based Authentication

Ticket-based authentication is a key part of the service. Ticket-based authentication allows the time-consuming database validation to take place only once, at the beginning of a session. Upon a successfully login, the client is issued a ticket that can be used to quickly authenticate the client for the remainder of a session. It's up to you to define when a ticket expires, and how it expires. Ticket-based authentication is introduced in Chapter 5.

The first step when using ticket-based authentication is to define a class that encapsulates all the ticket details. In this example, the ticket stores the user ID, the user's IP address, the time the ticket was created, and the client key:

```
public class TicketInfo
{
    public int UserID;
    public DateTime LastUsedDate;
    public string IPAddress;
    public byte[] ClientKey;

    public TicketInfo(int userID, string IPAddress, byte[] clientKey)
    {
        this.UserID = userID;
        this.LastUsedDate = DateTime.Now;
        this.IPAddress = IPAddress;
        this.ClientKey = clientKey;
    }
}
```

Tracking the IP address won't necessarily add security, because in many cases an entire organization will sit behind a proxy server or use network address translation to map multiple computers to a single IP address. However, tracking the IP address won't lower security, and it also raises some interesting information you can record with your logging code if a security problem occurs.

Let's get back to the `VirtualWebDriveService` class. The `Login()` method is quite straightforward, thanks to the encryption and database components we've created. The `SecureServerSession` class is used to decrypt the login data, which is then passed to the `DatabaseServices` component for validation. If the user cannot be validated, a generic exception is thrown. Otherwise, a new ticket is generated using a new GUID and the key information from the `LoginInfo` object.

```
[WebMethod()]
public string Login(byte[] loginData)
{
    LoginInfo loginInfo = session.DecryptLoginData(loginData);
```

```
        // An unhandled, generic exception will halt the process here if
        // the user is not found.
        int userID = DB.ValidateLogin(loginInfo);

        // Create a cryptographically random ticket.
        byte[] ticketBytes = new byte[16];
        RNGCryptoServiceProvider rng = new RNGCryptoServiceProvider();
        rng.GetBytes(ticketBytes);
        Guid ticketGuid = new Guid(ticketBytes);
        string ticket = ticketGuid.ToString();

        // Store this ticket in application state.
        Application[ticket] = new TicketInfo(userID,
          Context.Request.UserHostAddress, loginInfo.ClientKey);

        // Return the ticket.
        return ticket;
    }
```

The Logout() method simply removes the ticket:

```
    [WebMethod()]
    public void Logout(string ticket)
    {
        Application.Remove(ticket);
    }
```

The ticket-based authentication system needs one more detail: a private function that will verify that a submitted ticket is valid. This function verifies that the GUID corresponds to a valid ticket, that the ticket hasn't expired (which could indicate an attempted replay attack), and that the user's IP address hasn't changed (which could indicate an attempted session hijack). If any of these criteria are not met, a generic "Invalid ticket" exception is thrown.

If the criteria are met, the client's session key is submitted to the SecureServerSession object, where it can be used to decrypt or encrypt any exchanged data.

```
    private TicketInfo ValidateTicket(string ticket)
    {
        TicketInfo ticketInfo = (TicketInfo)Application[ticket];
        if (ticketInfo == null)
        {
            throw new ApplicationException("Invalid ticket.");
        }
```

```
    // Check IP address.
    if (ticketInfo.IPAddress != this.Context.Request.UserHostAddress)
    {
        throw new ApplicationException("Invalid ticket.");
    }

    // Apply expiration policy allowing up to twenty minutes
    // between requests.
    // This information could be read from the configuration file.
    if (ticketInfo.CreatedDate.AddMinutes(20) < DateTime.Now)
    {
        throw new ApplicationException("Invalid ticket.");
    }
    else
    {
        ticketInfo.LastUsedDate = DateTime.Now;
    }

    session.SetClientKey(ticketInfo.ClientKey);
    return ticketInfo;
}
```

Note that the ValidateTicket() method is the location where you define your expiration policy. In the VirtualWebDrive, tickets expire after twenty minutes of disuse. Every time a request is received it is checked for age, and if it's valid the created date is updated to the current date.

Managing Files

All that remains for the VirtualWebDriveService class are the three web methods for managing files and file information: GetFileInfo(), GetFile(), and SaveFile(). Each method begins by validating the ticket, which also sets the corresponding client key into the ServerSecureSession, so it can be used for encrypting and decrypting data.

The GetFileInfo() method simply returns the file information using the GetFilesForUser() method, and encrypts it using EncryptObjectForClient().

```
[WebMethod()]
public byte[] GetFileInfo(string ticket)
{
    TicketInfo ticketInfo = this.ValidateTicket(ticket);

    return session.EncryptObjectForClient(
            DB.GetFilesForUser(ticketInfo.UserID));
}
```

The `GetFile()` method retrieves information for a specified file, reads the file from the hard drive, and returns the content as a byte array. This data is not encrypted before transmission, because it has already been encrypted by the client.

The `GetFile()` method performs two additional security checks after the ticket is verified:

❑ Verifies that the requested file was in fact created by the requesting user.

❑ Verifies that the hash stored in the database matches the hash of the file. This ensures the file hasn't been modified since it was uploaded, assuming the information in the database hasn't also been tampered with.

If either of these checks fails, a generic exception is returned. The client has no way to determine whether the failure is a security exception, database problem, or a file I/O error. You could customize this if required, or add logging code so that information can be retrieved after the fact on the server.

```
[WebMethod()]
public byte[] GetFile(string ticket, string fileID)
{
    TicketInfo ticketInfo = this.ValidateTicket(ticket);
    FileInfo fileInfo = DB.GetFileInfo(new Guid(fileID));

    if (fileInfo.UserID != ticketInfo.UserID)
    {
        throw new ApplicationException("Cannot return file.");
    }

    byte[] fileData;
    try
    {
        FileStream fs = File.OpenRead(fileInfo.ServerPath);
        fileData = new byte [fs.Length];
        fs.Read(fileData, 0, (int)fs.Length);
        fs.Close();
    }
    catch
    {
        throw new ApplicationException("Cannot return file.");
    }

    if (!session.VerifyHash(fileData, fileInfo.Hash))
    {
        throw new ApplicationException("Cannot return file.");
    }

    // No encryption needed. Data is still encrypted.
    return fileData;
}
```

Finally, the SaveFile() method saves a new file on the server's hard drive and creates the corresponding database record. The file information is passed as an encrypted FileInfo object, along with encrypted file content. The FileInfo data has been passed with the current session key, and can be decrypted by the server. The encrypted file content, however, is not decrypted at the server end, and is written to disk in encrypted form. The SaveFile() method also calculates a hash value for the file, which is stored in the database record.

```
[WebMethod()]
public string SaveFile(string ticket, byte[] fileInfoData,
  byte[] fileContent)
{
    TicketInfo ticketInfo = this.ValidateTicket(ticket);
    FileInfo fileInfo =
      (FileInfo)session.DecryptObjectFromClient(fileInfoData);

    fileInfo.UserID = ticketInfo.UserID;

    // Add the hash information.
    fileInfo.Hash = session.CalculateHash(fileContent);

    // Generate the ID.
    fileInfo.ID = Guid.NewGuid();

    try
    {
        // Save file.
        // No encryption needed. Data is already encrypted.
        string path = ConfigurationSettings.AppSettings["FilePath"] +
          fileInfo.ID.ToString();
        fileInfo.ServerPath = path;
        FileStream fs = new FileStream(path, FileMode.CreateNew);
        fs.Write(fileContent, 0, fileContent.Length);
        fs.Close();

        DB.AddFile(fileInfo);
    }
    catch (Exception err)
    {
        // Log error.

        System.Diagnostics.Debug.WriteLine(err.ToString());
        throw new ApplicationException("Cannot save file.");
    }
    return fileInfo.ID.ToString();
}
```

As currently written, the SaveFile() method has one limitation. If a database exception occurs, it could write an "orphaned" file to disk without creating a corresponding database record. To remedy this problem, you could delete a file if a database exception occurs, or use a COM+ transaction and reverse the order of operation. This way, after a file I/O error you could roll back the database changes.

The Windows Client

The last part of this system is the Windows client that interacts with the VirtualWebDrive service. This client is shown below:

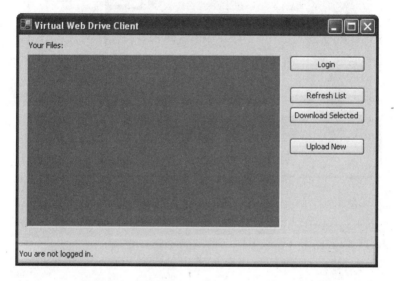

The client uses several member variables to reference the web service proxy, the current session, and an instance of the FileEncryption class. It also tracks the current ticket and a flag that indicates whether the client is logged in.

```
public class MainForm : System.Windows.Forms.Form
{
    private localhost.VirtualWebDriveService proxy =
    new localhost.VirtualWebDriveService();
    private VirtualWebDriveComponent.SecureClientSession session;
    private VirtualWebDriveComponent.FileEncryption FileUtil =
    new VirtualWebDriveComponent.FileEncryption();
    private string ticket;
    private bool loggedIn = false;

    // (Designer code and event handlers omitted.)
}
```

When the Login button is clicked, the Login() click event handler creates a new LoginForm as shown below. The user ID and password are then retrieved, and submitted to the web service in encrypted form. Note that the client does not need to be aware of how the data is encrypted, whether a timestamp is used, or even the fact that a new symmetric key has been generated for a key exchange. The form is updated after the login attempt with the ticket information.

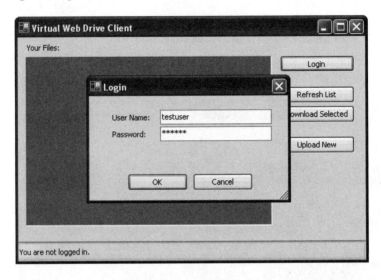

```
private void Login(object sender, System.EventArgs e)
{
    LoginForm login = new LoginForm();
    if (login.ShowDialog() == DialogResult.OK)
    {
        try
        {
            session = new SecureClientSession(proxy.GetKey());
            ticket = proxy.Login(session.EncryptLoginData(
                login.UserName, login.Password));
            status.Panels[0].Text = "You are logged in as " +
                ticket + ".";

            loggedIn = true;
            RefreshList();
        }
        catch (Exception err)
        {
            MessageBox.Show(err.ToString());
            loggedIn = false;
            status.Panels[0].Text = "You are not logged in.";
        }
    }
    else
```

```
    {
            ticket = null;
            gridFiles.DataSource = null;
    }
}
```

The `RefreshList()` method of `MainForm` automatically downloads the most recent list of files and displays it in the grid. Note that the retuned information is decrypted seamlessly using the `SecureClientSession` class.

```
private void RefreshList()
{
    DataSet ds = (DataSet)session.DecryptObjectFromServer(
        proxy.GetFileInfo(ticket));
    gridFiles.DataSource = ds.Tables[0];
}
```

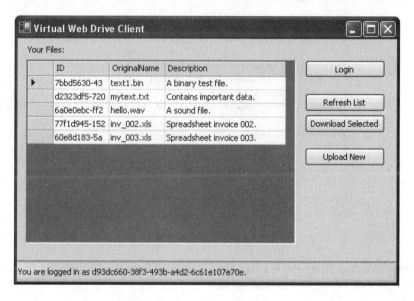

When the form closes, the client is logged out, if required:

```
private void MainForm_Closed(object sender, System.EventArgs e)
{
    if (loggedIn)
    {
        proxy.Logout(ticket);
    }
}
```

All that's left is to implement the functionality for uploading and downloading files. Once again, the encryption components will make this work easy. The client simply needs to use the `OpenFileDialog` or `SaveFileDialog` component to prompt the user for the file source or destination. The file is encrypted or decrypted using the `FileUtility` class.

```
private void cmdUpload_Click(object sender, System.EventArgs e)
{
    OpenFileDialog dlg = new OpenFileDialog();
    if (dlg.ShowDialog() == DialogResult.OK)
    {
        try
        {
            Stream fs = dlg.OpenFile();
            byte[] fileContent = new byte[fs.Length];
            fs.Read(fileContent, 0, fileContent.Length);
            fs.Close();

            // Encrypt file.
            fileContent = FileUtil.EncryptFile(fileContent);

            FileInfo fileInfo = new FileInfo(
               Path.GetFileName(dlg.FileName), dlg.FileName);
            proxy.SaveFile(ticket,
               session.EncryptObjectForServer(fileInfo), fileContent);

            // Refresh list.
            RefreshList();
        }
        catch (Exception err)
        {
            MessageBox.Show(err.ToString());
        }
    }
}
```

When downloading a file, the selected file is retrieved from the `DataGrid`, and then the same process takes place, but in reverse:

```
private void cmdDownload_Click(object sender, System.EventArgs e)
{
    DataTable dt = (DataTable)gridFiles.DataSource;

    SaveFileDialog dlg = new SaveFileDialog();
    dlg.FileName =
       dt.Rows[gridFiles.CurrentRowIndex]["OriginalName"].ToString();
    if (dlg.ShowDialog() == DialogResult.OK)
    {
        try
```

```
        {
            byte[] fileContent = proxy.GetFile(ticket,
                dt.Rows[gridFiles.CurrentRowIndex]["ID"].ToString());

            // Decrypt file.
            fileContent = FileUtil.DecryptFile(fileContent);

            Stream fs = new FileStream(dlg.FileName, FileMode.Create);
            fs.Write(fileContent, 0, fileContent.Length);
            fs.Close();
        }
        catch (Exception err)
        {
            MessageBox.Show(err.ToString());
        }
    }
}
```

You can test this logic out by creating a simple text file, as shown here:

When the text file is uploaded to the server, it is given a unique filename (in this case, dafd059e-27eb-4ae1-b959-ca6326e91c8a). If you attempt to open this file in Notepad, you'll see contents that look something like this:

Finally, when the file is downloaded back to the client hard drive, it is decrypted back to its original form.

Possible Improvements

The VirtualWebDrive service developed in this chapter uses a significant amount of cryptography code to secure data on the wire and in the database. In this example, we haven't made use of any security service (like Windows authentication or SSL) and it shows in the layers of code we have needed to add. But even with these details, there are still several security risks in the solution, some of which are easier to resolve than others.

❑   There isn't enough defense against a malicious authenticated user. In particular, an authenticated user could upload thousands of files to eventually fill the server's hard drive. This is, in essence, a denial of service attack. To remedy this problem, you would have to implement some sort of policy rules, or better yet, use isolated stores. Isolated stores allow data to be stored securely using a virtual file system provided by the .NET runtime. Isolated stores can enforce size limits.

❑ Some data is stored in the database as plaintext, including the original filename, description, and so on. This is a fairly minor risk, because an attacker would require access to the server computer before they would be able to access this information (at which point they could probably retrieve more valuable data). However, you can tighten security by encrypting this information. You can use the client's key, in which case the server can never examine this information, or you can use the server's public key, in which case this key must not change.

❑ Some replay attacks may be possible, inside the bounds of a particular session. For example, a replay attack can't be used with the login data (because it incorporates date information), but it could be used with a file upload or download request, provided the symmetric session key hasn't changed and the ticket hasn't expired. To counteract this possibility, all encrypted packages could incorporate date information.

❑ There is no identity verification. Because we are not using SSL or certificates, clients have no way to be sure they are communicating with the server. This opens up the possibility of a man-in-the-middle attack. Unfortunately, there is no easy way to resolve this problem, because there is no .NET API for verifying certificate information. One option would be for the client to pre-configure a list of public key's for the servers it trusts, and refuse to communicate with any others.

In addition to these security limitations, there are also a number of improvements that can be made to the code:

❑ The client application could be signed with a strong name and Authenticode signature. This could be used to reduce the chance that it could be replaced with a malicious Trojan application.

❑ Logging and auditing code could be added. Instead of writing error messages using the Debug object, you could call a Log() method in a third-party component, which could then store the information in an event log or database.

❑ Many improvements are possible in the Windows client. For example, you could add niceties that disable buttons to prevent the client from attempting to retrieve a list of files while not logged in.

Summary

One of the most significant application design issues with secure code is the complexity. To implement encryption, you often have to add lengthy additional code, troubleshoot unusual problems, and even change the interface of the system by modifying the data types of parameters and return values. In order to successfully implement secure code, you will need to carefully control this complexity with helper classes and dedicated components. Otherwise, as your application grows with new features and methods, it will become increasingly difficult to spot where security flaws might appear.

This chapter presented an end-to-end demonstration of a secure distributed application. It used a multi-layered design that separates the database and encryption logic into separate components, and allows the client and web service code to be simplified dramatically. It also demonstrates a step-by-step approach you might want to use when designing a new application, beginning with a security analysis.

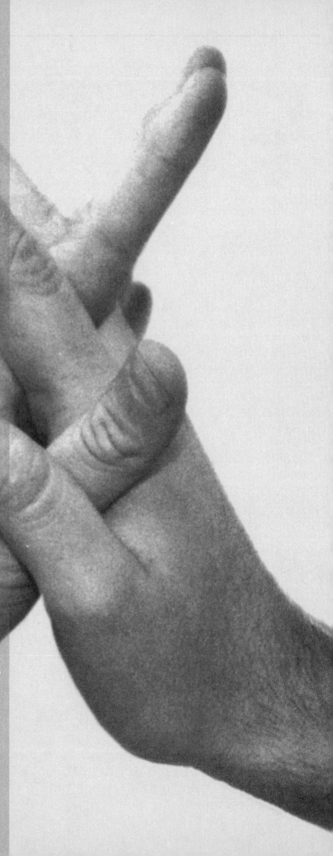

C#

Data Security

Handbook

Appendix A

Transport Layer Security

This appendix briefly discusses alternative ways of securing transported data 'below' your application, that is, your application can rely on data being secured by the transport mechanisms instead of securing them in your application. One common way of securing individual channels is using SSL (like one HTTPS session for example), which has already been discussed. Although SSLv3 is very secure, there is already an intended successor to SSL called Transport Layer Security (TLS), which is also used to secure individual channels. Both these techniques do, however, affect the application to some extent, like specifying HTTPS instead of HTTP in a URL, but it is still a very reasonable method for establishing a secure channel.

The need for securing transported data is becoming increasingly important, both within a corporation and especially over the Internet. Secure channels over the Internet are a requirement for e-commerce for example, because customers are reluctant to post their credit card information otherwise for example.

> **You need some basic knowledge of TCP/IP terms and definitions to fully understand what is discussed in this appendix.** *Professional .NET Network Programming* **(Wrox Press, ISBN 1-86100-735-3) provides a good introduction to network programming and terminology.**

There are yet other techniques that are discussed later in this appendix, like IP Security (IPSec) and Layer 2 Tunneling Protocol (L2TP) or Point-to-Point Tunneling Protocol (PPTP) to establish secure 'tunnels' between two nodes. These 'tunneling' techniques, which are also called Virtual Private Networks (VPN), will secure all traffic going in that tunnel. This is a very attractive solution for home-to-office networks, where an employee may sit at home, and then establish secure communication with the office network using their usual ISP making office network resources available from home.

In order to better understand how these techniques work and where they are implemented, you need an idea of how computer network communication is described, which the subject of the next section.

Reference Models

There are two major approaches to describing the communication layers today; one called the ISO/OSI 7-Layer Reference Model and the TCP/IP 5-Layer Reference Model. The nomenclature may be a little confusing here since TCP/IP actually only represents two of the layers in the 5-layer model, and OSI (Open System Interconnection) was a working group within ISO (International Standards Organization)!

The implementations (and sometimes the models themselves) of layered models are also called 'stacks'. Every layer in the stack has a dependency on the layer below. You may already have heard the term TCP/IP stack, which probably refers to the TCP/IP implementation in your system.

ISO/OSI 7-Layer Reference Model

The generic nature of this model makes it impractical to use it in specific cases, like TCP/IP. It may be used to describe TCP/IP as well, but is normally used only as the base model when describing protocols in general.

Layer	Name	Description
7	Application	End-user and end-application protocols, like FTP, SMTP, HTTP etc.
6	Presentation	The actual protocol representation is implemented here, like rules for packing and unpacking data.
5	Session	This layer is responsible for keeping the session consistency, making sure all packets travels between the right equipment. It is this layer that ensures packets to take the correct route through load-balancing hardware for example.

Layer	Name	Description
4	Transport	Responsible for ensuring data reliability and integrity (according to the protocol headers, does not protect data from being tampered with).
3	Network	Sets up address assignments and packet forwarding.
2	Data Link	Manage data into frames and communicates them through the physical layer.
1	Physical	This is where hardware transmits the actual data, normally through a wire but also through fiber, air or other media.

TCP/IP 5-Layer Reference Model

This model is modified to describe the specific nature of TCP/IP.

Layer	Name	Description
5	Application	End-user and end-application protocols, like FTP, SMTP, HTTP etc.
4	Transport (TCP)	Responsible for ensuring data reliability and integrity (according to the protocol headers, does not protect data from being tampered with).
3	Internet (IP)	Formats packets and specifies routing.
2	Network	Frame organization and transmission specification.
1	Physical	This is where hardware transmits the actual data, normally through a wire but also through optical fiber, air or other media.

Example Protocol Stack

SSL/TLS and IPSec operate on different levels, which are illustrated by the example stack diagrams below.

Figure 1

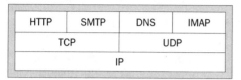

This is what a normal TCP/IP stack looks like, including application-level protocols such as HTTP, FTP, DNS, and IMAP.

The application-level protocols may all use both TCP and UDP, so you should only use this as a very rough map of how the protocols depend on each other.

Figure 2

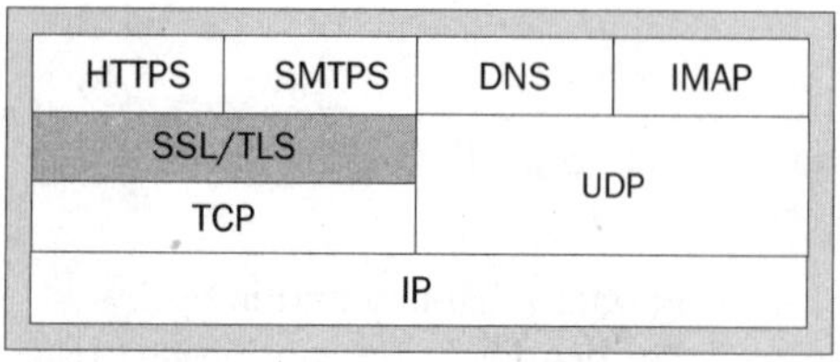

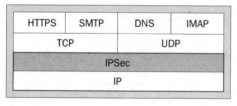

This example shows how SSL/TLS is implemented on top of the TCP box.

Note that application protocols must be adapted to SSL/TLS (implied by the last S in HTTPS and SMPTS).

Figure 3

This example shows how IPSec makes it possible for all protocols above to be secure without modifying them.

Note that IPSec must be configured through policies; it doesn't automatically provide secrecy to any of the application-level protocols for example.

Using IPSec also mean the TCP/IP stack implementation must support it as opposed to SSL/TLS implementations that do not affect the TCP/IP stack, but require each application to be adapted instead.

> **The remainder of this appendix will refer to the 5-layer model unless explicitly stated otherwise!**

Transport Layer Security (TLS)

The TLS protocol is defined in RFC 2246 (http://www.ietf.org/rfc/rfc2246.txt) and is built on the SSLv3 specification. An excerpt from the RFC document perhaps best describes the intentions of the TLS specification:

> *"This document and the TLS protocol itself are based on the SSL 3.0.*
> *Protocol Specification as published by Netscape. The differences between*
> *this protocol and SSL 3.0 are not dramatic, but they are significant*
> *enough that TLS 1.0 and SSL 3.0 do not interoperate (although TLS 1.0*
> *does incorporate a mechanism by which a TLS implementation can back*
> *down to SSL 3.0)."*

As the proposed successor of SSLv3, TLS is implemented in the SSPI (Security Support Provider Interface), which isn't directly available in the .NET Framework, at least not yet. There are, however, a couple of downloadable samples from Microsoft that implement two assemblies (written in C++) to help you gain access to SSPI in .NET. You can read more about this and download the code from:
http://msdn.microsoft.com/library/?url=/library/en-us/dndotnet/html/remsspi.asp.

IPSec

Internet Protocol Security was designed by the IETF (Internet Engineering Task Force). IPSec is included with Windows 2000 and later systems, and Microsoft-provide IPSec-based VPN clients are available for older systems; see the VPN section for downloads. The IP security specification provides cryptographic services like secrecy and authentication at the IP packet level – it works at layer 3 in the TCP/IP model. IPSec consists of several complementary security protocols:

❑ **Authentication Header** (AH) – provides authenticity

❑ **Encapsulating Security Payload** (ESP) – provides confidentiality guarantee for packets

❑ **IP payload compression** (IPCOMP) – provides a way to compress packets before ESP

❑ **Internet Key Exchange** (IKE) – ensure safe exchange of secret keys (optional)

Windows XP Professional includes local management of IPSec policies using an MMC snap-in, and it is possible to set up group policies using Active Directory with Windows 2000 or .NET server. IPSec is not inherently available directly on older (than Windows 2000) platforms, although it is available in some VPN client distributions (available to older platforms) mentioned later in this appendix.

Network Address Translation (NAT)

There are some considerations regarding Network Address Translation (also known as port forwarding) that you must be aware of before setting up an IPSec environment. The NAT services work as gateway between the local network and Internet, and translate the local address to the Internet address for requests and the reverse for the responses. For example, Microsoft's Internet Connection Sharing technology uses NAT to enable several computers to access the internet from one IP address.

Figure 4

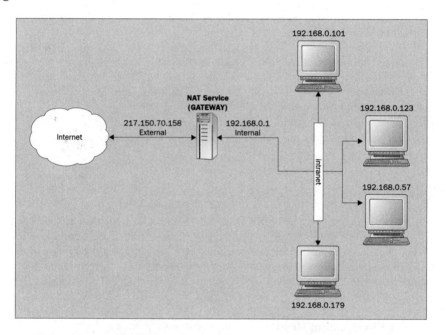

IPSec is based on IP and therefore using it depends on knowing the relevant IP addresses of the computers that are communicating. You may have realized by now that NAT is incompatible with IPSec as it is impossible to have local systems (inside the gateway) establish IPSec communication with computers outside the gateway.

Fortunately, there are already suggested solutions to this problem. Read the IETF drafts: *UDP Encapsulation of IPSec Packets* (http://www.ietf.org/internet-drafts/draft-ietf-ipsec-udp-encaps-04.txt) and *Negotiation of NAT-Traversal in the IKE* (http://www.ietf.org/internet-drafts/draft-ietf-ipsec-nat-t-ike-04.txt) for more information.

Microsoft has implemented these suggested solutions in its VPN software, which at least makes it possible to use its L2TP/IPSec VPN to your office even if you use ICS at home, as long as you connect to a server that also implements these suggestions.

Authentication Header (AH)

The authentication header is described in RFC 1826 (http://www.ietf.org/rfc/rfc1826.txt), and was designed to provide strong integrity and authentication of IP datagrams. The AH does not provide confidentiality or protection from network analysis, ESP does that. It is possible to combine these security protocols to you own liking.

The AH includes a cryptographically strong checksum of all data in the datagram including the static fields in all headers. The checksum is calculated using an algorithm and key(s) which both sender and receiver have previously agreed upon (using IKE for example) – very similar to a MAC in many ways. Such an agreement is called a "Security Association", and the parameters are stored locally referred to by a Security Parameter Index (SPI).

Encapsulating Security Payload (ESP)

The encapsulating security payload is defined by RFC 1927 (http://www.ietf.org/rfc/rfc1927.txt), and provide a mechanism for both integrity (like the AH) and confidentiality for IP datagrams. It can encrypt either the transport-layer segments, like TPC, UDP, ICMP or IGMP (transport or transit mode), or an entire IP datagram (tunnel mode).

The sender and receiver must agree on security parameters like keys beforehand, in the same manner as for the AH security associations.

IP Payload Compression (IPCOMP)

This protocol is defined in RFC 3173 (http://www.ietf.org/rfc/rfc3173.txt), and is designed to reduce the size of IP datagrams in order to increase the overall communication performance. It may also be very useful as a pre-processor to ESP for example, since encryption renders compression at lower layers (like PPP compression) ineffective.

> **Since encryption makes data more random in nature, compression should always take place before encryption.**

Internet Key Exchange (IKE)

As defined in RFC 2409 (http://www.ietf.org/rfc/rfc2409.txt), the IKE is a hybrid protocol designed to negotiate, and provide authenticated keying material for, security associations in a protected manner. This hybrid protocol uses parts of other specifications, like Internet Security Association and Key Management Protocol (ISAKMP, RFC 2408 http://www.ietf.org/rfc/rfc2408), the OAKLEY Key Determination Protocol (RFC 2412 http://www.ietf.org/rfc/rfc2412) and SKEME (*SKEME: A Versatile Secure Key Exchange Mechanism for Internet*, by H. Krawczyk, http://www.research.ibm.com/security/oldpubl.html).

IKE is often implemented on the server as a separate process and does not directly affect the TCP/IP stack. It does, however, provide the means for establishing the security associations and security parameter indexes used by AH and ESP, which are necessary to run the IPSec parts of the TCP/IP stack.

Virtual Private Network (VPN)

The purpose of a VPN is to establish a secure point-to-point tunnel, through which data can be sent securely from application level over a public (insecure) network. This is a well-established method of enabling secure network communications over the Internet. This is a common way to establish a secure link to you office network from home. Just connect to the Internet as usual, then connect to your office VPN server and alas, you have the office network securely accessible from home.

There are two popular tunneling protocols today:

❑ PPTP – Point-to-Point Tunneling Protocol

❑ L2TP – Layer 2 Tunneling Protocol

Point-to-Point Tunneling Protocol (PPTP)

It is often said that Microsoft invented PPTP, but it was actually developed by a consortium led by Microsoft including U.S. Robotics, ECI Telematics, 3Com, and Ascend Communications. However, the Microsoft implementation dominates the PPTP arena today.

PPTP encapsulates PPP (Point-to-Point Protocol, RFC 1661 http://www.ietf.org/rfc/rfc1661.txt) packets in GRE (Generic Routing Encapsulation, RFC 1701 http://www.ietf.org/rfc/rfc1701.txt and 1702). PPTP clients are available from Windows 95 onwards, but older implementations should be updated due to security weaknesses (see the Windows Update site, http://windowsupdate.microsoft.com/ for updated versions).

Layer 2 Tunneling Protocol (L2TP)

This protocol is defined in RFC 2661 (http://www.ietf.org/rfc/rfc2661.txt), and merges the best features from PPTP and L2F (Layer 2 Forwarding specification from Cisco).

Most current PPTP implementations have several disadvantages;

❑   All network communication is encrypted making it relatively slow (or expensive if you buy special hardware to speed things up).

❑   Most current implementations use weak encryption when compared to IPSec, which uses Triple-DES.

❑   Security associations are usually set up manually on each computer; with IPSec these can be performed automatically.

LT2P/IPSec VPN software was introduced in Windows 2000, and VPN servers are included in W2K Server and .NET Server. The .NET Server implementation also includes the proposed NAT traversal solutions mentioned in the IPSec section. L2TP/IPSec client software (including support for NAT traversal) is available from Microsoft for Windows 98, Windows Me (Millennium Edition) and Windows NT Workstation 4.0 at: http://www.microsoft.com/windows2000/server/evaluation/news/bulletins/l2tpclient.asp.

C#

Data Security

Handbook

Appendix B

B

Generating Secure Randomness

Random numbers are a critical part of cryptography. They are used in key generation, as initialization vectors, in SSL, and in challenge/response protocols.

There are a number of tests that numerically score how random a given sequence of numbers is. They consider how often a given number appears in the sequence, and more subtle measurements, including how often runs of identical numbers or other repeated pattern occur. The requirements for statistical randomness differ from those of cryptographic randomness. A sequence of numbers can be statistically random but cryptographically insecure if an attacker can predict the series of the numbers by understanding the algorithm and the random seed that was used, which wouldn't be too good when we want to hide and make data secure.

The .NET Framework includes two random number generators:

- ❏ The `System.Random` class is a pseudo-random number generator, and isn't suitable for cryptographic applications.

- ❏ The `System.Security.Cryptography.RNGCryptoServiceProvider` class is a cryptographically secure random number generator. This random number is created using the CryptoAPI `CryptGenRandom()` function.

We'll examine the reasons that you should always use `RNGCryptoServiceProvider` instead of Random (for cryptography) in this appendix, and demonstrate how you use the `RNGCryptoServiceProviderClass`.

Pseudo-Random Numbers

The most common description of a random series of numbers is one where there is no mathematical way to predict the next number from the previous numbers. The best random numbers are obtained from a physical process (anything from flipping a coin to monitoring the radioactive decay of an atom), because the physical processes appear truly random in practice. In fact, some random number generators use a hardware device for this purpose, like audio input or a noisy diode.

Computers are designed to be deterministic, and thus are not a good source of random numbers. They usually fall back on an algorithm that generates a statistically random series of numbers. In order to determine what input values to use in this algorithm, they require a user-supplied seed value, which is often derived from the system clock, network interface card MAC address, and other variable systems parameters.

These random numbers work well for sample data or modeling physics in a computer game. However, they aren't suitable for cryptographic purposes. Some of the weaknesses include:

❑ Pseudo-random numbers are periodic. Eventually, the sequence of numbers will repeat.

❑ If you use the same seed number, you will receive exactly the same sequence of "random" numbers. Thus, there can only be as many random sequences as there are seed values.

❑ Random numbers can be reverse-engineered. With knowledge of the algorithm, a brute force attack can be mounted to guess the seed value. If a correlation is made between the seed value and time, the attacker will be able to predict all future "random" numbers.

When creating an instance of the Random class, you can specify a seed value (using a 32-bit integer), or specify nothing, in which case a value will be used from the current system timer. You can then call the NextBytes() method to fill a byte array with a pseudo-random sequence of data, or the Next() method with parameters that specify the range of values. The following code shows a few different ways to create pseudo-random numbers with the Random class.

```
// Create a random generator and specify the seed value
Random rand = new Random(DateTime.Now.Millisecond);

// Create a random generator and use the default
// (current millisecond) seed.
rand = new Random();

// Generate an integer number between 0 and 10.
int number = rand.Next(10);
```

```
// Generate an integer number between 1 and 10.
number = rand.Next(1, 10);

// Fill a byte array with random data.
byte[] data = new byte[100];
rand.NextBytes(data);
```

Here's a simple Console example that uses the Random class in a loop. It demonstrates one of these weaknesses.

```
class RandomNumberTest
{
    [STAThread]
    static void Main(string[] args)
    {
        do
        {
            Random rand = new Random();
            Console.Write(rand.Next(1, 10));
        } while (true);
    }
}
```

Because the Random class is seeded with current time each time it is instantiated, it is possible to receive the same number if the class is instantiated rapidly (before the millisecond changes). Here is the partial output from this application:

```
88888888888888888888888888888888888888888888888888888888888888888888888888
88888888888888888888888888888888888888888888888888888888888888888888888888
8888888888811111111111111111111111111111111111111111111111111111111111111
11111111111111111111111111111111111111111111111111111111111111111111111111
11111111111133333333333333333333333333333333333333333333333333333333333333
33333333333333333333333333333333333333333333333333333333333333333333333333
33333333333333335555555555555555 ...
```

You can correct this problem by instantiating Random outside of the loop. In this case, each call to Next() will move to the next pseudo-random number that is generated by the algorithm. This is one reason why you need to instantiate the Random class before you can use it retrieve a random number—it is a stateful object that remembers its "position". However, the sequence of random numbers will still be repeated if the same seed is used.

Pseudo-random numbers have been the basis on many infamous attacks. One proposed attack was against a gambling application that used a random number seed to sort a deck in such a way that the number of possible shuffles was dramatically limited. After examining the first few cards, a user would be able to match the current draw against one of the possible shuffles, and determine the order for the rest of the pack. Another infamous example was a time-dependent random number generator in an early version of Netscape Navigator, which compromised the dynamically generated key used to encrypt data in a session with SSL. If you're interested in this you can read detailed description of this vulnerability at http://www.cs.berkeley.edu/~daw/papers/ddj-netscape.html

Cryptographic Random Numbers

In order for a series of random numbers to be deemed cryptographically secure, it must be computationally infeasible for a user to regenerate the same series of random numbers. Unfortunately, with pseudo-random numbers it's easy to reproduce the sequence. All the user needs is knowledge of the pseudo-random number generator algorithm (or a copy of the .NET Framework) and the seed value.

Cryptographically secure numbers are based on cryptographic algorithms, and a much more random seed value. .NET defines an abstract base class for cryptographically strong random number generators called RandomNumberGenerator, which defines methods like Create() and GetBytes(). It also includes one derived class, RNGCryptoServiceProvider, which uses the CryptGenRandom function from CryptoAPI.

To form the seed value, various values are combined into a system-wide seed. These include bits that the calling application may provide, such as the user latency between mouse or keyboard actions, and system and user data like the process ID and thread ID, the system clock, the system time, the system counter, the number of free disk clusters, and the hashed user environment block. This value is then hashed using SHA-1, and the output is used to create a stream of random data (and used to update the system seed). This works because hash values produce data that appears to be random, and changing only a single bit in the source document (the seed) statistically, the hashes of any two inputs have only 50% of their bits in common, even if the two inputs differ by only a single bit. Of course, it is still theoretically possible that some of these processes might be periodic in nature. For example, disk seek times appear random but actually depend on easily identifiable factors, and can be predictable. For even better random number generation, CryptoAPI can be used with a hardware generator for random numbers, like Intel's random number generator (see http://www.intel.com/design/security/rng/rngppr.htm).

> It takes *much* more time to create a cryptographically secure random number, which means it may not be suitable if you need to rapidly generate a large number of random numbers (for example, millions of numbers) in a short time frame. In a simple test, it took less than a second to generate one million random numbers with the Random class, and approximately eight seconds to do the same with RNGCryptoServiceProvider.

Here's the code needed to fill a byte array with random data using the RNGCryptoServiceProvider. Note that the programmer does not specify the seed.

```
byte[] randomBytes = new byte[100];
RandomNumberGenerator rand = RandomNumberGenerator.Create();
rand.GetBytes(randomBytes);
```

Unlike the Random class, neither RNGCryptoServiceProvider or RandomNumberGenerator provides any convenience methods for generating numbers that fit inside a certain range. However, you can simulate these calculations by using a class like BitConverter, which can convert the binary data into another data type. Here's an example that creates a random 32-bit integer:

```
// Four bytes are needed for a 32-bit integer.
byte[] randomBytes = new byte[4];

RandomNumberGenerator rand = RandomNumberGenerator.Create();
rand.GetBytes(randomBytes);
int randomInt = BitConverter.ToInt32(randomBytes, 0);
```

A similar technique could be used to fill a string with data, and even apply Base64 encoding through the BitConverter.ToString() or Convert.ToBase64String() methods.

Following is a code example that uses the RNGCryptoServiceProvider to generate random numbers in a Console application. It's equivalent to the earlier example with the Random class.

```
class RandomNumberTest2
{
    [STAThread]
    static void Main(string[] args)
    {
        byte[] randomBytes = new byte[0];

        do
        {
            RandomNumberGenerator rand;
```

```
      rand = RandomNumberGenerator.Create();
      rand.GetBytes(randomBytes);

      // Convert the random byte into a decimal from 1 to 10.
      Console.Write(
        (int)(((decimal)randomBytes[0] / 256) * 10) + 1);
    } while (true);
  }
}
```

In order to convert the random byte value (from 0 to 256) into a number from 1 to 10, you use the following formula:

```
value = (int)((decimal)RandomByte / 256 * MaxValue) + 1
```

The output appears more random than the earlier test, and will pass the statistical tests for randomness. More importantly, malicious users can't guess subsequent random numbers, even if they know the technique that is used to generate these numbers and have a list of recently generated values.

```
1011132391819716792861223655191323261714725535265441026887469582783912
7231113104741031094354161042691104878739910937788487107148109699184367
3978346162610915526222710856189911547564469316783595235162210454291064
646293593944498953246283658787286210594 ...
```

You can use a similar technique to create a cryptographically random GUID by seeding the Guid class with a truly random number:

```
byte[] randomBytes = new byte[16];
RNGCryptoServiceProvider rng = new RNGCryptoServiceProvider();
rng.GetBytes(randomBytes);
Guid randomGuid = new Guid(randomBytes);
```

Keep in mind that when you dynamically generate keys by creating a new instance of a SymmetricAlgorithm or AsymmetricAlgorithm class, .NET will use RNGCryptoServiceProvider to generate secure random values, which will then be used to fill key fields and the initialization vector.

> **It is not sufficient to use a number generated with RNGCryptoServiceProvider to seed the Random class, although this will improve security to a point. This technique ensures that it is impossible to predict where the random number sequence will begin. However, given a sequence of numbers generated by the Random class, an attacker could still be able to determine subsequent numbers.**

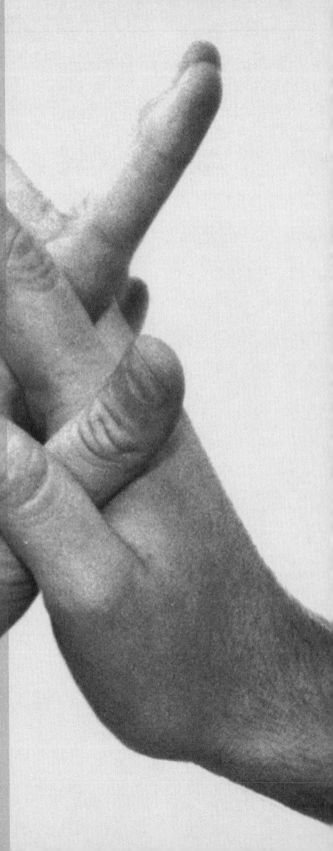

C#

Data Security

Handbook

Appendix C

Support, Errata, and Code Download

We always value hearing from our readers, and we want to know what you think about this book and series: what you liked, what you didn't like, and what you think we can do better next time. You can send us your comments, either by returning the reply card in the back of the book, or by e-mailing us at feedback@wrox.com. Please be sure to mention the book title in your message.

How to Download the Sample Code for the Book

Log on to the Wrox site, http://www.wrox.com/, and simply locate the title through our Search facility or by using one of the title lists. Click on Download Code on the book's detail page.

The files that are available for download from our site have been archived using WinZip. When you have saved the archive to a folder on your hard-drive, you will need to extract the files using WinZip, or a compatible tool. Inside the Zip file will be a folder structure and an HTML file that explains the structure and gives you further information, including links to e-mail support, and suggested further reading.

Errata

We've made every effort to ensure that there are no errors in the text or in the code. However, no one is perfect and mistakes can occur. If you find an error in this book, like a spelling mistake or a faulty piece of code, we would be very grateful for feedback. By sending in errata, you may save another reader hours of frustration, and of course, you will be helping us to provide even higher quality information. Simply e-mail the information to support@wrox.com; your information will be checked and if correct, posted to the Errata page for that title.

To find errata, locate this book on the Wrox web site (http://www.wrox.com/books/1861008015.htm), and click on the Book Errata link on the book's detail page.

E-Mail Support

If you wish to query a problem in the book with an expert who knows the book in detail then e-mail support@wrox.com, with the title of the book, and the last four numbers of the ISBN in the subject field of the e-mail. A typical e-mail should include the following:

❑   The name, last four digits of the ISBN (8015), and page number of the problem, in the Subject field

❑   Your name, contact information, and the problem, in the body of the message

We won't send you junk mail. We need the details to save your time and ours. When you send an e-mail message, it will go through the following chain of support:

❑   **Customer Support**

    Your message is delivered to our customer support staff. They have files on most frequently asked questions and will answer anything general about the book or the web site immediately.

❑   **Editorial**

    More in-depth queries are forwarded to the technical editor responsible for the book. They have experience with the programming language or particular product, and are able to answer detailed technical questions on the subject. Once an issue has been resolved, the editor can post the errata to the web site.

❑ **The Author**

Finally, in the unlikely event that the editor cannot answer your problem, they will forward the request to the author. We do try to protect the author from any distractions to their writing (or programming); but we are quite happy to forward specific requests to them. All Wrox authors help with the support on their books. They will e-mail the customer and the editor with their response, and again all readers should benefit.

The Wrox support process can only offer support for issues that are directly pertinent to the content of our published title. Support for questions that fall outside the scope of normal book support, is provided via our P2P community lists – http://p2p.wrox.com/forum.

p2p.wrox.com

For author and peer discussion, join the P2P mailing lists. Our unique system provides Programmer to Programmer™ contact on mailing lists, forums, and newsgroups, all in addition to our one-to-one e-mail support system. Be confident that the many Wrox authors and other industry experts who are present on our mailing lists are examining any queries posted. At http://p2p.wrox.com/, you will find a number of different lists that will help you, not only while you read this book, but also as you develop your own applications.

To subscribe to a mailing list follow these steps:

❑ Go to http://p2p.wrox.com/

❑ Choose the appropriate category from the left menu bar

❑ Click on the mailing list you wish to join

❑ Follow the instructions to subscribe and fill in your e-mail address and password

❑ Reply to the confirmation e-mail you receive

❑ Use the subscription manager to join more lists and set your mail preferences

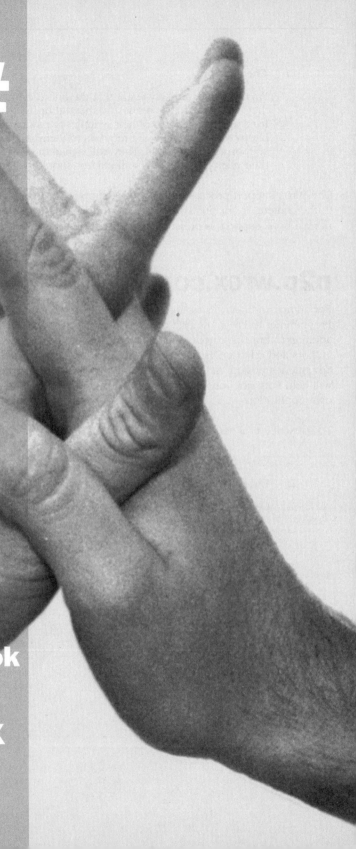

C#

Data Security

Handbook

Index

Index

A Guide to the Index

The index is arranged hierarchically, in alphabetical order, with symbols preceding the letter A. Most second-level entries and many third-level entries also occur as first-level entries. This is to ensure that users will find the information they require however they choose to search for it.

U

V

W

X

Z

Free C#Today Article

www.CSharpToday.com is a web site dedicated to providing informative material on the C# language. C#Today provides you with a weekly in-depth case study, giving you solutions to real-world problems that are relevant to your career. Every case study is written by a leading professional, tackling a problem that occurs in the real world, meaning that you benefit from their expertise as you read about cutting edge techniques and methods that enable you to get the skills that you need to survive in the C# world. As well as our weekly case study, we also offer you access to our archive of over 200 high quality articles and case studies, which cover every aspect of the C# and .NET development. C#Today is the tool for the C# professional.

Throughout this book we have been discussing various uses for cryptography (secrecy, data integrity, etc.), this bonus C#Today article discuss yet one more interesting use, zero-knowledge proof. This article by Walter Schoellmann was originally published in January 2002. You can view this article online at http://www.csharptoday.com/info.asp?view=DataSecurity.

Abstract

.NET makes far-flung distributed processing a real possibility. While .NET provides a rich framework of enabling technologies, the responsibility is on us to recognize the issues and design patterns of distributed processing and to be able to implement them using the framework. A primary issue of distributed systems is the authentication of users and system components. Authentication, privacy, integrity, and non-repudiation are the domain of modern cryptography. Cryptography provides several ways to implement authentication based on a mutual secret. This article demonstrates how components can prove they know a mutual secret without revealing or compromising it in the process. In cryptographic circles, this concept is known as the **Zero-Knowledge Proof**. A Zero-Knowledge Proof may seem like an impossible notion, but the scheme is really pretty simple, easy to implement, and very useful in distributed applications.